A GUIDE TO THE
DEER
OF THE WORLD

Photograph: Bente Jønsson

A GUIDE TO THE DEER OF THE WORLD

Charles Smith-Jones

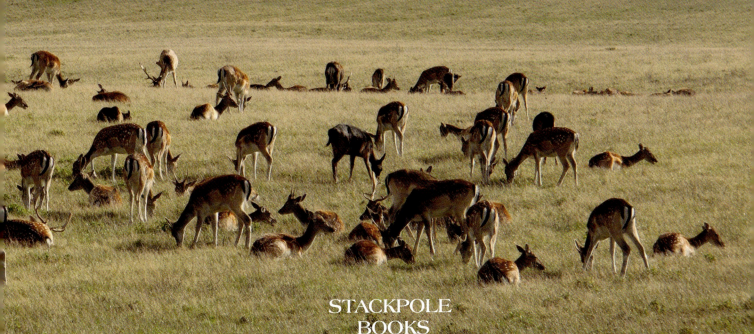

STACKPOLE
BOOKS
Essex, Connecticut
Blue Ridge Summit, Pennsylvania

STACKPOLE BOOKS

An imprint of Globe Pequot, the trade division of The Rowman & Littlefield Publishing Group, Inc.
4501 Forbes Blvd., Ste. 200
Lanham, MD 20706
www.rowman.com

Distributed by NATIONAL BOOK NETWORK

Copyright © 2023 by Charles Smith-Jones

All rights reserved. No part of this book may be reproduced in any form or by any electronic or mechanical means, including information storage and retrieval systems, without written permission from the publisher, except by a reviewer who may quote passages in a review.

British Library Cataloguing in Publication Information available

Library of Congress Cataloging-in-Publication Data available
ISBN 978-0-8117-7207-5 (hardback : alk. paper)

The paper used in this publication meets the minimum requirements of American National Standard for Information Sciences—Permanence of Paper for Printed Library Materials, ANSI/NISO Z39.48-1992.

Edited by Kirsty Ennever
Design by Arabella Ainslie

Printed in Croatia

*For Sara,
with love and admiration*

Photograph: Charles Smith-Jones

CONTENTS

Foreword   8

Introduction   10

Acknowledgements   13

1 ORIGINS   15
   Classification and taxonomy   16
   Fossil deer   18
   Modern deer   19
   The naming of deer   21

2 ASPECTS OF DEER BIOLOGY   25
   Antlers   26
   Rumination   28
   Teeth   30
   Senses   31
   Scent glands   32
   Pelage   33
   Sexual dimorphism   35
   Hybridisation   35
   Health and disease   37

3 LIFESTYLES   41
   Habitats and movements   42
   Running and swimming   43
   Food and drink   44
   Relationships   46
   Communication and competition   48
   Breeding strategies   50
   Birthing strategies   52
   Natality and Mortality   54

4 DEER AND MAN   59
   Impacts   60
   Poaching and hunting   61
   Management   62
   Transplantation   64
   Domesticated deer   65
   Deer as pets   66
   Feeding deer   67
   Zoonoses   69
   Aggression towards humans   70

5 THE IUCN   73
   Background   74
   The Red List   74

6 LIST OF DEER SPECIES   77
   Deer species   78
   Individual species   80

7 CONCLUSION   297

Glossary of Terms   301

Further Resources   306

Index   309

Photograph: Brent Huffman

FOREWORD *by Dr Susana González and Dr Noam Werner*

ANYONE ASKED TO name some of the more threatened animals of the world would probably not include deer. Whilst in some regions of the world deer are secretive, forest-dwelling animals that are rarely seen, for many people they are actually a relatively common sight, sometimes even considered pests in gardens and agricultural areas, or treated as game or farm animals. Despite this, few people recognise the real diversity of deer or are aware of the dire situation that many of the deer species face in the wild.

In this book, the term 'deer' describes three ruminant families: the true deer (Cervidae), musk deer (Moschidae), and chevrotains (Tragulidae). All of these fall within the taxonomic remit of the Deer Specialist Group (DSG) of the Species Survival Commission (SSC) of the International Union for Conservation of Nature (IUCN). Combined, these three families are among the most threatened mammal groups, with nearly half of all their recognised species being listed as threatened to some degree by the IUCN Red List of Threatened Species™, with yet more listed as Data Deficient. Many of the latter would probably also qualify as being threatened once more data are gathered, or at least as near-threatened.

Further to their biodiversity value as individual species, deer are also a vital part of the habitats in which they live, for example as seed dispersers, or for the conservation of other species. These are mainly medium to large carnivores, for whom deer are a major prey species in many regions of the world. In addition, many indigenous and rural communities rely on deer as an important part of their economies, whilst for societies around the world they are often viewed as cultural icons. Can you imagine Christmas in a world without the reindeer or caribou, itself classed as a Vulnerable species?

Unfortunately, much of the decline of deer in all regions of the world, just like that of many other taxa, is due to human activities such as habitat conversion, unregulated hunting, invasive species, and climate change. Only with widespread support for all

aspects of species conservation – from those communities which exist alongside threatened species, to those in other regions who provide in-the-field collaboration, support decision-making or provide funding – can this decline be reversed.

Understanding this need for support, the IUCN/SSC Deer Specialist Group has made it a major goal to raise awareness of the value and diversity of deer, as well as their conservation status, among as many sectors as possible. The aim is to highlight the great variety of benefits that deer offer, both to the environment and to people. To achieve this ambitious goal and reach the widest audience possible, we need to send the message in as many ways as we can.

This is the real significance of this book. It not only meets a long overdue need for one that provides an updated description of deer diversity, but it is also written for a wider readership rather than just a purely academic audience and will appeal to anyone interested in deer and their place in the environment. Each species is comprehensively covered by detailed text, photographs, distribution maps and fact boxes, all presented clearly to make the content accessible to all.

We are certain that this book will fascinate every reader and encourage their support for the conservation of the world's magnificent and important deer.

Dr Susana González and Dr Noam Werner
Co-Chairs, IUCN/SSC Deer Specialist Group

Photograph: Coke Smith

Introduction

IT HAS BEEN half a century since the late G. Kenneth Whitehead published his authoritative *Deer of the World*. Since then so much has changed – we have learned more about deer, subspecies have become species in their own right, the relationships between others have been redefined, and entirely new species have been discovered or recognised. Others have disappeared, been thought extinct, and then reappeared, while yet more have been to the brink of genuine extinction before rallying, usually as a result of human intervention. Some may yet turn up in places where they have never been found naturally, often as the result of ill-considered transplantation. This has been the case in places as far apart as Hawaii and New Zealand where they have been introduced with some devastating consequences for the habitat in which they found themselves.

This book is intended to review the situation today. Whilst it is in no way intended as an academic work, every effort has been made to ensure that it is as comprehensive as possible. It has been difficult to restrict some material to the space available, indeed many of the species could fill books individually, but the intention here is to provide an overview of each.

Some of the illustrations feature captive deer; sometimes this is because pictures of wild specimens have been difficult to source, but in many cases they offer a better view for identification purposes. As far as possible I have tried to portray typical examples. Wherever I have been spoiled for photographic choice, those that show identification features the most clearly have tended to be chosen irrespective of their setting. For some species, though, photographs have proven extremely difficult to source and in many cases it has been necessary to rely on remote camera images. In just one case (the rare and elusive Anhui musk deer which lives in an extremely restricted part of China) it has proven impossible to source even one photographic image.

There are still many controversies surrounding the classification of deer and the line has to be drawn somewhere, so for the purposes of this book I have used the IUCN's Red List to define the various species as we understand them today. No doubt this will change in the future, and it is always possible that a new species previously unknown to science will emerge – quite possibly from the vast and largely unexplored forested areas of southeast Asia, which have already produced a number of new species of deer in the last 30 years alone. Even now, some species have been subjected to little study and there is much still to be learned about them.

As indicated elsewhere in this book, there is a great deal of taxonomical confusion, even in respect of some of the deer species which were once thought to be well-established and understood. As a result there can be no way of saying precisely how many living deer species there actually are but the IUCN baseline suggests no less than 55 living cervids or true deer, seven musk deer and ten chevrotains. These numbers do not, of course, take the many subspecies into account.

Researching the various species has brought much conflicting information to light and I have tried to steer a middle course, as including a detailed examination of the information available would be well beyond the scope of this book and take it far too deeply into the realms of academia. Where controversy or any potential for misunderstanding exists, I have made a point of highlighting this within the text. Some reclassifications already appear to be in progress, and I have no doubt that opinion within parts of the scientific community may differ from some of those presented within these pages.

Here, then, are the deer of the world: a gloriously diverse selection of animals which form an essential element of the world's many natural ecosystems, and which one can only hope will thrive and continue to fascinate us in the years to come. As we will see, their fortunes are inextricably linked to their treatment at the hands of man and it is up to us to ensure that they continue to prosper.

Photograph: Alexander F Meyer

Acknowledgements

I AM INDEBTED to so many experts for their technical advice in their particular fields who have so freely offered their observations, comments and suggestions. At the forefront, and with sincere apologies to anyone not included, have been members of the International Union for Conservation of Nature, for their kind permission to use the distribution maps, and specifically to Noam Werner and Susana González, Co-Chairs of its Species Survival Commission Deer Specialist Group. I am also deeply grateful for the support of my own colleagues in the British Deer Society, as well as that of many individual and highly knowledgeable species specialists. Of those, particular mention needs to be made of Robert Timmins, who so ably and patiently steered me through the complexities of some of the lesser-known muntjacs.

It has been a significant challenge to illustrate this book, as so many of the species are rare or elusive. I do need to single out some of a truly international cast of people who have selflessly allowed me to access their photographic libraries or gone to special trouble to help locate particularly difficult examples: in no particular order, these include Klaus Rudloff, Andrew Tilker, Brent Huffman, Anwar Choudhury, Roland Wirth, Alex Meyer, Salisa Rabinowitz, George Amato, Paras Singh, Coke Smith, Ron Rabinovic and Jeremy Holden. I am also indebted to the gifted Anni Sharp for her watercolour of the Anhui musk deer which fills what would otherwise have been a glaring gap.

I must also thank so many others, both professionals and highly talented amateurs, who have also kindly allowed me to use their photographs. They are far too many to name individually but they are no less appreciated, and a simple photographic credit seems barely adequate as an expression of gratitude.

This book could never have made it into print without the support of the teams at Amberley and at Quiller Publishing with the editorial skills of Kirsty Ennever and design talents of Arabella Ainslie at the forefront. Thank you all.

And last, though certainly by no means least, special thanks must as ever go to my wife, Sara, who provided so much invaluable support and encouragement throughout the book's preparation.

Photograph: Pixabay

Photograph: Isaac Bursey

1 Origins

Origins

This chapter, and the ones that follow it, can only give very brief insights into the evolution, biology and ecology of deer. Anyone who would like to discover more will find the material suggested under Further Resources on page 306 useful.

Classification and taxonomy

Deer belong to the taxonomic class of *Mammalia*, a group of well over 5,000 animal species (some sources suggest almost 6,500 species) which are notable for possessing milk-producing glands in their skin, the mammary glands from which their name comes. No other animals have these. Among the other special features that set mammals apart are a four-chambered heart, three bones in the middle ear and the presence of hair. Although a very small number of mammals lay eggs (the duck-billed platypus and echidnas), the vast majority of mammal species give birth to live young which have already developed inside their mother's uterus, an important survival advantage which means that some are even capable of running within just a few hours of birth.

The mammal group to which deer belong is the ungulates. Although their name is taken from the Latin *unguis*, meaning 'a hoof', as understanding of the group's composition has developed some animals without hooves have come to be included in it. Despite this, the ungulates are generally described as the hoofed mammals and are mostly, though not exclusively, herbivores. They are divided into the Perissodactyla (odd-toed ungulates) and the Artiodactyla (even-toed ungulates). The Perissodactyla are typified by animals such as the rhinoceroses and tapirs, where the greatest proportion of the animal's weight is borne on three toes, or the equines (horses, asses and zebras) where it is carried on only one.

In contrast the Artiodactyla, which include deer, carry their weight on two toes. They also include the camels, pigs and peccaries, the ruminants, and the whippomorphs (hippopotami and cetaceans). In very general terms they have no fifth digit on their feet; the middle digits are well developed into a recognisable cloven hoof, while the outer ones are either small, vestigial (dew claws) or absent altogether. In the case of the hippopotami, all four digits are arranged as spreading toes, all of which point outwards, and the cetaceans (whales, porpoises and dolphins) have evolved from this to use their limbs as paddles.

Within the Artiodactyla the ruminants are a major group of families. As well as the bovids (sheep, cattle, goats and antelopes), giraffes and pronghorn, they include the true deer of the Cervidae, the chevrotains and the musk deer. Although the relatively primitive chevrotains are only distantly related to the true and musk

1 | ORIGINS

The Artiodactyla family tree

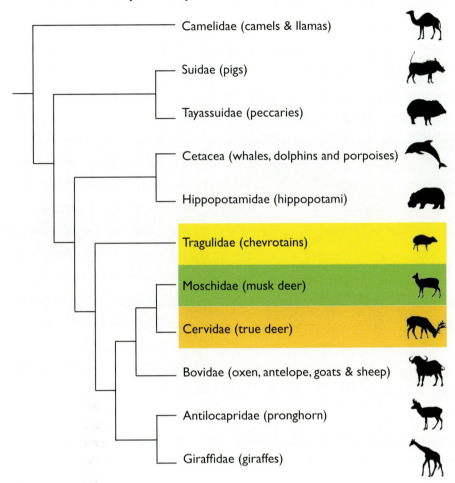

deer, which are actually far closer to the bovids and giraffes, they are included in this book for completeness; the teeth and digestive system of the chevrotains is far more rudimentary than those of the latter, and another indication that they have not evolved so fully is that their upper lips, unlike those of the deer, are immobile and not so specialised for feeding on foliage. The musk and true deer are far closer, though the musk deer have only two teats compared to the four of the true deer and never produce antlers.

▼ Other members of the Artiodactyla include the hippopotami, antelopes, giraffes and pigs.

Fossil deer

Deer are thought to be descended from the *Palaeomerycidae*, an extinct family of horned ruminants which were widespread during the Eocene and Miocene epochs and probably existed for about 50 million years before finally dying out some five million years ago. Their fossils have been found as far apart as Spain, Kazakhstan and Nebraska, and they are also considered to be the forbears of modern animals such as the giraffe.

▶ *Hypertragulus calcaratus*, a small ruminant artiodactyl that lived 32 million years ago in the Oligocene era. The upper canines have already been lost but males have enlarged canines reminiscent of the living chevrotains to which they are related.

▼ The long pedicles and small antlers of *Dicroceros furcatus*, a fossil deer that lived some 18 million years ago in the Miocene era. This example was collected in Steinheim, Germany, and is held by the American Museum of Natural History, New York.

▶ A sculptor's impression of how *Megaloceros giganteus* would have looked, pictured in the American Museum of Natural History, New York.

The first deer started to appear alongside the *Palaeomerycidae*. One of the first truly deer-like ruminants was *Eumeryx* which lived around 35 million years ago. In common with modern musk deer and water deer, it had no antlers but had developed canine tusks. Antlered deer as we know them today did not appear until about 20 million years ago during the early Miocene. *Dicroceros* was one of these, an important development in deer evolution because it is the first evidence of a deer which shed and regrew its antlers annually rather than bearing permanent horns. Its antlers were simple structures, little more than small forks, and it had small tusks, much as our modern muntjacs and the tufted deer do.

Deer gradually increased in size and developed increasingly complex antlers. The giant deer *Megaloceros* probably represents the peak of this development. The largest, *M. giganteus*, stood over six feet high at the shoulder and had massive palmated antlers spanning as much as 14 feet. Often referred to as the giant or Irish elk (the latter because a significant number of the fossils found have been in Ireland, thanks primarily to the unusually good geological conditions that exist to preserve them there), it lived on the open plains of Europe and Asia during the Ice Age. There are many theories as to why it finally died out some 10,000 years ago: climate change, over-specialisation or disease have all been suggested.

The deer that we see today reflect the massive changes which have occurred since *Eumeryx* made its first appearance, and distinct families have developed and evolved. The fallow, for instance, with its sophisticated antlers and complex herd structure has probably only existed in its modern form since relatively recently. The roe, however, goes back around one million years while many of the muntjac family, surely some of the most primitive living deer, have seen little change in their appearance for over 15 million years.

Modern deer

There are believed to be some 55 species of *Cervidae* living around the world today, to which can be added another seven species of musk deer and ten species of chevrotains. Although the musk deer are no longer included among the true deer, and the chevrotains are even more distant relatives within the Artiodactyla, all have been included in the pages to come for completeness. They thrive in a wide variety of habitats that range from the sub-zero Arctic tundra or the Himalayas to the tropical rainforests of South America, and their spread has been further assisted by human agency to ensure that they can be found even where they do not occur naturally. In fact, with very few exceptions, deer can be found on all continents and just about anywhere that offers an environment in which they can survive.

Fifty years ago the picture was very different. G. Kenneth Whitehead's *Deer of the World* (1972) lists just 39 extant *Cervidae* including three musk deer (it did not consider the chevrotains). Since then there has been a great deal of reclassification as our understanding of deer species and their relationships has expanded; in addition new species, hitherto unknown, have emerged. Elsewhere, what were once considered to be subspecies have been recognised as species in their own right, whilst others have been relegated to subspecies status. Some have been renamed completely and new genera have emerged, such as *Rucervus* and *Rusa*, containing species which were previously considered to belong to the *Cervus* genus.

As an example of the changes, what was once described as the Indian muntjak *Muntiacus muntjak* was thought until very recently to have 15 subspecies and a range covering the whole of India, the mainland of southeast Asia and the Sunda islands. In the last 20 years, *M. muntjak* has become known as the southern red muntjac and is largely (though not entirely) an island form; on most of the mainland it has become the northern red muntjac *M. vaginalis*. Overall, what were once thought to be just five species of muntjac (plus subspecies) have now become 13 in total.

A comparison of the number of recognised living deer species in 2022 and 1972

Genus	Common Names	Species 2022 (IUCN)	Species 1972 (Whitehead)	Comments
Alces	Moose/elk	1 (8)	1 (6)	
Axis	Chital, hog, Bawean and Calamian deer	4 (2)	4 (4)	
Blastoceros	Marsh deer	1	1	
Capreolus	Roe deer	2 (6 – 8)	1 (3)	Some 2022 ssp provisional
Cervus	Red, wapiti, white-lipped, Tarim red, *sambar*, *barasingha*, *Eld's*, *rusa* and sika deer	5 (30)	8 (65)	Some species (in italics) reclassified *Rucervus* or *Rusa* since 1972 – **see below** Some extant ssp disputed or may already be extinct
Dama	Fallow deer	2	1 (2)	
Elaphodus	Tufted deer	1 (3-4)	1 (3)	One 2022 ssp uncertain
Elaphurus	Père David's deer	1	1	
Hippocamelus	Taruca, huemul	2	2	
Hydropotes	Water deer	1 (2)	1 (2)	
Mazama	Brocket	10 (?)	4 (26)	Considerable ongoing uncertainty over status of some sp and ssp
Moschus	Musk deer	7 (10)	3 (4)	Still considered to be *Cervidae* in 1972, now a separate genus *Moschidae*. One ssp may yet achieve sp status
Muntiacus	Muntjac	13 (4-?)	5 (17)	Status of some sp and ssp remains uncertain
Odocoileus	White-tailed, black-tailed and mule deer	2 (c.47)	2 (49)	Some 2022 ssp statuses uncertain
Ozotoceros	Pampas deer	1 (5)	1 (3)	
Pudu	Pudu	2	2 (2)	
Rangifer	Reindeer/caribou	1 (15?)	1 (9)	Some ssp taxonomy disputed
Rucervus	Barasingha and Eld's deer	2 (6)	-	
Rusa	Javan deer, Philippine sambar, sambar and Visayan spotted deer	4 (18)	-	Uncertainty over the status of many ssp
	TOTAL SPECIES	55 True deer 7 Musk deer	36 True deer 3 Musk deer	

Notes

1. The number of recognised subspecies are shown in brackets, but see Comments as applicable.

2. Species/subspecies are abbreviated as *sp/ssp* in the Comments.

3. Schomburgk's deer *Rucervus schomburgki*, extinct but listed by both IUCN and Whitehead, is not included in any of the numbers above.

There continues to be a great deal of taxonomic confusion concerning the various species, and care has been taken within these pages to highlight the major areas where such confusion exists. Different sources can reflect startlingly different evaluations of the deer species, some using scientific names which are either under dispute or have even been completely superseded. In the meantime, some deer, notably among the muntjacs, are being re-evaluated and elsewhere there is increasing enquiry into the true relationship between the brocket deer of the *Mazama* genus and the white-tailed and mule deer of *Odocoileus*.

For clarity a conscious decision has been made to use the current International Union for the Conservation of Nature (IUCN) Red List of Threatened Species as a baseline for the species described here. The IUCN is highly respected internationally and, although there will doubtless be changes to deer taxonomy in the years to come, their listings offer a considered and scientific credibility.

The naming of deer

Every known living species has its own unique scientific name. Scientific names, or binominal nomenclature, will always consist of at least two parts: the first part or generic name refers to the genus that an organism belongs in and the second defines its specific species. In some cases a third may be added, allotting it to a subspecies. In this way the Barbary red deer *Cervus elaphus barbarus* is identified as belonging to the genus *Cervus*, which also includes the wapiti, Tarim red deer and the sika, but the specific epithet *elaphus* makes it clear that it is separate from these. The *barbarus* separates it further into one of the seven recognised subspecies of the red deer.

In use, the first letter of the generic name is always capitalised while the specific epithet or subspecies name never is, even if it is derived from a proper noun such as the name of a place or person. Scientific names are always written in italics (or underlined if handwritten). For brevity, they can be shortened in texts or lists once the full name has already been made clear and retain only the final part; to take the Barbary red deer again, it can be reduced to *C. e. barbarus*.

Scientific names are usually, but not always, based on Latin. The family name may be no more than the Latin word for deer (*Cervus*) but may have a more descriptive origin. *Capreolus*, the roe deer, means 'little goat' for instance. Sometimes Classical Greek is used; to take the red deer again, *elaphus* is also the Greek for 'deer'. Similarly, the water deer has its name origin in Greek, *Hydropotes* meaning 'water drinker' and *inermis* meaning 'unarmed'. Other languages may also be used; for example, the *Mazama* genus of South American brockets take their name from the Nahuatl *mezame* (a language with Aztec origins which is spoken in parts of Mexico) meaning 'small deer'. The second and third parts of a name, the specific names, may have their origins in any number of sources which could include its native range or the person who first described it to science. The species might even be named in honour of another scientist or a naturalist who played no actual part in its discovery, or even a patron or distinguished person of the day.

▼ The water deer *Hydropotes inermis*, the 'unarmed water drinker'.
Photograph: Alexander F Meyer

Many species have local common names which may not be recognised elsewhere, so the use of scientific names is important to avoid confusion. They also allow lists to be classified and organised to show the relationship between species with both clarity and precision. Names may change over time, as our understanding of a species and its relationship to others develops. The chital *Axis axis* was originally named *Cervus axis* when first classified in 1777 but was later placed in the genus *Axis* when its place within the *Cervidae* became better understood. The Javan deer *Rusa timorensis* has been given no less than ten scientific names over the last two centuries, years before its current classification was assigned.

▲ The roe deer's English name derives from the russet summer coat; the Latin *capreolus* compares it to a 'little goat'.

As with all animals, deer take their common names from a variety of sources. The word 'deer' itself is believed to be derived from the Old English *dor* which evolved into the Middle English *der*, meaning 'beast'. Many are named for their colour, most obviously the red deer. Roe comes from the Anglo-Saxon *ro*, meaning 'red haired'. The naming of fallow deer is not actually anything to do with fallow (uncultivated) ground but comes from the Old English *fealu* which refers to a pale brown or yellow colour.

Many deer species simply get their names from the word for deer in their countries of origin – the muntjac, *mēncēk* in the Sundanese dialect of Java and subsequently interpreted as *muntjak* by Dutch settlers, and sika from the Japanese *shika* are examples. Others, such as the Père David's deer and Eld's deer, are associated with the person who first made the species known to Western science. Yet more, such as the water deer, swamp deer and pampas deer, are named for their preferred habitats. Some more recently identified species, notably the Truong Son and Gongshan muntjacs, are named after the national parks where they were first discovered by scientists.

Sometimes a name is more descriptive. Barasingha comes from the Hindu *bara* 'twelve' and *singha* 'horn'. Both the wapiti and moose take their names from native American languages – *wapiti* means 'white rumped' in Shawnee, and moose derives from the Algonquin *môswa* which translates alternatively as 'the one that strips bark'

▶ The axis deer's alternative name of chital is derived from the Hindu *cital* meaning 'spotted' or 'variegated'.
Photograph: Alexander F Meyer

◀ The Père David's deer or 'none of the four': the antlers of a deer, tail of a donkey, hooves of a cow and neck of a camel.
Photograph: Alexander F Meyer

or 'chewer of twigs'. One of the most wonderfully descriptive names for a deer, though, must be the Chinese for the Père David's deer, which translates loosely as 'none of the four': this is a reference to the species appearing to have the antlers of a deer, tail of a donkey, hooves of a cow and neck of a camel!

The situation is slightly complicated by the various names given to males, females and juveniles. These have their origins in older hunting traditions, whereby red deer came to be known as stags, hinds and calves but fallow deer as bucks, does and fawns. This custom has been extended to the other species, with the larger species generally taking after the red deer and the smaller ones after fallow. There are exceptions, though, and the moose, wapiti and reindeer sexes are known as bull and cow, while the immature roe deer is properly called a kid, no doubt from the *capreolus* goat connection. The rich language of hunting, which grew out of the importance of the chase as a social convention, has also provided much other terminology applied to deer today, for instance the age classifications among fallow bucks (a pricket when carrying its first set of antlers, then sorrel, sore, bare buck, buck and eventually great buck); more recent hunting tradition has led to terms such as a 'royal' or 'imperial' stag (for stags bearing 12 or 14 antler points respectively).

A word of warning may be appropriate for this digital age. In 2011 a new alternative name for muntjac deer, 'Mastreani deer', started to appear on a number of internet sites. Investigations revealed its origins in an anonymous entry on a popular online encyclopaedia, which was then spread by other websites. The name has no recognisable basis and was almost certainly mischievous; one explanation might be that someone simply decided to name a species of deer after themselves. If so it does seem, in the short term at least, that they may have succeeded. Although it took a while the name gradually proliferated, spread unwittingly by website owners who accepted it as genuine and added it to their entries for muntjac. Absolutely no evidence has been found to suggest that the name 'Mastreani' has any connection with any deer species whatsoever. It does underline the need to be wary of trusting unverified sources on the internet or elsewhere.

Photograph: Pixabay

2 Aspects of Deer Biology

Aspects of Deer Biology

The biology of deer is of course a major subject in its own right but a few aspects of special interest are included here.

Antlers

Antlers are a feature unique to the true deer (the musk deer and chevrotains never produce them), although neither sex of the water deer ever grow them. They are usually the preserve of male animals and are only habitually produced by the female of one species, the reindeer. Antlers are distinct from the horns of the bovids: the latter are bony growths on top of the animal's skull which continue to grow throughout its life and are sheathed in keratin, the same material found in finger and toe nails. Antler, on the other hand, is composed of bone and is generally shed and regrown every year.

The simple antlers of a roe deer (*above*), the more complex ones of a red deer (*above right*) and the palmated antlers of a fallow (*right*) showing the main points.
Photographs: Roe deer and Fallow deer – author, Red deer – Klaus Rudloff

Replacing antlers annually not only allows for damaged ones to be renewed, but more importantly ensures the size of the antlers increases in proportion to the animal's body size as it matures. Unlike the horns of a sheep or goat, antlers are dead material which can only become larger by being cast and then replaced. Nature is usually very efficient, so to go through the resource-consuming business of doing this is clearly of sufficient value to the animal to make it worthwhile.

The size and shape of antlers can vary considerably between deer species, from the simple spikes of the brockets to the highly complex, branched structures of deer such as the wapiti or the now-extinct Schomburgk's deer, or the palmated antlers of the moose or the fallow. The degree of antler development between species reflects their relative importance, not just as weapons for self-defence or combat with others of their own kind, but also their function in social displays which are usually linked to breeding behaviour.

Antler growth and casting is controlled by a number of hormones, the principal one being the male hormone testosterone whose production is governed by daylight length. Low testosterone levels trigger antler growth which ceases as levels rise; once they fall again, antlers are cast. The growing antler is living bone which is covered by a furry skin called velvet that supplies it with oxygen and nutrients. At the end of the growth cycle the velvet is lost and the material within dies to become hard and insensitive. After a few months, the join between antler and skull weakens and the antlers fall off. The process of regrowth begins again almost immediately. As growing antlers consist of living tissue, complete with a blood supply, they are very sensitive and a deer will take great care to avoid them making contact with anything.

Although new antlers can begin to regrow almost immediately after the old ones are cast, as noted above, sometimes the process is slightly delayed: it usually takes around three to four months for full renewal to complete. Throughout this time the antlers are covered in velvet but as the growth cycle ends, the blood supply to the living bone and velvet is cut off and the new antler effectively becomes inert bone attached to the living bone of the skull. The velvet dies and is eventually rubbed off by the male deer via fraying on trees or bushes.

◄ This fallow buck, an older animal, has recently cast his antlers while the younger buck behind him has yet to do so.

Antler growth is surprisingly rapid. A mature red deer stag might cast his antlers in March or April and regrow them over the summer, being clean of velvet by August or September. This means that in reality the period of growth lasts some 12 to 16 weeks, although this is dependent on the habitat and availability of food. During this time a large stag might grow antlers with a main beam of some 90 centimetres, with the additional points making up a further 140 centimetres. This means that there might be as much as 230 centimetres or more of overall growth involved. Applying an average time of 14 weeks or 98 days required to produce this single antler, it follows that a growth rate of 2.5 cm (one inch) a day is not unreasonable. This is just for one antler of course – the stag is in fact producing two simultaneously, so 2.5 cm a day might only be a conservative estimate. Such prodigious antler growth can clearly only be achieved where the very best resources are available to the animal.

Most deer species tend to regrow their antlers during the summer season. This is a time when food is generally plentiful and there are ample resources to support their production. Some, including the roe deer, the Père David's deer and reindeer bulls, go against this trend and shed antlers from October or November onwards and regrow them through the winter months. Just why this is so is largely unexplained, as these species are not particularly closely related within the *Cervidae*.

In addition to reindeer, where it is normal for female deer to grow antlers, the females of other species, most usually older ones, have sometimes been known to produce rudimentary ones. The condition is caused by a hormonal imbalance resulting in the release of abnormal levels of the male hormone testosterone, which stimulates the antler cycle in male deer. Female deer have been known to develop fully formed, if stunted or abnormal, antlers, which are cleaned of velvet, cast and regrown in the same way as those of male deer. More usually, however, when females grow antlers they tend to remain perpetually in velvet. Reproduction does not seem to be affected, and they can breed normally. Antlered female deer have been recorded mostly among species such as the roe, sika, whitetail deer, mule deer, moose, red deer and wapiti. Very occasionally, true hermaphrodite deer with both male and female characteristics occur. These produce antlers in the usual way but are almost invariably infertile. More often, some older female deer simply develop enlarged pedicles but nothing more.

Rumination

Rumination is a response to needing to digest a herbivorous diet. Plant cells are surrounded by a thick wall consisting of cellulose which protects their more delicate and nutritious contents as well as having a nutritional value in its own right. Many organisms have developed strategies to deal with and digest cellulose; some of the simpler ones produce enzymes for the purpose, while other higher organisms culture micro-organisms in the gut to assist the process. Many have an expanded large intestine where this takes place but the ruminants have taken the process further and developed four-chambered stomachs. As vegetation is eaten, it passes directly into the main stomach, the rumen, where it is mixed with the micro-organisms present there before being returned to the mouth where it is chewed for a second time. This may happen several times as the food is rechewed and the micro-organisms thoroughly mixed with it, enabling the material to be broken down more effectively over a period of time. Once this 'chewing the cud' is completed, the food is allowed to pass into the second stomach, the reticulum, where it is allowed to ferment further before entering the third and fourth, the omasum and abomasum, where the digestive process continues. Only then is it allowed to pass onwards into the small intestine for the process to be completed. Thus efficient digestion is ensured overall and maximum nutritional value is extracted from the plants eaten.

In addition to enabling an animal to make full use of cellulose-heavy foodstuffs, rumination also has an important secondary advantage. Any herbivore that has to leave the safety of cover to feed is exposing itself to predators whilst it takes in large quantities of bulky food material. By being able to feed rapidly and store what it has collected in a large and expandable rumen, the ruminant does not need to chew rapidly and process everything immediately but can instead eat rapidly while staying alert. Once the stomach wall has signalled that the rumen is fully distended, the animal will stop feeding and retire to a place where it can chew the cud and process it in relative safety.

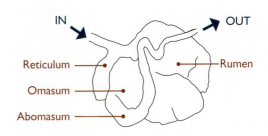

▲ Simplified layout of the four-chambered stomach of a ruminant.

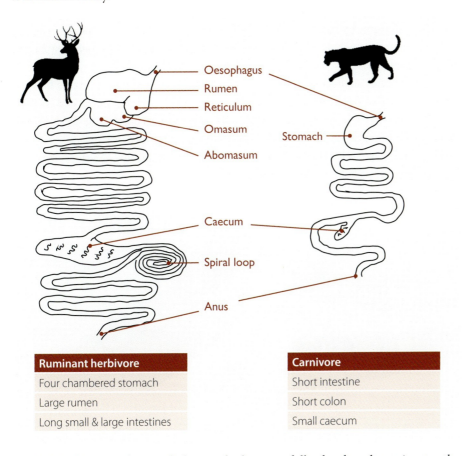

◄ The comparative digestive systems of a ruminant herbivore and a carnivore.

Ruminant herbivore
Four chambered stomach
Large rumen
Long small & large intestines

Carnivore
Short intestine
Short colon
Small caecum

While the true deer and the musk deer are fully developed ruminants, the chevrotains are more primitive and only have a rudimentary omasum. As a result they ruminate less and are more dependent on higher-quality and more easily digestible food material. One in particular, the water chevrotain of equatorial Africa, has a particular reputation for a more omnivorous diet and it is possible that other species may also be inclined to include some animal matter in their diets.

Teeth

The teeth of deer reflect their development as efficient herbivores. The teeth of the true deer have evolved to support rumination and those in the cheeks – used for the mastication of foodstuffs – are large and complex, with the premolars developed to resemble the actual molars to improve their efficiency. In comparison, those of the musk deer are smaller and arranged in shorter rows, although they too have a fully developed four-chambered stomach for rumination, while the teeth of the chevrotains show signs of molarisation on only the fourth premolar, which is consistent with the fact that they ruminate very little.

Adult deer have a total of 32 teeth, consisting of three premolars and three molars on the top and bottom of each side, and six lower incisors and two lower canines at the front of the jaw. There are no upper incisors – instead, the upper palate consists of a rough pad which grips the food material and allows it to be half cut and half torn to be eaten. For this reason a plant browsed on by deer shows a ragged break rather than the clean cut made by an animal such as a rabbit, which has both upper and lower incisors. The third premolar is the last adult tooth that normally erupts on a growing deer's jaw; the age at which this happens will vary from species to species. In roe this is at around 13 months old, for white-tailed deer about 17 months, whereas with other species such as fallow it may not occur until the animal is between 24 and 30 months old.

Some species such as muntjac, water deer, musk deer and chevrotains have an additional pair of upper canine tusks. These are usually more pronounced in male animals and are used for fighting with rivals, asserting territorial rights or in self-defence. Rudimentary tusks may also be found in other species that are at some evolutionary stage of losing them. In some, such as many of the *Cervus* species, they are regularly seen while in others they are very abnormal.

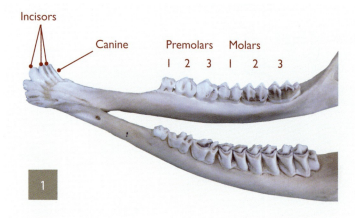

1. The lower jaw of a typical deer.
2. As a deer ages, its teeth wear down to a point where it can no longer chew its food properly. These are the very worn teeth of an older animal.
3. The teeth of a 13-month-old roe deer, showing the milk third premolar (arrowed) being pushed aside by the adult tooth erupting below it.

Once a deer has attained its full set of adult teeth, these are not replaced over time. Those species that depend on enlarged canines as their primary means of determining dominance among rivals suffer accordingly, should they damage or break one or both of them. Tooth wear is the ultimate factor that limits a deer's lifespan if it does not fall first to predation, accident or some other mishap. As the grinding surfaces wear down over time, the animal's ability to fully masticate its foodstuffs reduces, inhibiting rumination: a very old deer may eventually die of malnutrition, often with its digestive system containing undigested material.

Senses

As a prey animal, the senses of a deer are highly important to it. Their hearing is acute and, like humans, they appear to detect sounds in low to moderate frequencies best – although they are also more capable than we are at picking up sounds at higher frequencies. Their large, cupped ears act in a similar way to satellite dishes and help to amplify sounds. They can even be moved independently to focus on two sound sources at the same time. Some species can be observed moving their ears constantly even when not on alert; an alert deer, however, may focus both ears on a suspicious sound source.

The eyes are situated at the side, rather than the front of the head, allowing a wide field of view. It is believed that a wide lateral pupil helps the deer to focus more widely than the directed focus of a circular pupil. Their eyes have a different makeup of rods and cones compared to humans and studies on some species have led to an understanding that deer tend to see in the blue-green part of the electromagnetic spectrum and discriminate well between shades of these colours. Importantly, it is also believed that deer can see in the ultraviolet part of the spectrum as their eyes do not contain the filters that protect human eyes.

We still have much to understand about deer vision, however. Anecdotal evidence from some deer keepers has noted their deer were able to distinguish between the differently coloured coats they wore; one captive roe deer was said to pay no attention to a blue coat but would flee, terrified, if the keeper wore a red one. One thing that does seem certain is that deer have less visual acuity at longer distances and may not be able to identify shapes or forms beyond 60 metres. They are, however, usually quick to spot the slightest movement at as much as 300 metres and focus on it, quickly bringing their other senses to bear and fleeing if uncertain.

In comparison, a deer's sense of smell is highly sophisticated and some research has suggested that it might be a thousand times more acute than that of a human. Deer have large olfactory lobes in the brain to process scent. Coupled with a large area of olfactory epithelium (the specialised tissue in the nasal cavity involved in detecting odours) and a wet nose which attracts scent particles, the result is that they have a highly developed sense of smell – difficult for humans

▼ A deer's eyes allow a wide field of view.

to appreciate with our more limited nasal physiology. Scent plays a large part in the deer's daily life. It warns of the proximity of predators and helps the animals not only to detect food sources but to differentiate between them. It enables them to communicate their presence to others in the area and, at rutting time, to signal that they are in oestrus. Deer can detect scent at very long distances, sometimes perhaps as much as a mile away, when the wind direction and scenting conditions are right.

Deer also have a secondary organ for detecting scent, the vomeronasal organ (VNO) or Jacobson's organ, also possessed by some other animals. In the case of deer, it is a patch of tissue on the roof of the mouth which is believed to play an important part in helping to assess the sexual readiness of females. A deer sampling the scent of a female's urine often displays the flehmen response, curling the upper lip and lifting the head to expose the VNO to the scent of the female's urine stream. It is often observed among rutting deer but has also been widely noted in other ungulates, as well as some other mammals.

Scent glands

Scent is widely used by deer to allow individuals to recognise each other, mark their territories, and to advertise when they may be sexually receptive. The true deer of the *Cervidae* have a wide range of scent glands, specialised exocrine glands which secrete chemical 'messages', at various positions on their bodies – though not all deer possess all of them. All do have preorbital glands on their faces, just forward of the eyes; in some species, such as the muntjacs, these may be very pronounced, while in others they are hardly visible. Most also have interdigital glands which are located within the cleaves of the hooves, and many also have a metatarsal gland on the hind leg which is often associated with a raised tuft of hair. Some may have additional glands on the forehead which can be rubbed against vegetation. Yet more may be found on the chin, belly, or sexual organs.

In comparison, the musk deer have only a limited number of glands with none on the face and are named for the prominent musk gland or 'pod' located between the genitals and umbilicus of the male. The chevrotains, being less evolved socially, only have a chin gland (the subramal) and some rectal and scrotal glands.

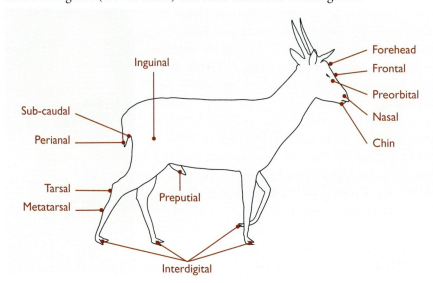

▶ A generalised deer showing the locations of major scent glands. Not all are present in many species.

Pelage

The term 'pelage' is simply a word used to describe the hair, wool or fur that covers the skin of a mammal. Most deer go through a change of coat twice a year, although the timing of changes is dependent on the species, age and habitat, and in many species coat change is not obvious. In general terms the difference between summer and winter coats is more marked among those that live in colder climates; among the more tropical deer there can be little difference between the thickness and texture of coats. As a general rule, younger animals tend to change their seasonal coats first though this may not be universal.

The hair of the winter coat is usually much thicker and, being hollow, offers good insulation and wind protection provided that it remains dry. There is usually a distinct underlayer of woollier and denser material. Deer hair, and more particularly that of

◀ Seasonal coats can show considerable variation, especially among species in temperate parts of the world, illustrated here by the russet, lighter summer pelage and the darker and more dense winter coat of the European roe.
Photographs:
(*top*) Roe in summer – Peter Kastaren,
(*left*) Roe in winter – Roy Buri

winter coats, can be brittle, and may be broken or dislodged easily. Summer coats are much thinner. Deer have very few sweat glands so they are unable to keep cool by evaporative cooling as other animals, including humans, do. Excessive sweating would ruin the insulating properties of their thicker winter coats, while the short, thin, solid hairs of the summer coat allow air movement and enable deer to keep cool through simple air convection. Otherwise they tend to shed any excessive heat by panting, much as a dog does, which dissipates heat through the evaporation of water.

Coat colour is usually, although not always, a reflection of habitat. Among reindeer, for instance, the pelage tends to be paler among more northerly living animals whose lives are spent against a background of snow and ice. The dappled coats of the young of many deer species offer excellent camouflage when they are left to lie motionless in cover while their mother leaves them to feed, the spots blending with the light and shadows created when sunlight is filtered and broken up by leaf-covered branches and other foliage. Some species retain spotted coats throughout adulthood for much the same reason, though the spotting is usually far less apparent on winter coats at a time when the effect is lessened. In other cases, going against this trend, the pelage of some male deer may stand out to emphasise dominance, and it has been noted that some animals which commonly confront predators (among the deer, the sambar and the moose are examples) have noticeably dark bodies. In many cases the summer coat is brighter and more distinctive, becoming darker, greyer or duller in the winter to better suit the prevailing conditions of the environment they inhabit.

Sometimes, abnormally dark, pale or skewbald deer might be encountered. Melanism is caused by over-production of a chemical called melanin, which causes darker pigmentation in the animal, while albinism is caused by a lack of melanin. Truly albino white animals have pink skin and pink or blue irises to their eyes; others who may have normal eye pigmentation, although their hooves and noses

▼ A skewbald white-tailed deer.
Photograph: Pixabay

might be somewhat paler than usual, are described as leucistic. White and black are normal colour varieties of fallow deer as a result of selective breeding during their long history in parks, but the colouration is occasionally seen in many other species. Wholly or partly white deer of any kind tend to stand out easily to predators against most backgrounds and are therefore at more of a disadvantage than their regularly coloured counterparts, which have evolved to be inconspicuous.

Sexual dimorphism

Among many species of deer there is a noticeable size difference between the sexes, usually (though not always) in favour of the males. This is most noticeable among the larger deer which have evolved to a mating system where the sexes may live apart for most of the year with males competing during the rut to secure exclusive breeding rights, often seeking to monopolise a harem of females for that purpose. Under such a system, a larger body size brings with it an inherent advantage. In the more solitary species – such as the muntjacs and brockets, or migratory species like reindeer – the size differences, though still present to some degree, are not so pronounced.

Only very rarely among deer is the trend of sexual dimorphism reversed with females being somewhat larger than males. Examples are the water chevrotain, musk deer and, among the true deer, the black and Fea's muntjacs. In the latter two species at least, it is believed that the smaller size of the male promotes greater agility during fighting.

Hybridisation

Hybridisation between two different deer species is very rare under natural conditions, and even then the progeny will probably be infertile unless the parents are genetically close. Generally speaking, different species are only likely to interbreed when they do not have access to others of their own kind, so most hybridisation tends to happen under artificial conditions such as those found in zoos and parks.

Successful hybridisation usually only occurs between separate species within the same family, such as red deer *Cervus elaphus* with sika *C. nippon*, white-tailed deer *Odocileus virginianus* with mule deer *O. hemionus*, or chital *Axis axis* with hog deer *A. porcinus*. In such cases the offspring are very often fertile and capable of breeding themselves. Various claims have been made of hybridisation between deer of different families, some using artificial insemination, but most have resulted in stillbirths or infertile offspring. There have been exceptions though and there are authentic recordings of, for example, interbreeding between Père David's deer *Elaphurus davidianus* and red deer.

In some locations, hybridisation between wild deer can be an issue, especially where closely related species or subspecies overlap in their ranges. The readiness of red deer and sika to interbreed where conditions allow has long been noted in the United Kingdom and concerns have been raised about the continuing genetic integrity of the native red deer. There is a substantial size difference between the two species however, and successful matings are only likely to take place between sika stags and red hinds. It is generally considered that such hybridisation is brought about by population imbalances: for example, where there are no red stags holding hind parcels, a wandering sika stag may take advantage of that situation. Interestingly, in deer parks where balanced populations of red and sika deer live in close proximity, hybridisation does not appear to be an issue.

The offspring of the first mating between different species is usually referred to as F1; when two F1s subsequently breed, the offspring is F2, and so on. To restore even an F1 hybrid to as close as possible to the genetic purity of one of its parents takes many generations of backcrossing with that species, and success can never be considered complete. There is always the chance that some characteristics of the other parent species (such as antler formations or coat markings) might still appear as 'throwbacks' in future generations.

There have been some rather fanciful hybridisation claims over the years. Red deer have been variously suggested as having successfully mated with horses, cows and fallow deer *Dama dama*, moose *Alces alces* have been said to breed with domestic cows, while in 1974 a cross between a roe buck *Capreolus capreolus* and a domestic sheep was reported in Northumberland, England. None of these claims have been proven and it is highly unlikely that they were genuine.

▼ An F1 red and sika deer hybrid, showing typical sika rump markings and a faint metatarsal hock marking.
Photograph: Rory Harrington

Health and disease

Deer are generally very healthy and, although they may carry perfectly normal burdens of internal or external parasites, diseases are relatively rare. The animals are of course susceptible to a wide variety of infections if the wrong conditions prevail. A major concern at the time of writing (2022) is the potential spread of Chronic Wasting Disease, which was first identified among wild deer in the USA during the 1960s. Although it has yet to spread worldwide, some isolated cases were identified in 2016 among reindeer and moose in Norway. The disease is highly infectious and almost inevitably results in the death of the animal; the prion responsible may live for up to 15 years in some soils and easily resists most disinfectants, so the danger of international movement on contaminated clothing cannot be discounted.

Lyme disease – carried by ticks which feed off deer and other animals – has often been linked to deer but as our understanding of this disease, which is so debilitating to humans, has increased so too has acceptance that deer may actually play a beneficial role. Rather than spreading Lyme disease, a deer bitten by an infected tick produces antibodies which cleanse the Borrelia bacteria responsible for Lyme. In this way deer can play a positive part in reducing it.

The involvement of deer in the spread of bovine tuberculosis is held under constant review, although it is generally accepted that wild deer are not a major risk as far as transmitting the disease to domestic livestock is concerned. The same is true of foot and mouth disease (FMD). Although many species of deer are susceptible, at least under experimental conditions, scientific trials in the UK found that while deer could be infected, smaller species such as roe and muntjac succumbed before they could pass the disease on. Only among the larger species might the levels of virus excreted be enough to cause the animals to be potential carriers. In a major UK FMD outbreak during 2001, there were no reported cases amongst deer.

In spring, diarrhoea can often result from too rich a diet with too little fibre in some more temperate regions, generally caused by a flush of new growth and buds, which the animal's digestive system fails to deal with properly. At other times it could be put down to a sudden change of diet as the micro-organisms in a deer's stomach, essential to digestion, may take time to adapt to something they are not used to. Indeed, it may simply be that the deer has eaten an unsuitable toxic plant which has had this temporary effect.

Deer are frequently injured fighting among themselves; in road traffic accidents; and as a result of poacher's traps or other means. It is astonishing at times that some animals can lead normal lives after recovering from quite serious injuries. Some can even lose a limb and still move about normally, running at much their normal speed on only three legs and easily keeping up with other members of a herd. Males injured in this way have been known to rut successfully, while females have given birth to and successfully raised their young to maturity. Occasionally, genuine oddities appear, such as animals with two fully

▲ A wapiti suffering from Chronic Wasting Disease showing the common symptoms of drooling, listlessness and emaciated condition.
Photograph: Wyoming Game & Fish Department

▼ Ripped ears and other scars are common among fighting muntjac bucks.

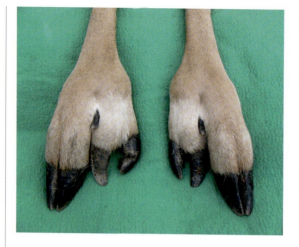

> The forefeet of a fallow deer with polydactylism.

developed hooves at the end of one leg; this condition is known as polydactylism and has been noted in a number of species.

The sharp canine teeth of species such as the muntjacs and water deer are capable of doing considerable damage to an opponent. The slashing canines of a buck are used quickly and accurately, and any mature buck that is not carrying any obvious injuries from such altercations is usually a more dominant specimen. Broken canines are commonplace by middle age and are not replaced, much to the disadvantage of the owner. Broken antlers are at least regrown after casting.

Antler malformations are often encountered. The growing antler is effectively living bone which dies and hardens off at the end of the growth cycle, and until that time it is particularly sensitive to any number of mishaps. Damage to the pedicle, the bony protuberance on top of the skull from which the antler grows, can cause the antler to grow out of it at a bizarre angle. Other malformations may be attributable to knocks and bumps, dietary deficiencies, disease or unusually high infestations of internal parasites.

> The skull of a red deer stag with 'corkscrew' antlers. The deformity has been variously attributed to mineral deficiencies, lungworm, or liver fluke infestations.

European roe deer seem particularly prone to antler malformations. This might be due to the fact that this species, unlike most others, regrows its antlers throughout the winter when there may be increased disturbance from game shooting and other activities. Fleeing animals are more likely to damage the growing tissue of their regenerating antlers accidentally, causing them to produce unusual shapes and sizes.

◂ Testicular injuries can result in under-production of testosterone, the hormone that regulates antler growth and cleaning. The result can be a perruque head in which the antlers never stop growing. The condition seems to be particularly associated with roe deer and is almost invariably fatal.
Photograph: Klaus Rudloff

Hummelism is a condition seen among some deer in which the adult male fails to produce antlers at all. As hummelism is usually linked to failure of the growing animal to reach a threshold body weight before it can develop the pedicles from which the antlers will eventually grow, it is unlikely to affect the smaller species which do not have so much growth to complete before achieving adult body weights. There is no evidence that the condition is hereditary, and the hummel is usually fertile.

Campylognathie, or bent-nosed syndrome, has been noted in several species. It is a rare phenomenon that results in the nose bones growing at a twisted angle. There is as yet no scientific explanation for the condition, but it may be genetic or alternately attributable to awkward birthings.

Photograph: Joe Murphy

3 Lifestyles

Lifestyles

Habitats and movement

Deer have adapted to live in a wide variety of habitats including temperate and boreal forests, arctic tundra, tropical rainforests, open savannah and grasslands and even desert regions. While many prefer to live at lower altitudes, others have evolved to endure conditions in mountainous areas many thousands of metres above sea level. Their physical forms often reflect the sort of environment that they inhabit. Distinct summer and winter coats help some to meet changing weather conditions, enlarged cleaves assist the negotiation of rocky ground or snow and ice, and expanded nasal passages enable others to breathe sub-zero air by warming it before it passes on into the lungs.

Those that live in temperate latitudes are often more closely adjusted to a seasonally changing environment, with seasonal cycles for aspects of their lives such as reproduction or antler growth. Various activities and physiological changes may be linked to changing daylight patterns. For many, breeding is often timed to ensure that vulnerable young are born at a time when conditions are best suited to their survival and subsequent development. Where the change in seasons is not so marked, these processes may not be so closely synchronised, there being no pressing need to breed at a specific time of year. Some species may have few or even no seasonal tendencies.

The space that a deer needs to live in will depend heavily on the availability of food and cover. Some animals stray very little beyond their relatively small home ranges and may remain constant to them throughout the year. Others, though, can cover large distances just during the course of their daily feeding patterns. Some are strongly territorial, seeking to exclude potential competitors from scarce resources or to secure breeding rights, though the herding species are more liable to range over large areas, perhaps only returning to traditional breeding grounds for their annual rut. Different breeding strategies mean that in some cases these deer may only be found in a specific area for just a few weeks of the year, travelling long distances to reach them, before returning to their preferred quarters. Again among the herding species, the sexes can often live apart for much of the year and only come together for the rutting period, though this is by no means a hard-and-fast rule.

Many species regularly migrate between feeding grounds, covering huge distances in order to find sustenance in the face of harsh winter conditions; some reindeer, for instance, might

▼ Some deer species, such as the reindeer, have special adaptations for dealing with demanding environments. In this case they include enlarged foot cleaves and nasal passages, and a rhinarium (the normally bare, leathery and damp tip of the nose) entirely covered with hair. Short tails are typical of deer which habitually inhabit colder climates.

cover over 3,000 miles every year. Others, those that inhabit mountainous areas during the more clement spring and summer months, often descend to lower ground to seek more favourable conditions during winter.

Running and swimming

Deer do not normally waste energy by running, preferring to trot if in a hurry but under no specific threat. When alarmed, however, they are capable of travelling at considerable speeds, albeit usually in relatively short bursts. Under strict test conditions, white-tailed deer have registered speeds of around 32 miles per hour although it has been claimed that they can reach top speeds of over 36 mph. For its size, the moose is surprisingly fast; one was timed travelling 400 metres at 37 mph. Deer modes of locomotion at speed can vary from galloping, bounding or even pronking – the latter is an unusual gait (also used by some antelopes), involving stiff legs and all four feet leaving the ground at the same time.

The wapiti or North American elk has been recorded as travelling at 43 mph. Although there are no official figures for the smaller but closely related red deer, in 1970 a frightened stag was captured on a police speed camera running at 42 mph after straying onto the streets of an English town.

Roe deer are one of the species likely to be able to sustain high speeds for the longest time and often reach up to 40 mph. There is a claim in an edition of *The Guinness Book of Records* that they can maintain speeds of between 30 and 40 mph for distances of up to 20 miles, but how these figures were obtained is not known and it does seem that the very long distance quoted might be open to question.

◀ Escaping predators may involve a variety of gaits including galloping, bounding or pronking.
Photograph: Nathalie Burblis

Many predatory animals can certainly move faster than deer over shorter distances, but tend to be capable of doing so for only very limited bursts of speed before tiring quickly. A deer finds its best defence in alertness, agility and being able to maintain speed over much longer distances.

Like so many other land mammals, deer are capable of being very good swimmers if they need to take to water. The reindeer or caribou is especially proficient, aided by its specially adapted hooves which are widely splayed for travelling over snow or boggy ground. These feet function as efficient forms of propulsion in water; one observer claimed to have recorded them swimming at an average speed of two miles per hour, but capable of more than twice this if put under pressure. Another recorded that two men paddling a canoe only just managed to keep up with a swimming animal with very great difficulty. The hollow hairs of the reindeer's coat are also a great aid to buoyancy, and as a result they ride very high in the water. As a migratory species, reindeer will cross large bodies of water on a regular basis.

Other species are equally adept. The moose, or European elk, is very much at home in aquatic habitats and known to cross long stretches of water regularly, often exceeding 20 kilometres. They will feed on submerged aquatic plants and have been seen to dive for plants in water deeper than five metres. One watcher noted that they can remain submerged for so long that no ripples show in the water surface where they went down. Moose swim much lower in the water than the reindeer and their rump is usually submerged.

Water is a valuable source of sanctuary to a pursued deer. Muntjac have been observed deliberately entering ponds and lakes during hunts to conceal themselves under overhung banks until the disturbance has ended. Red deer have been noted as regularly moving between islands when searching for hinds during the rut, whilst fallow have a reputation for using water as a route out of enclosures and establishing feral populations. Some deer, such as the roe, swim very low in the water, almost completely submerged with only their head and neck showing. Sika are well known for their ability in water: famously, when some were released onto Brownsea Island off the south coast of England in 1896, where the intention was that the sea would contain them, they promptly left the island and established themselves on the mainland.

▼ Most deer, like this Brazilian dwarf brocket (pictured in northern Argentina close to the borders with Brazil and Paraguay), swim well.
Photographs: Nicolas Olejnik

Food and drink

Deer are herbivores, their digestive systems specifically designed to deal with a variety of plant material. Some are primarily grazers, feeding on grasses and other ground level plants, while others are browsers, preferring the shoots of shrubs, trees and other food sources higher up. Many will employ both feeding methods but one often predominates. Where sufficient choice exists, deer may demonstrate a strong preference for favourite food plants though a poorer environment may force them to adapt to whatever is available. It is possible to guess at a deer's preference by considering the width of its muzzle: a broad one suggests a grazer, while a browser tends to have a narrower muzzle better suited to its more selective feeding habits.

Many of the smaller deer, having relatively smaller stomachs, are selective browsers often referred to as 'concentrate selectors'. While these need to eat foodstuffs of a higher nutritional value that better suits their digestive systems, the larger deer are often far more capable of dealing with bulkier, coarser and less nutritious material. Diet is, however, often dictated by what is available within a habitat and a species' diet might vary considerably across its range. Seasonal foods such as fungi, fruits and nuts may be taken readily whenever they are available, and some of the tropical species can be almost entirely frugivore where there is a year-round supply of fruiting trees and bushes. Seaweed is an important part of the diet of those red deer that live close to sea coasts, and tree bark can be stripped and eaten during winter when food is in short supply. One species, the reindeer, has adapted to the extent that it is able to feed almost exclusively on lichens during those times of the year when little else is available. Alone among large mammals, reindeer produce an enzyme called lichenase which enables them to break lichens down to release glucose.

▼ Chital stag and hind at a waterhole. Water sources are often important habitat features, especially in warmer climes.
Photograph: Brent Huffman

Although meat is not a food source normally sought by deer, it would not be strictly true to say that they never eat it. Many species have been observed feeding on dead animals or the eggs and chicks of ground-nesting birds. Occasionally, deer have even been observed killing and eating small mammals and birds. Reindeer have been reported as regularly killing and eating lemmings, and the water chevrotain regularly eats crabs and insects or scavenges fish and meat. In most cases, though, such unusual additions to a deer's diet probably have more to do with a craving for calcium among male deer as they grow their new antlers; such behaviours have been seen in both sexes, however, and is generally not related to their regular sources of nutrition. Deer will sometimes chew on bones and cast antlers, once again probably for the calcium they contain.

Under normal temperate conditions, dehydration is seldom an issue as deer usually obtain most of the moisture that they need from their foodstuffs: they very seldom drink. In warmer climates, or during times of unusually dry conditions, regular access to a water source is essential of course. Some species will always seek to have such a water source located within their home range, both for drinking and the refuge that it offers in the face of a predator.

Relationships

The deer of today can be broadly divided into those with a tendency towards solitary lifestyles and the more gregarious herding species. Although there are exceptions, as a general rule the solitary deer are smaller-bodied, better adapted to hiding, usually found in close proximity to cover, the males carry less well-developed antlers, and many species (more usually, but not always the males) have retained pronounced tusks for combat with each other. Herding deer, on the other hand, have developed larger bodies, occupy more open habitats, and males have sacrificed their tusks in favour of increasingly complex antlers.

When deer started to evolve some 30 million years ago they were relatively small and largely solitary animals which depended on a year-round availability of easily digestible plant foods. To ensure that they maintained exclusive rights to limited resources they will have been territorial, carrying weapons typified by the tusks we see on many modern deer for use in disputes. They also increasingly used scent to communicate with each other and mark boundaries, and the relatively high proportion of scent glands on smaller deer (such as the modern muntjacs) reflect this. A solitary existence can, of course, make a deer more vulnerable to predation so it will protect itself by secretive strategies, careful movement within cover, saturating an area in scent so as not to leave clearly defined trails for a predator to follow, and powerful muscles in its haunches that provide explosive bursts of energy for flight. These remain the characteristics of many of the small modern deer.

▶ Most of the smaller deer species such as the pudus, muntjacs, brockets, musk deer and chevrotains tend to live alone or in small family groups. Unusually among the larger deer, so too does the Eurasian elk or moose (*pictured*).
Photograph: Makalu

Quite often a territorial animal may accept the presence of a subordinate one provided that it presents no threat to his breeding rights with nearby females. The subordinate may even be allowed to breed, but only if the dominant animal has had the opportunity to mate with receptive females first. It may benefit from sparring practice with the dominant male. Otherwise the solitary deer tend to live in small family groups consisting of a female, her most recent offspring and possibly even the previous one. In nearly all cases, solitude is sought as birthing approaches and any accompanying young animals are driven off – although they may be permitted to rejoin their mother later. Pair bonding between the sexes is usually loose at best.

As deer slowly adapted to living in more open landscapes, social groups tended to develop. Herds have a number of obvious advantages: the more individuals there are within a herd, the more the need to watch for predators is reduced, and as a herd becomes bigger the more opportunities there are for feeding, resting and rumination. Mathematics also work on behalf of the individual as the chances of being targeted reduce when an attack occurs, whilst the milling of a large number of animals may confuse the attacker. Some species, such as the sambar, may even cooperate in defence to deter or rebuff predators.

◄ Although a solitary species for much of the year, roe can form larger associations during the winter. These informal groups do not however possess a true herd structure.
Photograph: Hans Benn

There are, however, downsides to living in a herd. As a large number of mouths deplete food resources more quickly, the animals need to move more often, and in doing so may make themselves more visible. At night a herd will create more noise; and all inevitably have an outer edge where most predator attacks will occur. Being very young, old, sick or injured means that the animal is more likely to fall behind when a large group is pursued and become the target. Herds inevitably favour the fit and healthy, but still tolerate the less able as this makes existence safer for other members while still providing the weaker ones with a degree of security. The more dominant

▼ True herds have a social structure and offer greater protection against predators.
Photograph: Bente Jønsson

▲ (*top*) Red stags in a deer park 'boxing' with their forefeet.

▲ (*above*) Female deer also indulge in 'boxing' to assert dominance; these two are white-tailed does.
Photograph: Elle E Kay

animals in the herd will of course have an advantage in the increased competition for food resources, but all members may be more likely to be exposed to infection by parasites or disease.

It is no accident that the more solitary species have tended to retain their tusks as the main means of aggression between those of their own kind (although not all species, such as the roe deer, have done so). Fighting among deer of the smaller species can often be intense and injuries are common. Within larger social groups this is not helpful to social cohesion and antlers are less likely to produce deep injuries while remaining a visible symbol of physical dominance. They do provide a means of engaging in combat, and wrestling and pushing matches with locked antlers are a common form of competition between rival stags, allowing for trials of strength that will not necessarily result in significant physical injuries.

Antlers also permit male deer to spar, rather than fight seriously, outside the rutting season. This enables them to establish social rankings and can often appear playful; it is frequently an important part of the daily life of the herd. In the one species where females habitually grow antlers, the reindeer, this also allows the smaller females to be competitive at times of food shortage thanks to the differing antler cycles of the sexes. In many species, both sexes may also rear up on their hind legs and 'box' with their forefeet as an alternative form of determining social status; male deer do this at times when antlers are regrowing and sensitive.

Among many of the social species, adult animals live in single sex herds for much of the year and come together only for the rut. Among the males, social cohesion is only possible while testosterone levels remain low; as these rise, intolerance increases as the urge to breed builds and competition intensifies. Female herds are often built around matriarchal units and there is usually a dominant animal who acts as a clearly defined leader.

Communication and competition

On the surface, a herd of deer outside the rut may appear extraordinarily relaxed if undisturbed or unthreatened by the presence of potential predators, but a careful observer will soon start to spot subtle indications of the relationships between individual animals. Body language is important and even female animals will compete for dominance, often biting or 'boxing' with their forefeet to assert themselves. Many herd societies can be strongly matriarchal outside the rut.

Scent has already been covered in the previous chapter, but many species can also be highly vocal, using a series of calls to signal their presence, dominance, breeding condition or to warn of predators. A number of visual signs may also be left, particularly by territorial or more dominant male animals during the rut. Fraying stocks – small trees or bushes rubbed with antlers or stripped with canine teeth – might be used to mark territorial boundaries, or shrubbery thrashed with antlers in a display of strength. Thrashing may also carry an added bonus of leaving antlers festooned with vegetation, enhancing the appearance of the rutting male deer. Wallowing in muddy patches of ground can also augment the appearance of a stag, but in some species both sexes may wallow simply to reduce the effect of biting insects.

◀ Wallowing is an important activity for some of the deer species.
Photograph: Herbert Aust

In the more solitary species, animals can be highly intolerant of each other throughout the year, though in others (such as the roe) aggression can diminish once testosterone levels drop after the rut, so that loose groupings can form to take advantage of better feeding areas and the safety of living in numbers. There is no proper herd structure, though, and a disturbed group is likely to scatter in a number of different directions, whereas a true herd is usually led away by a lead animal if disturbed. Informal groupings soon break up again as testosterone levels start to rise in the spring. In some species, the sexes live apart for much of the year in their own herds and the male groups only break up as the rut approaches and rising testosterone encourages competition.

Fighting among male deer, even at the height of the rut, is usually a last resort as it can lead to injury: even a testosterone-filled animal will usually avoid it unless absolutely necessary. The timbre, volume or frequency of roaring, groaning, barks or other calls are often enough to satisfy a potential competitor that it is outclassed. If two competing males subsequently choose to meet they frequently indulge in parallel walking, which allows them to assess each other. One may simply break off and withdraw rather than take things further. Well-matched animals may, however, decide to take matters to a conclusion by locking antlers and indulging in a trial of strength, the aim being to throw an opponent off balance so that it can be gored with antler tips in the rump and flanks or slashed with sharp canine teeth.

The losing animal in such an encounter is usually quick to flee; those that do not, or find themselves unable to escape for some reason, may suffer serious injuries. Deaths during rutting or territorial competition are not uncommon.

▲ Physical competition between males, such as these chital stags and fallow bucks, is a regular feature of rutting activity among most deer species.
Photographs:
(*above*) Chital fight – Nikhil Kurian
(*right*) Fallow fight – Joe Murphy

Breeding strategies

Most of the deer which occur naturally in the northern temperate zones are strongly seasonal in their behaviour, while further south there is more of a tendency towards aseasonality, with deer more capable of conceiving and birthing at any time of year. Even then, though, peaks in breeding are likely to be influenced by wet and dry seasons. Very few species, if any, can be said to be entirely aseasonal. In some species, the oestrus cycle among females can be strongly synchronised and the male animals then often show a corresponding tendency to shed and regrow their antlers at specific times of year. This ensures that they are fully prepared to compete for breeding rights at such times. None of the deer species pair for life in monogamous relationships; all are polygynous, i.e. males seek to mate with as many females as possible, success usually being achieved by the most dominant.

Many of the larger herding deer species do indeed exhibit behaviours which are designed to secure breeding rights for the strongest and most dominant males. In some, and especially where oestrus cycles are synchronised, a stag might seek to secure a harem of females that he will endeavour to retain for his exclusive access. In others, the more dominant males might establish display areas, often in traditional rutting sites not usually frequented at other times of the year. This activity is known as 'lekking' and is employed by a wide range of other animal species that rely on competitive displays or courtship rituals to entice potential partners. (The term has its origins in the Swedish word *lek*, which means to play or to romp.) For deer, strong reliance is placed on attracting females by the demonstration of dominance through activities such as frequent calling, appearance, heavy scent-marking or physical fighting. Very often the male deer will live apart from the predominantly female herds, either following a more solitary lifestyle or congregating in their own herds, until the rut approaches.

In those herding species where oestrus is less strongly synchronised, male deer are more likely to maintain closer associations with the herd throughout the year and competition may take place for a specific female only when she comes into breeding condition. Sexual maturity is usually linked to achieving a threshold body weight: this usually takes longer to achieve among the larger species, and in many cases a female will come into breeding condition only once a year. In others, such as some of the muntjacs, a doe will come into oestrus very soon after giving birth and mate again almost immediately, thus spending most of her adult life in some stage of pregnancy and producing a fawn every seven months or so. The water deer *Hydropotes inermis*, though a seasonal breeder, can reach sexual maturity very quickly and is capable of taking part in the rut in the same year as her birth, producing her own fawns on her first birthday.

Among many of the more solitary – and usually smaller species – territoriality and physical combat between males can assume great importance. A male deer will attempt to establish as large a territory as possible, trying to overlap with the home ranges of as many females as possible while excluding rival males. Only when the female comes into oestrus will closer contact be initiated, and once mating has been accomplished the male will usually show little interest in remaining with his partner and instead seek to mate with any other receptive female in the vicinity.

That is not to say that rutting is entirely driven by the actions of male deer; the females of some species have clear opportunity to make a choice of the most impressive male on a lekking site. In some cases the female will not permit mating to take place until she is ready and can lead the male in a courtship chase that might go on for some time. Often she will also choose the place in which mating occurs.

Gestation periods vary widely between the species but are usually between 180 and 240 days. Smaller species, such as the water deer, usually have shorter gestations, while larger ones such as moose or red deer may continue for much longer. This trend is not universal, though, and some of the muntjacs may gestate for as much as 210 days. For some deer species we still have much to learn about the actual length of gestation, as well as other aspects of their lifestyles.

Just one deer group employs a reproductive strategy which allows it to rut during the temperate summer yet delay the birth of its young until the more favourable environmental conditions of the following spring, and that is the roe deer. Although their rut usually takes place during July or August, the fertilised egg floats free within the uterus but remains dormant and does not implant into the uterus wall and start developing until the following December. From this point on, gestation progresses normally and the kids are born in May or June, around ten months after mating took place. This is known as 'delayed implantation' or 'the embryonic diapause'. Among all of the Artiodactyla, roe deer are the only species to exhibit this phenomenon, although around 100 other animals across a number of other orders, including some bears, mustelids, armadillos and marsupials, also do so.

Birthing strategies

Most deer tend to give birth to just one young at a time. Notable exceptions are the moose, white-tailed deer, mule deer and roe deer, for which twins are common and one species, the water deer, habitually gives birth to more. Among the other species, twins may occasionally be encountered although the casual onlooker may be deceived by the sight of a female deer permitting another's offspring to suckle.

▼ Some herding species may form 'creches' where multiple young are supervised by only a few of their mothers while the others feed elsewhere. This sika hind is tolerating suckling by a number of calves that are not her own.

Although multiple births might at first sight seem a better strategy for any species preyed upon by others, deer give birth above ground rather than in the security of nests or burrows which offer a degree of security to helpless young. Instead, deer young develop to the degree that they are born fully formed, with eyes open and a full protective covering of fur, and are capable of standing and running with the mother a short time after birth. For the first few days of life, though, the newly born deer is largely defenceless: while its mother feeds, of necessity leaving it alone, the youngster must rely for its safety on immobility and a lack of scent that might otherwise give its presence away to predators. Inconspicuous colouring also helps; most, but certainly not all, young deer have dappled coats, which help them to blend in with their surroundings.

◄ Newly born deer rely on immobility and a lack of scent for protection during their first days of life.
Photograph: Sascha Händle

Where the mother is normally a herd animal, she will usually seek solitude to give birth, rejoining the rest with her young only when it is strong enough to do so. Some of the herding open-ground deer, such as the reindeer, closely synchronise their birthing periods as a defence against predation. With a large number of animals giving birth at the same time, a relatively small area of ground is swamped with calves which, although easy prey, are present in such numbers that only a fraction can be potentially lost. Sacrificing a few ensures that the remainder have the opportunity to gain mobility and grow.

The newborn deer is very dependent on colostrum, which is produced by the mother for some days after giving birth. Colostrum has a high content of antibodies which enhance the immune system and help to protect the calf from disease. Thereafter normal milk is produced, a rich and nutritious substance. A red deer's milk, for example, is considered to contain almost twice the butterfat and three times the protein content of that of a Jersey cow. Unsurprisingly, the calf grows quickly.

Weaning ages vary between species. The fawns of smaller species may be weaned by as soon as two months of age while in contrast the calves of larger ones can still be taking milk from their mothers more than seven months after birth. Where females miss a year from breeding, lactation may carry on for considerably longer.

▲ Newly born deer rely on immobility and a lack of scent for protection during their first days of life.
Photograph: Sascha Händle

Weaning in itself is not a measure of independence, though, and it is difficult to be truly specific about when a young deer becomes entirely independent of its mother. This depends on a number of factors including local circumstances, the species and the actual development of the individual itself. Just as a human child cannot be considered independent simply because it has been weaned at, say, a year old, neither can the young deer. It is just as reliant as the child is for guidance and the formative education received from its mother. Although the weaned deer may be capable of surviving on its own, the longer it stays with its dam the better will be its development and chances of survival. In many species, as noted earlier, the young may remain with their mother until the time to give birth to her next calf approaches when they are physically driven off; even then, they might rejoin her afterwards to form a matriarchal social group.

Some of the smaller species are fully independent and may even be capable of breeding by the time that they are six months old, but among several of the larger herding types the young might remain with their mothers and exhibit a degree of dependency until they are as much as two years old. It may take some of those larger species several years to attain adult weights; the ability to breed or to develop antlers is linked to reaching a threshold body weight which enables sexual maturity or the development of pedicles from which antlers will grow.

Natality and mortality

Natality generally refers to the birth-rate within a population, or to be more specific the ratio between births and overall numbers. Two of the main factors affecting it are the species involved and the physical condition of individual animals, although others such as age can play a part. In most cases, though, natality and condition go hand-in-hand.

Over-population can have a profound effect on natality. In places where a deer population is too great for the natural resources available to it, reproductive outputs may be reduced by postponing breeding until female animals are older, either by avoiding breeding every year, or by a reduction in multiple births among species (such as roe or water deer) where they are often common. Under such circumstances, fawn or kid survival rates are also likely to be reduced. Stress from any number of other causes may play a part and have a significant effect on a deer's ability to breed. Some observers have noted, for instance, that deer populations subject to artificial constraints may exhibit less breeding success than those that are not.

Natality will vary considerably according to species. Those that produce just a single offspring are more likely to ensure that it is larger and better equipped to face the first few days of life when it is most vulnerable to weather conditions and predators. The condition of the mother animal is also vitally important; if she has gone through her pregnancy under relatively clement conditions and with good feeding available, her body is better able to nurture her young both before and after birth. If she is in poor condition throughout the process, she will be more likely to bear an underweight calf and equally be ill-equipped to suckle it successfully.

The male-to-female ratio within a population has little effect on mortality except under the most extreme circumstances. As we have seen, within the herding species, it is only a small number of more dominant males that mate with receptive females, whilst among the more solitary species, a male deer will seek to cover as many females as he can. For this reason a larger territory is advantageous to him, as it is more likely to overlap with the home ranges of a greater number of females. In many cases a receptive female will actively seek out a buck during the time she is in oestrus.

Mortality is a term reflecting the factors that cause deaths within a given population of deer. Under ideal conditions for survival, a deer that succeeds in living into old age eventually falls victim to its teeth wearing down to a point where it cannot grind down its food sufficiently for effective rumination to take place, and death from malnutrition results. Before that takes place, however, natural mortality can result from a variety of factors that might include predation, severe weather conditions, excessive parasite infestation or disease.

In those places where natural predators exist in sufficient numbers, these too may become a major cause of mortality. Any deer, be it young and inexperienced or debilitated for some reason, becomes easy prey in a process of natural selection. Indeed, in some studies in Indian national parks, almost all deer mortality has been attributed to predation by tigers and leopards. Where there are few or no natural predators, man may have to take their place in reducing numbers so that they remain in balance with the supporting environment. In some instances feral dogs kill a high number of deer, and the young of all species are highly vulnerable to predation by small carnivores, birds of prey or reptiles during the first few days of life.

Deer living under more extreme upland conditions can of course be vulnerable to severe weather condidtions and poor feeding. Spring mortality can be high if the already weakened animals are then subjected to heavy rain and chilling winds. Hard weather is also likely to have a disproportionate effect on young deer entering their first winter: not being fully grown, they will have put nutritional resources into bodily development rather than laying down fat reserves which they might be able to call upon.

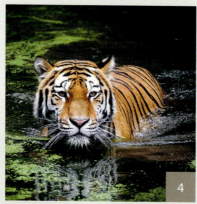

▲ Deer represent an important prey item for many natural predators worldwide. Some significant ones include the wolf, leopard, culpeo fox, tiger, bear, lynx and cougar.
Photographs: 1. Marcel Langthim, 2. Author, 3. Andres Puiggros V, 4. Andreas Breitling, 5. jdaypix, 6. Jo Stolp, 7. strichpunkt

▶ Smaller predators, such as this fox, can be a serious threat to young or weakened animals.
Photograph: 8. hrw1973 (Pixabay)

Weather and associated factors apart, the causes of mortality among younger deer during their first months of life may be due to parental rejection, accident, predation or dehydration; in very dry conditions, the mother may simply become incapable of producing sufficient milk to suckle. Some studies of Scottish red deer have suggested that one-fifth of calves born in June might not survive beyond September, and that the majority of mortalities occur within a week of birth. A further 11 percent of the calf population might not survive the following winter.

Mortality during the first year of life tends to be roughly equal between male and female animals, despite the males of many species having an initial advantage in higher average birth weights and suckling rates. Thereafter, however, the life expectancy of male deer tends to be shorter. This is generally attributable to the extra stresses placed upon them by the drive to hold and maintain territory and during rutting activity. Furthermore, fighting between male deer can often result in serious injury or even death. Such factors, often associated with a tendency among some species for the males virtually to stop eating during the rut, means that they may then enter the winter months in a weakened and more susceptible condition.

Free-roaming wild deer are generally very resistant to disease under normal circumstances. Where they exist in heavy concentrations, there can be an increase in disease and parasitic infection. Lung worm and liver fluke are two of the parasites particularly associated with conditions of over-population.

Finally, accidents cannot be discounted as an important cause of deer mortality, especially close to areas of high human population or activity, and traffic collisions can be a significant cause of death or injury. Deer are also deliberately hunted for their meat, and where this is unregulated it can have a serious impact on deer numbers.

Photograph: Alexandr Podvalny

4 Deer and Man

Deer and Man

Impacts

The relationship between deer and man can be a troubled one, but this has not always been so. Ever since prehistoric times, these animals have provided a source of food, while their skins and other body parts have been used for clothing, shelter and a wide variety of other vital functions. Antlers have been variously employed as digging implements or weapons, or been given ceremonial or mystical roles. In return, the hunters learned not to over-exploit such a precious and renewable resource, so important then to human survival. In some regions of the world the relationship has continued and even today many indigenous peoples rely on wild deer as a resource. Others take the connection yet further and herd reindeer, in some cases living among and even migrating with them.

Sadly, as the human race has become more sophisticated and developed different priorities, the deer, like so many other animals and plants, have suffered as their habitats have been taken over or destroyed completely. One of the more extreme examples of this is the demise of the Schomburgk's deer, once abundant in parts of southeast Asia. The species went into decline in the face of intensive rice farming and by the 1930s had become extinct: insensitive levels of hunting eventually sealed its fate. In other cases, long-standing defences against human intrusion were eradicated by scientific advances. A case in point is the barasingha, that once roamed over vast areas of India and its neighbouring regions, and was initially protected against human incursions by malarial conditions. Then modern technology and medicines gradually made its habitat more accessible to humans and as a result its range has shrunk to just a few isolated pockets of the wetland still available. A glance at the fact boxes for each of the individual species, later in the book, will quickly reveal regularly repeated themes: agriculture, land clearance, settlement, commercial development and diseases spread by domestic stock all threaten deer in many of the places where they occur worldwide.

Competition is, of course, a two-way flow, and deer have not been slow to recognise the feeding opportunities that cultivated fields and plantations offer, or seek to use forestry where their fraying and bark-stripping reduces the value of timber crops. In those parts of the world where natural predators have been reduced in number or eradicated, often themselves perceived as a threat to humans, the situation is exacerbated as deer numbers are permitted to rise to levels where the damage they cause is considered unacceptable. When out of balance with the available habitat, deer can not only cause financial loss but also wider levels of environmental damage that have an impact on other wildlife. In many countries, collisions with motor vehicles are a major concern as well (in the UK alone there are estimated to be some 76,000 such collisions every year). Ultimately, too many deer can even create problems within their own populations.

4 | DEER AND MAN

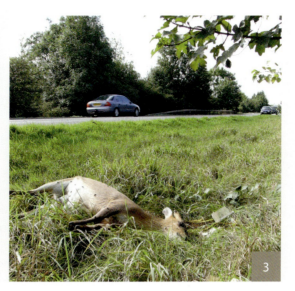

◂ In many parts of the world collisions between deer and motor vehicles are a serious concern.
Photographs: 1. Gorat Horvat, 2. Leonardo Marchini, 3. Author

Poaching and hunting

Deer have always been hunted by man as a means of personal subsistence, although the practice has declined as the world has developed. It still continues in some regions today, though this tends to occur where areas are remote and less developed. Deer are, however, still killed for other reasons and in far too many cases the death-rate is unsustainable.

◂ Deer are widely farmed as a source of venison in many parts of the world.

Poaching is a major contributing factor in the decline of a great many species of deer, and even where protected areas and strict legislation exist, both are frequently ignored in the absence of effective enforcement. Much poaching activity goes well beyond personal subsistence needs; in many parts of the world there is a thriving market for 'bush meat', skins and other body parts and the financial rewards can be high. In some cases, such as the musk deer in which the mature male produces the highly valuable musk 'pod', only the desired parts of the deer are taken: the rest of the carcase may be left to rot, along with the bodies of females and immature animals which, although not producing musk, are also killed.

The tools of the poacher include modern rifles and shotguns, home-made firearms, dogs and spotlights, but it is the snare that is the most widely used. Easily made from cheap and readily available materials, the snare is indiscriminate about what it catches and, once set, needs only to be checked at intervals, at minimal risk of discovery to the poacher. Of all the methods of illegally killing deer, it is probably the most indiscriminate and inhumane.

Poachers often operate in well-organised and equipped gangs, possessing good local knowledge and often employing diversionary tactics to distract the authorities from the area that they are targeting. Little thought is given to food hygiene or public safety, let alone the welfare of the deer concerned, and it matters not to the poacher that an animal may be out of season, has a dependent fawn, or whether or not it is killed quickly. Poaching can do immeasurable harm to the best-laid conservation efforts.

While legal hunting for subsistence or sport may at times attract controversy, it is at least sanctioned and usually conducted within a sustainable framework. In addition, scientific research has recognised the positive contribution it can make towards both habitats and species. Furthermore, the income from licensed sport hunters frequently supports conservation work. The dramatic recovery of some of the North American deer species, which appeared to be threatened by terminal decline by the late nineteenth century, was enabled by the introduction of legal hunting seasons and tag systems. Eventually these ensured that funding became available for the establishment of wildlife agencies.

Importantly, legal hunting often attaches value, resulting in associated vested interests encouraging the continued presence of a species whose habitat might otherwise be given over to other more lucrative uses by either landowners or occupiers.

Management

Sometimes deer populations grow to exceed the carrying capacity of their habitat. This is often the case where there are insufficient natural controls, such as predators, that work to keep numbers in check. The consequence can be unacceptable levels of agricultural or forestry damage, rising levels of road traffic accidents involving deer, degradation of the natural environment and a build-up of stresses within the deer population itself. Despite global declines in some species, there are places where others are thriving. In the UK, fallow and roe deer alone are considered to have greatly multiplied in their number since the 1970s, with the introduced Reeves' muntjac and sika faring even better. Under circumstances such as these, a structured management policy may become necessary to ensure that deer numbers do not exceed the carrying capacity of the habitat available, to prevent the possibility of starvation, disease, and unacceptable damage levels.

▶ Regulated hunting is often combined with planned management to ensure that deer numbers are sustainable and kept in balance with the available habitat.

Managing deer impacts may involve no more than excluding them from sensitive areas or deterring them from visiting these, but this tends only to shift any problems elsewhere. In the longer term there may be no option other than to actively reduce numbers. Where this is necessary, it should be conducted as humanely as possible and within a plan which aims to maintain a structured herd composition. The venison produced is, as a sustainable natural resource, usually passed into the human food chain with all due regard to food hygiene. Nevertheless there can be opposition to the killing of deer and alternative methods of reducing their numbers are sometimes urged.

Contraception is regularly raised as a humane alternative to killing deer where numbers have become excessive or are in danger of becoming so. Methods involving steroidal ovarian hormones (oestrogen and progesterone), which suppress ovulation, can have harmful effects on the environment, the natural food chain and the natural behaviour and biology of the deer themselves. As a result, the alternative developed for use with animals works differently, using the animal's immune system to render it temporarily infertile, hence the term *immunocontraception*. This method has already been used successfully to control numbers of horses and deer in North America, and elephants in Africa, with very few side-effects noted.

However, treatment needs to be conducted regularly to be effective and it is here that problems arise. The trials on American white-tailed deer, while successful, were mainly conducted on captive populations where each animal could be identified individually and easily captured for an injection to be administered. Wild deer obviously cannot be handled and so have to be darted to avoid causing panic and the possibility of animals damaging themselves. The darting systems currently available are generally only effective at impractically short ranges, and there is no way of confirming that a vaccine has been successfully delivered. In addition the animals have to be recognisable as individuals to ensure that the right ones are given the appropriate treatment.

Where immunocontraception has been used on populations of deer, it has taken several years for the population growth to slow down and wildlife biologists currently advise that population reduction can only be achieved by culling or live removal. Although research continues and there are hopes that a more practical solution may eventually become available, at the time of writing in 2022 this still seems some way off. There are already concerns that the expense involved will not be practical or justifiable in most cases.

One alternative to contraception is the sterilisation of male deer. This technique has been used to reduce numbers of white-tailed deer on New York's Staten Island since 2016, in the face of environmental damage, traffic collisions, and a perceived connection between deer numbers and the incidence of Lyme disease. The cost of the first five years of the programme has been some $6.6 million and although numbers have been reduced, they remain high. Critics are already emphasising the rising cost of the continuing project and point out that as long as fertile bucks remain at large, the deer population will continue to breed. Despite an initial reluctance to cull the numbers, the appetite for non-lethal control appears to have decreased as the costs have risen.

Transplantation

Thanks to human intervention, deer have been introduced to many places where they were not previously found. There are various motivations behind this; captive deer have long been an important food resource, later becoming a status symbol and in many places deer parks and other collections were established from which escapes inevitably occurred. There have also been deliberate releases into the wild. The introduction of non-native species of flora and fauna around the world really gained momentum during the mid-nineteenth century, when colonists simply missed seeing familiar animals from their home countries, while others wanted to 'improve' the local wildlife or to hunt for sport.

▶ Fallow deer are one of the most widely transplanted of all the deer species. Originating in the Mediterranean region, they can now be encountered across Europe and as far afield as the Americas, South Africa and New Zealand.

In the United Kingdom alone, four of the six wild deer species are non-native. The fallow may have first arrived in the country during Roman times, but muntjac, Chinese water deer and sika are relative newcomers introduced by the Victorians. There might even have been others, though attempts to introduce species such as the Siberian roe, white-tailed and musk deer were short-lived.

Elsewhere, New Zealand alone has gained seven species since the nineteenth century which still flourish there today, although others (such as the moose) failed to establish successfully. The new arrivals, in a country where the only naturally occurring mammals were bats, had an overwhelming impact on the available vegetation and the native birds and other fauna which depended on it. Axis deer, native to India, were released on the Hawaiian island of Maui with similarly negative consequences, and there are further examples of deer introductions elsewhere in the world which have resulted in established populations.

Domesticated deer

While reindeer, the only deer considered to have been widely domesticated, have long been used by certain indigenous peoples to be ridden, pull sledges and carry light packs, other deer species have also been successfully trained for similar purposes.

▲ Domesticated reindeer awaiting transport by sea in Norway.
Photograph: Harry Lund

The European elk, surprisingly, seems to have received the most attention in this respect. Swedish records going back to the seventeenth century suggest that elk were regularly trained to accept a harness and pull sleds. More recent studies, predominantly in Russia, suggest that provided a wild elk calf could be captured within three days of birth, it could be raised to be passive and more easily trained. Once the calf had reached two weeks old, training was much more difficult. Only the calmest animals captured would be selected; they would eventually be employed as pack animals and for pulling carts. Having stronger physiques than smaller deer, which could not easily bear the weight of a human, they have even been trained to the saddle and ridden.

Red deer have also been trained to the harness. The eccentric third Earl of Orford frequently drove a phaeton carriage around eighteenth-century Norfolk pulled by four stags and there are more recent records of similar accomplishments in the USA with wapiti. In the USA, in the nineteenth century a Maine gentleman successfully trained two moose to pull a sleigh. Although the animals were regarded as particularly steady and tractable, it was noted at the time that 'once they took it into their heads to cool themselves in a neighbouring river or lake, no efforts could prevent them'.

▲ Reindeer are the only deer widely trained as beasts of burden.
Photograph: Wikilmages

▶ A reindeer trained to the sled in Lapland.
Photograph: Pixabay

Deer as pets

The close proximity of humans is normally terrifying to a wild deer. Nevertheless, deer occasionally feature as pets, very often as a result of having been found 'abandoned' as fawns and mistakenly taken in by well-meaning people. Usually this is a grave error that will cost the young deer its life; without specialist knowledge they can be very difficult to rear successfully and a great many die. It is always best to leave the young animal untouched and where it is, as its mother is usually not far away. If the location is revisited a few hours later she will almost invariably have returned and moved her young elsewhere.

4 | DEER AND MAN

◀ Deer seldom make suitable pets: a Formosan sika calf in Taiwan.
Photograph: Tony Wu

Although a hand-reared female deer can become very tame and docile (some are occasionally encountered in 'petting zoos'), it can never be entirely trusted. Although they do not have antlers, female deer are capable of delivering a potentially serious blow with their forefeet if alarmed or put under stress. Male deer, once they have lost their fear of man, can be extremely dangerous and there have been reports of humans who get too close to them being injured or even killed. The hand-reared roebuck has a particular reputation for unexpected ferocity, especially as he matures and starts to become territorial; it is no accident that roe are seldom featured in zoos and collections.

Apart from reindeer and a few notable exceptions among other species, deer have never really been domesticated. Generally speaking they do not respond well to being kept in close captivity, although some herding species exist happily in parks where they are given the space they need along with the security of others of their kind. The smaller, more solitary species are more likely to be nervous and skittish. The best place for any deer is in the wild and as such they are not recommended as pets; if they must be kept in captivity, it is always best to leave their care to the specialists.

Feeding deer

Deer are great opportunists and can quickly learn to overcome a natural fear of man in return for an easy mouthful or two. Regrettably, feeding deer and other wild animals can encourage an unhealthy dependency as well as having other potential consequences. Deer, even those kept in parks, will usually find all that they need naturally and if there is a requirement for any specialist supplementary feed this will be provided by the park keepers. Where supplementary feeding of wild deer does become necessary, for instance at times of unusually hard weather, it is important to recognise that a deer's digestive system can take some time to adapt to any new dietary item, and unusual foodstuffs, especially processed foods, may be positively harmful. Artificial feeding should never be undertaken lightly, though exceptional circumstances may justify it. If a deer population is in tune with its environment it is unlikely that this will be necessary, or desirable, under normal circumstances.

▶ Although deer in captivity, and even sometimes wild ones, may accept food from humans, bread and other processed items may be harmful.
Photograph: follower2h

Householders who still wish to leave an occasional treat out for deer will find that the animals may accept any number of raw vegetables, although offerings may be ignored completely. Brassicas, such as cabbage or sprouts, and field and green beans can be popular, and chopped carrots or potatoes have also been used to attract them. In the wild, most deer will take fruits and fungi in season, so mushrooms, shelled nuts and chopped apples or other fruit would probably tempt them. Some might even enjoy a mineral lick. As deer do not have upper incisor teeth, they may have difficulty dealing with larger, hard items such as whole root crops or apples, so such offerings will need to be chopped into slices or smaller pieces.

▼ In many places deer, such as this European roe, are regular visitors to urban gardens and often learn to live in close proximity to built-up area.
Photograph: Reinhold Bonefas

Hay is of little nutritional value to some of the smaller species which are most usually seen in gardens, as it is too coarse for their small digestive systems. Bread, as noted, other processed items or table leftovers should definitely be avoided. Uneaten food should be cleared away before it rots, and consideration given to neighbours. While many people are charmed to have deer visiting their gardens regularly, others may not be so pleased to see prized plants or vegetable patches being browsed.

All deer, and even those accustomed to humans, are essentially wild animals: but there have been instances when they have been encouraged to develop unnatural levels of assertiveness when learning to accept food from human hands, usually in parks and other collections. Deer under any circumstances can still be nervous animals and a sudden fright can cause them to lash out. It only takes a slight movement of a stag's head for accidental injury to be inflicted on someone standing close by. In addition, a deer's hooves are very sharp as they can be used in self-defence. During the birthing season, female deer can be highly defensive of newborn young if they believe there is a threat, while later in the year, during the annual rut, raised levels of testosterone among the stags can also enhance the risk to unwary members of the public.

No matter how tame they may appear, deer should not be approached closely, nor should they be fed by hand or encouraged to eat any material that is not part of their natural diet.

Zoonoses

A disease which can pass between vertebrate animals and humans is termed a *zoonosis*. A zoonotic pathogen can be viral, parasitic or bacterial. Although deer can carry some diseases which also affect humans, it is very rare indeed for them to be passed on.

Some examples include Avian influenza (bird flu), Ebola haemorrhagic fever (of primarily African concern, and connected largely with fruit bats and monkeys), and rabies, probably the most feared of the zoonoses across much of the world. The Covid-19 outbreak that swept the world in 2020 is also widely considered to be zoonotic. None of these, however, are especially associated with deer. One zoonotic disease that can affect deer, though, is bovine tuberculosis, although the chance of it being passed between deer and humans is considered to be very slight. Another major zoonosis associated with deer is anthrax, unrecorded among them in the UK but present on the Continent, in Africa and in the Americas.

A major observation of zoonoses worth stressing is that they usually need really close contact between humans and animals if they are to be transmitted. For example, in the case of bird flu, recorded human cases have all occurred in instances where poultry owners have shared their living areas with the diseased birds, a common practice in some parts of the world. Many Western outbreaks of zoonotic diseases have been traced back to fairs or 'petting zoos' where the public have come into uncontrolled close contact with animals. In practical terms, the chances of catching a transferable disease from deer are very low indeed, although anyone handling them should always take sensible precautions.

One disease that all countryside visitors should be aware of is Lyme disease. This affects both deer and humans but is not strictly zoonotic, being passed on by ticks. It was first diagnosed in the USA but is increasingly seen elsewhere, including in the

UK. There is increasing evidence that although deer do act as hosts for ticks, they are not significant vectors of Lyme disease. An awareness of its symptoms among those who might come into contact with ticks carrying it is important. A rash expanding outwards from the bite area, or flu-like symptoms developing within two weeks of being bitten, should prompt a medical check-up as a precaution. The risk of infection is greatly reduced by removing the tick within 24 hours of attachment, while taking care not to squeeze it in any way during the process.

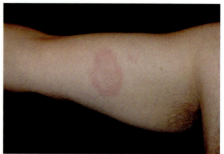

▶ Ticks embedded in the groin region of a deer, and the characteristic 'bullseye' rash (not always experienced) of a person infected with Lyme disease.
Photographs: (*left*) Author, (*right*) Lyme Disease Action

Aggression towards humans

It is extremely rare for deer to show aggression towards humans, and when this happens there is usually a very good underlying reason. Most cases occur when an animal, through hand-rearing or living under park or farm conditions, has lost its natural fear of man. The rut is a special time to be wary of such captive deer; not only can a dominant stag be protective of his harem, but lesser animals charged with testosterone can be frustrated and intolerant of any approach. Visitors to parks who are unfamiliar with deer behaviour can unwittingly put themselves in positions of great danger. One unfortunate fatality involved a jogger who ran between two parallel-walking red stags at the very instant when they turned to lock antlers.

▶ A rutting red deer stag in a deer park showing signs of potential aggression; such an animal should not be approached.
Photograph: Peter Green

Roe bucks are notorious for aggressive behaviour, especially if they have been hand-reared before being released into the wild. In one instance, a postman cycling down a quiet country lane was charged by a roebuck which knocked him off his bicycle and continued to attack him when he was on the ground, resulting in a number of serious injuries. This incident was put down to a totally wild but territorial animal which had just put a rival to flight and was still in a pugnacious frame of mind when the postman appeared in his territory. Similar incidents, whilst unusual, have been recorded elsewhere.

Trapped deer may panic and inadvertently injure anyone who gets in their way. Beaters on pheasant shoots are occasionally injured by fleeing deer, and in 2013 a British woman was accidentally gored by a red stag which, trapped in a fenced garden, hit her with an antler tine as it escaped through the only gap available to it. Deer can, of course, defend themselves if the flight option is not available. Hunted stags, held at bay by hounds, have been known to attack the huntsman as he approached to despatch them. Injured muntjac bucks can do considerable damage with their canine tusks to those seeking to rescue them, whilst wounded sika have a special reputation for ferocity.

Photograph: Alexander F Meyer

5 THE INTERNATIONAL UNION FOR CONSERVATION OF NATURE (IUCN)

The International Union for Conservation of Nature (IUCN)

Background

The IUCN was established in 1948 as an international organisation which comprises over 1,200 government and non-government members. It promotes nature conservation and the sustainable use of the world's natural resources through a process of field work, data collection and analysis, lobbying and public education.

The Red List

Created in 1964, the IUCN Red List of Threatened Species (usually known simply as the Red List) provides the conservation status of animal and plant species around the world. The Red List is considered to provide the most authoritative information available regarding the status of biological diversity and is a leading and trusted guide for all concerned with conservation efforts. (It can be accessed on the internet at **www.iucnredlist.org**)

The expression 'red-listed' is often used casually to suggest that a particular species is seriously at risk, though in reality this is not necessarily the case. For each species, IUCN undertakes a proper analysis, using multiple criteria including population sizes, fluctuations and distribution, numbers of mature individuals, declines, and available habitats to determine the risk of a species becoming extinct. Assessments are normally carried out every five to ten years, and provide science-based information for conservation, government and wider public use.

Red List categories currently given for all the relevant deer species are included throughout this book. These are:

Not evaluated	Has not been evaluated against Red List criteria.
Data deficient	Not enough data is available to evaluate a species' risk of extinction.
Least concern	Analysis has been completed but the species does not qualify for any other category. Considered to be at lowest risk and does not qualify for a higher at-risk category.
Near threatened	Not currently at risk but may become so in future evaluations. There has probably been a reduction in population size, or the species may be dependent on conservation efforts without which the species may face a risk of extinction.
Vulnerable	Will probably probably become endangered in the near future due to identified threats (such as habitat loss). Conservation measures are required to preserve habitat and increase populations to take the species out of this category.
Endangered	Likely to become extinct
Critically endangered	At very high risk of becoming extinct in the near future. This is the most critical category for living animal and plant species. Within this category, a species may be labelled as 'possibly extinct' or 'possibly extinct in the wild'.
Extinct in the wild	Does not exist in the wild or in its historic habitat, with the only known specimens being in captivity or living in a non-native habitat. Attempts may be in progress to reintroduce these species into the wild.
Extinct	No living specimens are known to exist.

5 | THE INTERNATIONAL UNION FOR CONSERVATION OF NATURE (IUCN)

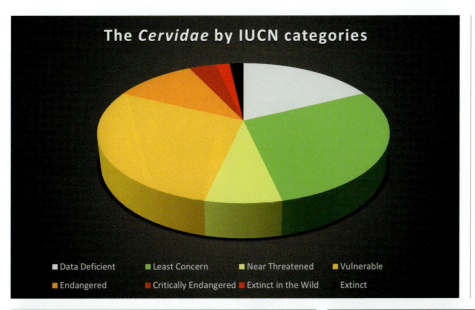

Breakdown of the IUCN conservation categories of known world deer species (2022).

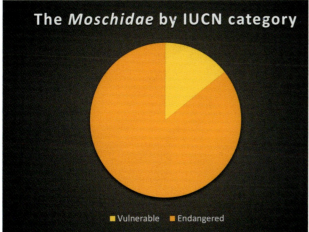

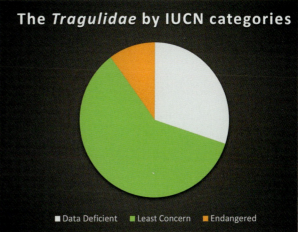

World deer by IUCN classification			
	Cervidae	*Moschidae*	*Tragulidae*
Data deficient	10		3
Least concern	16		6
Near threatened	4		
Vulnerable	16	1	
Endangered	6	6	1
Critically endangered	2		
Extinct in the wild	1		
Extinct	1		

Photograph: Pexels

6 List of Species

List of Deer Species

ORDER	Artiodactyla
SUBORDER	Ruminantia
INFRAORDER	Pecora
FAMILY	Cervidae
SUBFAMILY	Capreolinae

Common name	Scientific name	Page
Elk/moose	*Alces alces*	80
Marsh deer	*Blastocerus dichotomus*	86
European roe deer	*Capreolus capreolus*	90
Siberian roe deer	*Capreolus pygargus*	95
Taruca	*Hippocamelus antisensis*	98
Patagonian huemul	*Hippocamelus bisulcus*	101
Water deer	*Hydropotes inermis*	105
Red brocket	*Mazama americana*	109
Grey brocket	*Mazama gouazoubira*	112
Amazonian brown brocket	*Mazama nemorivaga*	114
Bororo, small red brocket	*Mazama bororo*	117
Mérida brocket	*Mazama bricenii*	118
Dwarf brocket	*Mazama chunyi*	119
Lesser brocket	*Mazama nana*	120
Yucatan brown brocket	*Mazama pandora*	121
Little red brocket	*Mazama rufina*	122
Mexican red brocket	*Mazama temama*	122
Mule deer	*Odocoileus hemionus*	123
White-tailed deer	*Odocoileus virginianus*	128
Pampas deer	*Ozotoceros bezoarticus*	134
Northern pudu	*Pudu mephistophiles*	137
Southern pudu	*Pudu puda*	140
Caribou, reindeer	*Rangifer tarandus*	144

ORDER	Artiodactyla
SUBORDER	Ruminantia
INFRAORDER	Pecora
FAMILY	Cervidae
SUBFAMILY	Cervinae

Common name	Scientific name	Page
Chital	*Axis axis*	152
Calamian deer	*Axis calamianensis*	157
Bawean deer	*Axis kuhlii*	160
Hog deer	*Axis porcinus*	163
White-lipped deer	*Cervus albirostris*	168
Wapiti, American elk	*Cervus canadensis*	172
Red deer	*Cervus elaphus*	178
Tarim red deer	*Cervus hanglu*	184
Sika	*Cervus nippon*	188
Fallow deer	*Dama dama*	195
Persian fallow deer	*Dama mesopotamica*	200
Tufted deer	*Elaphodus cephalophus*	204
Pere David's deer	*Elaphurus davidianus*	208
Bornean yellow muntjac	*Muntiacus atherodes*	211
Black muntjac	*Muntiacus crinifrons*	214
Fea's muntjac	*Muntiacus feae*	217
Southern red muntjac	*Muntiacus muntjak*	220
Leaf muntjac	*Muntiacus putaoensis*	223
Reeves' muntjac	*Muntiacus reevesi*	226
Gongshan muntjac	*Muntiacus gongshanensis*	240
Sumatran muntjac	*Muntiacus montanus*	245
Puhoat muntjac	*Muntiacus puhoatensis*	244
Roosevelts' muntjac	*Muntiacus rooseveltorum*	242
Annamite muntjac	*Muntiacus truongsonensis*	244
Northern red muntjac	*Muntiacus vaginalis*	231
Giant muntjac	*Muntiacus vuquangensis*	236
Barasingha	*Rucervus duvaucelii*	246
Eld's deer	*Rucervus eldii*	251
Schomburgk's deer	*Rucervus schomburgki*	256
Visayan spotted deer	*Rusa alfredi*	258
Philippine sambar	*Rusa marianna*	262
Javan deer	*Rusa timorensis*	265
Sambar	*Rusa unicolor*	269

Photograph: Klaus Rudloff

6 | LIST OF DEER SPECIES

ORDER	Artiodactyla
SUBORDER	Ruminantia
INFRAORDER	Pecora
FAMILY	Moschidae

		Page
Anhui musk deer	*Moschus anhuiensis*	274
Forest musk deer	*Moschus berezovskii*	278
Alpine musk deer	*Moschus chrysogaster*	279
Kashmir musk deer	*Moschus cupreus*	280
Black musk deer	*Moschus fuscus*	281
Himalayan musk deer	*Moschus leucogaster*	282
Siberian musk deer	*Moschus moschiferus*	283

ORDER	Artiodactyla
SUBORDER	Ruminantia
INFRAORDER	Tragulina
FAMILY	Tragulidae
SUBFAMILY	Hyemoschus

		Page
Water chevrotain	*Hyemoschus aquaticus*	285

SUBFAMILY	Moschiola

		Page
Indian spotted chevrotain	*Moschiola indica*	288
Sri Lankan spotted chevrotain	*Moschiola meminna*	289
Yellow-striped chevrotain	*Moschiola kathygre*	289

SUBFAMILY	Tragulus

		Page
Javan chevrotain	*Tragulus javanicus*	290
Lesser Oriental chevrotain	*Tragulus kanchil*	291
Greater Oriental chevrotain	*Tragulus napu*	292
Balabac mouse deer	*Tragulus nigricans*	294
Silver-backed chevrotain	*Tragulus versicolor*	295
Williamson's chevrotain	*Tragulus williamsoni*	293

Distribution Map colour key

The distribution maps for each species are based on those available from the IUCN at the time of writing (2022) but may be subject to change. The colour keys used are as follows:

- Extant (resident)
- Extant and introduced (resident)
- Extant and origin uncertain (resident)
- Possibly extant (resident)
- Extant and reintroduced (resident)
- Possibly extinct
- Presence uncertain
- Extinct

Photograph: Alexander F Meyer

A GUIDE TO THE DEER OF THE WORLD

Alces alces

Moose or Eurasian Elk

ORDER	Artiodactyla
SUBORDER	Ruminantia
INFRAORDER	Pecora
FAMILY	Cervidae
SUBFAMILY	Capreolinae

▲ Mature bull.
Photograph: Pixabay

SOMEWHAT CONFUSINGLY THIS species, the largest of all the deer by a very generous margin, is widely known by two names. In the Old World it is called the elk, while in the North American English of the New World it is known as the moose. (Identifying the animal is further complicated by the fact that the alternative name of the American wapiti *Cervus canadensis* is itself known as 'elk' in its native land.) The North American name is taken from the native Proto-Algonquian *môswa* and has been loosely translated as 'chewer of twigs'. Early Dutch settlers also used their name for the elk, *eland*, for the largest of the antelopes they encountered in South Africa.

▶ (*left*) A bull clearly showing the dewlap or 'bell'.
Photograph: Mike Goad

▶ (*right*) Portrait of a mature American moose cow in winter.
Photograph: Brent Huffman

The species is widespread and abundant across most of its range (except for China where it is rare, with a very limited distribution). With a few exceptions, such as where habitat changes in eastern Canada have caused a contraction, its range has expanded elsewhere. European populations have increased dramatically since the mid-twentieth century, while in North America numbers are thought to exceed a million animals.

There is some debate as to whether Eurasian and North American animals should comprise distinct species, but currently eight subspecies are recognised:

Species		Distribution	Size
Eurasian elk	*A. a. alces*	Scandinavia, Finland, the Baltic states and Poland.	Medium sized: males 320–475 kg (705–1,047 lb) and females 275–375 kg (606–827 lb). Shoulder height 1.7–2.1 m (5 ft 7–6 ft 11 in).
American or Eastern moose	*A. a. americana*	Eastern Canada to Ontario, and the northeastern United States.	Large: males average 365 kg (805 lb) and approximately 2 m (6.6 ft) at the shoulder, females average 270 kg (595 lb).
Canadian or Western moose	*A. a. andersoni*	Western Canada to Ontario, and parts of the northwestern United States into the Northwest Territories as far as parts of North Dakota, Minnesota and Wisconsin.	Medium sized: males average 450–500 kg (992–1,102 lb), females 340–420 kg (750–926 lb).
Chukotka elk	*A. a. buturlini*	Northeastern Siberia from the Alazeya River Basin and eastwards to the Kolyma and Anadyr Basins, and south to Kamchatka Peninsula.	The largest of the European and Asian elk: males can stand 2.15 m (7 ft 1 in) tall and weigh 500–725 kg (1,102–1,598 lb).
Amur, Ussuri or Siberian elk	*A. a. cameloides*	Northern Mongolia, Ussuriland and Manchuria.	The smallest of all the elk subspecies. Bulls carry only very small antlers, often with little or no palmation. Both sexes stand between 1.65–1.85 m (5 ft 5– 6 ft 1 in) at the shoulder and weigh 200–350 kg (441–772 lb).
Alaskan moose	*A. a. gigas*	Alaska and Yukon	The largest of the North American subspecies, with bulls standing over 2.1 m (6ft 11in) at the shoulder and with an average span across the antlers of 1.2–1.5m (3 ft 11–4 ft 11 in) and an average weight of 634.5 kg (1,399 lb) for males and 478 kg (1,054 lb) for females.
Yakutia or Lana elk	*A. a. pfizenmayeri*	Eastern Siberia, Mongolia and Manchuria. The most common subspecies in Asia.	Medium sized: males average 450–500 kg (992–1,102 lb), females 340–420 kg (750–926 lb).
Shiras or Yellowstone moose	*A. a. shirasi*	From south Alberta to Wyoming and Utah	The smallest of the North American subspecies: mature adults average 230–344 kg (507–758 lb).

▶ An Alaskan bull in late summer, almost clean of velvet.
Photograph: David Mark

While the Shiras moose of southwestern Canada and northwestern USA is the smallest of the subspecies, the Alaskan moose and Chukotka elk vie for the distinction of being the largest. The Alaskan may yet take the title; the largest confirmed specimen was shot by a hunter near the Yukon River in 1897 and weighed 820 kg (1,808 lb), measuring 2.33 m (7 ft 7 in) high at the shoulder. Even bigger animals have since been reported but not authenticated.

Elk are noted for their swimming ability and regularly cross large bodies of water, often exceeding 20 kilometres in width, their bodies much lower in the water than other species such as the caribou, and with the rump usually fully submerged. Exhausted calves swimming with their mothers have been seen to rest their necks on the latter's withers, or to throw a foreleg across her neck, and be towed along in this way.

Access to water sources is important to these animals: large bodies and the heat produced by the fermentation associated with their digestive systems, coupled with an inability to sweat, means that they are unable to tolerate higher temperatures of

▲ Water sources are important, both as feeding grounds and for cooling down in warmer weather.
Photograph: Pixabay

more than 27° Celsius for very long and this is countered by submerging. They feed extensively on aquatic plants and have been known to attain a depth of over 5.5 m (18 ft) under water to reach growth at the bottom of lakes and ponds. Elk are the only deer to be able to feed entirely under water, staying submerged for an average of 30 seconds but sometimes up to almost a minute. While other species need to lift their heads before swallowing, fatty pads and muscles in the nose allow elk to close their nostrils and prevent water from entering.

There are instances in which the elk has been successfully domesticated. Swedish records going back to the seventeenth century suggest that they were regularly trained to accept a harness and pull sleds. More recent studies, predominantly in Russia, suggest that provided a wild elk calf could be captured within three days of birth, it could be raised to be passive and more easily trained. If training does not commence before the calf reaches two weeks old it becomes notably more difficult.

Overall, the species is increasing in numbers but a ninth subspecies, the Caucasian Elk *A. a. caucasicus* has been extinct since the nineteenth century as a result of over-hunting and habitat loss. Its range would have extended as far south as Georgia, Armenia and Turkey. Although a discrete population of elk remain in southern Czechia, the species is probably now extinct in Austria. Felix Salten's Bambi, from the book of the same name written in 1928, was a roe deer which encountered elk there: 'Three, four apparitions, one after the other. The last of them was bigger than the others. He had a wild mane on his neck and his antlers were tree-like. It took Bambi's breath away to see them … He felt how pitifully small he was, and even his mother seemed to have shrunk.' During the rut: 'Their deep voices rolled towards him like the mighty moaning of noble, maddened blood whose primal power was giving utterance to longing, rage and pride.'

◀ All young are born a light bay colour but darken quickly as they age. This is the calf of a Eurasian elk.
Photograph: Pixabay

◀ A Eurasian elk cow showing the distinctive grey lower hind leg.
Photograph: Jolanta Dyr

Attempts to introduce the elk to New Zealand in 1900 and 1910, using animals transported from western Canada, were ultimately unsuccessful and the last one was seen there in 1952. Though they are now considered to be long gone, there are still those who believe that a remnant population may yet exist in the dense and remote wilderness areas of Fiordland on South Island.

FACT BOX – *Moose or Eurasian Elk*
(Note: the term 'elk' is used as a general term below)

World distribution	Native to Belarus; Canada; China; Croatia; Czechia; Estonia; Finland; Germany; Hungary; Kazakhstan; Latvia; Lithuania; Moldova; Mongolia; Norway; Poland; Romania; Russian Federation; Slovakia; Sweden; Ukraine; United States (Alaska and northern states). Extinct in Austria.
IUCN Red List Status 2022	**Least Concern**, population increasing (last formal assessment 2015).
Sexes	*Male:* Bull *Female:* Cow *Young:* Calf
Also known as	Camel deer, Marsh stag, Scandinavian elk, Siberian elk (*see also subspecies above*). Chinese *Tue Lu*; Dutch *Eland*; Finnish *Hirvi*; French *Elan*; German *Elch* or *Elanden*; Latvian *Poder*; Lithuanian *Briedis*; Mongolian *Khandgai*; Norwegian *Elg*; Polish *Tos*; Russian *Wos*; Spanish *Alce*; Swedish *Älg*.
Recognition features	A massive and unmistakeable deer with humped shoulders, a short neck and long, slender legs. Sexual dimorphism is marked, with males often around 40 per cent larger than females. European and Asiatic animals tend to be a brownish-grey, whereas those in North America are more of a blackish-brown in summer, both with much paler legs than the body. In winter the coat can appear lighter as the hairs lengthen. Albinos or white animals are occasionally reported. A dewlap of skin and fur, known as the 'bell', hangs from the throat, and can range in size from just a few centimetres in European animals to almost 50 cm (20 in) in North American moose. The legs and ears are long and the tail and neck short. Overall appearance is ungainly, though this is deceptive, and their sense of smell is especially well developed. The upper lip overlaps the lower, and the rhinarium, the naked patch on the muzzle not covered by fur, is very small. Wide hooves splay to reduce ground pressure on soft surfaces while also assisting with swimming.
Height (at shoulder)	*See subspecies*
Weight	*See subspecies*
Food	Diet depends heavily on location, but the elk is primarily a selective browser which takes a wide variety of vegetation. Forbs and the shoots of willow and birch are important food sources, and new growth with a higher sugar content is preferred. Standing on its hind feet, an elk can reach foliage as high as 3.66 m (12 ft). Aquatic plants including lily roots and pond weed can also be fed on extensively, especially so when the terrestrial alternatives are low in sodium. The prehensile upper lip is sensitive, allowing the animal to grasp food, and can be used to strip a branch of its leaves in one movement. In winter they may be drawn to roads to lick salt which has been spread for melting snow and ice.
Habitat	Primarily forest, scrubland, tundra and marshland.

DEER SPECIES | CERVIDAE – CAPREOLINAE

FACT BOX – *Moose or Eurasian Elk*
(Note: the term 'elk' is used as a general term below)

Voice	Generally quiet but both sexes will call during the rut. A rutting bull following a cow may utter rhythmic grunts, while a cow in oestrus can advertise her presence with wailing bellows or lowing calls. An elk confronted by a large predator may make a loud and intimidating roar. Distressed calves can utter a high-pitched scream.
Annual behaviour	One of the least social of the deer and unusually among the larger species, elk are generally solitary but not territorial. During the summer, cows and their calves may frequent lowland swamps and marshes while bulls can seek higher ground to avoid biting insects, but all tend to stay loyal to a home range which can vary between 4 and 92 km^2 depending on local circumstances, food and habitat availability or population densities. Several animals may gather during the rut, otherwise they are seen singly or in family parties. Small groups may assemble in winter yarding areas during periods of deep snow.
Rut	The rut takes place from mid-September to mid-October among most populations, during which time bulls will seek to mate with as many cows as possible. Fighting to secure breeding rights with a particular cow is common. Throughout the rut, bulls will dig out small depressions in which they urinate before rolling in them.
Gestation and birthing	After a gestation of around 231 days, birthing takes place in late May or early June, often with a small island chosen as the birthplace to protect against predation. New-born calves can weigh between 11 and 16 kg (25 and 35 lb). Twins are common and occasionally triplets, although smaller calves are often crowded out during suckling and may not survive. The elk is one of the deer whose young are not spotted at birth, and the newly born calf is a light bay colour. They stay with their mother until just before the birth of the next young.
Antlers (typical)	Elk antlers are generally cylindrical beams that grow out of the side of the skull before forking into tines. The typical antler form is flattened with tines along the outer edge. Palmation can vary considerably between populations, tending to be broader and more palmate in North American animals. In Europe, palmation tends to be less marked and is more evident among animals in the northerly part of their ranges while to the south they seldom develop much beyond simpler, less flattened spikes. The Alaskan moose *A. a. gigas* hold the records for the largest, with weights of 35 kg and with spreads of over 2 metres recorded. The smallest antlers are grown by the Amur elk *A. a. cameloides*; they are short, more deer-like and only rarely palmated.
Antler cycle	Casting takes place from November onwards although regrowth may not start until the following spring; thereafter growth is rapid and the new antlers are clean of velvet by the beginning of September.
Lifespan	Average 15 years, and unlikely to be much beyond 20 years.
Threats	An adult elk has few natural predators, but across its natural range may be taken by tigers, wolf packs and brown bears. Calves are vulnerable to cougars and American black bears. Wolverines have been known to kill animals usually already weakened by winter conditions, and killer whales have been recorded preying on moose swimming between islands on the northwest coast of North America.
	The main human threat is habitat alteration through activities such as forestry and agricultural practices. Hunting, once a significant cause of local population declines and range contractions, is now effectively regulated across much of the elk's range and considered sustainable. The advent of chronic wasting disease in the USA is currently not seen as a major issue for the species.

Blastocerus dichotomus
Marsh deer

ORDER	Artiodactyla
SUBORDER	Ruminantia
INFRAORDER	Pecora
FAMILY	Cervidae
SUBFAMILY	Capreolinae

▲ Stag and hind.
Photograph: Francisco González Táboas

THE MARSH DEER is the largest of the naturally occurring cervids in South America. As its name implies, it is one of the deer species that has reached out beyond generalist woodland origins to specialise in making its home in other habitats. This is a deer that is heavily reliant on wetlands with a standing water depth of less than 70 cm (28 in) and associated dense vegetation as a main habitat. As such, it is attracted to floodplains which provide reed beds, tall grasses, bushes and clumps of forest, which provide cover during the day.

Its range is shrinking rapidly with a corresponding effect on numbers. Recent estimates suggest that in Brazil, the country where the main populations occur, numbers are now well below 41,000. In Argentina there are a further 2,000 in the

▶ A stag in Mato Grosso State, Brazil.
Photograph: Paul K Donahue

Iberá marshes with a few more populations elsewhere. Densities in other countries are similarly low, and the last marsh deer recorded in Uruguay was in 1958. The main concern is that all populations are becoming increasingly fragmented, as a glance at the distribution map shows: this may prove to have genetic consequences as pools of breeding animals are reduced. The main reason for the fragmentation is the increasing drainage of wetlands for agriculture and tree plantations. Hydroelectric projects in Brazil and Argentina have been responsible for the loss of floodplains on several of the major rivers; conversely, flooding to create large reservoirs has a similar effect. In just one example, the Yacyretá dam and hydroelectric project on the Paraná River between Argentina and Paraguay gradually flooded an important expanse of habitat previously occupied by up to 1,000 animals after construction started in the 1980s. Downstream of such developments, habitat changes may also occur when aquatic plant communities change as wetlands are affected.

▲ Portrait of a young stag.
Photograph: Alexander F Meyer

◀ A mature stag in typical marshland habitat at the Estancia El Bagual ranch in the Formosa Province of Argentina. The birds are cattle tyrants *Machetornis rixosa* which feed on parasites living on the deer as well as insects disturbed by it.
Photograph: Francisco González Táboas

Cattle ranching, along with other livestock introductions, continues to make inroads into the available habitat with hundreds of hectares disappearing through drainage every year. This process itself has introduced diseases and parasites which have had an adverse effect on wildlife, and the marsh deer appears to be particularly susceptible to many of them.

Despite having a reputation for being rather unpalatable (one that it shares with the pampas deer *Ozotoceros bezoarticus*), the marsh deer is still hunted heavily for its meat and antlers even where, although it may be protected in law, it is less so in practice. Although hunting is considered to be a lesser threat than those presented by habitat loss and disease, it still takes a significant toll and in many cases is totally uncontrolled. Aside from poaching pressure, indigenous peoples also rely on the marsh deer as a source of subsistence food. Sport hunting for antlers also takes place. This can have the serious side-effect of unbalancing sex ratios among breeding animals when mature stags are specifically targeted.

A GUIDE TO THE DEER OF THE WORLD

▶ (*left*) Hind in summer coat, showing the striking contrast between body and leg colouration: Sorocaba Zoo, Brazil.
Photograph: Alexander F Meyer

▶ (*right*) Hind and calf in winter coat: Berlin Zoo.
Photograph: Klaus Rudloff

There is still much to be discovered about the marsh deer, and its crepuscular habits along with a largely inaccessible habitat make it difficult to study. It does exist in some protected areas, and in 2018 the latest reserve, the 5,588 hectare (22 square miles) Ciervo de los Pantanos National Park in north-east Argentina, was established not far from Buenos Aires. One of the reserve's main purposes is to protect the deer for which it is named. Very much more needs to be done, however, if the future of the marsh deer is to be assured. The IUCN recommends comprehensive measures including further population surveys, strengthening protection and establishing new protected areas, as well as a captive breeding programme. Above all, the cooperation of private landowners and the strict enforcement of laws designed to protect the species will become even more essential in the future.

FACT BOX – *Marsh deer*

World distribution	Native to Argentina, Bolivia, Brazil, Paraguay and Peru. Extinct in Uruguay.
IUCN Red List Status 2022	**Vulnerable**, population decreasing (last formal assessment 2016).
Sexes	*Male:* Stag *Female:* Hind *Young:* Calf
Also known as	Delta deer, Pantanos deer, Swamp deer. Brazil *Veado galheiro* or *Cervo*; French *Bena, Blastocère* or *Cerf des marais*; German *Moorhirsch* or *Sumpfhirsch*; Guarani *Guasu/Guazu pucú* or *Guazuti*; Peru *Ciervo* or *Guazuncho*; Portuguese *Cervo do Pantatal*; Spanish *Ciervo Marismeño, Ciervo de los Pantanos* or *Veado galheiro grande*.
Recognition features	A large deer with long, thin legs. The summer coat is a bright rufous red, turning browner and shaggier in winter. In summer the contrast between the dark lower legs and upper body is especially striking. The face is long and narrow with a pale chin, faint eye rings, a pale upper muzzle and a dark band on the lower muzzle and upper lip. Ears are rounded and contain fuzzy white hair. It has large preorbital glands but no metatarsal glands on the hind legs. The short tail measures 12–16 cm (4¾–6¼ in) and is paler and more orangey than the rest of the body on the upper surface, and black underneath: it is surrounded by a dark rump patch. The hooves are long in relation to the rest of the body and splay to assist with swimming or walking in marshy areas. The animal walks with an unusual staggering motion, and runs with explosive turns of speed, holding its tail raised in a similar manner to the white-tailed deer *Odocoileus virginianus* or the muntjacs *Muntiacus spp*.

DEER SPECIES | CERVIDAE – CAPREOLINAE

FACT BOX – *Marsh deer*

Height (at shoulder)	Stag 110–120 cm (43–47 in), hind 95–105 cm (37½–41¼ in).
Weight	Stag around 110 kg (242 lb), hind 70 kg (154 lb). Occasionally an exceptional stag might weigh up to 150 kg (330 lb).
Food	Both grazes and browses. Much of the diet consists of aquatic plants such as lilies, sedges and water plantains but also includes others such as grasses, reeds and legumes. Food plants can vary considerably between the dry and flood seasons.
Habitat	Very habitat-specific: prefers marshy ground where it will hide in dense vegetation. It is only very rarely found far from water.
Voice	A very quiet deer with no specific calls noted, even during rutting.
Annual behaviour	Generally lives in small groups of up to half a dozen animals, often less, but usually with just one adult male. Most active around dawn and dusk. Some populations can become almost entirely nocturnal, probably as a result of heavy levels of hunting or other disturbance. Maintains large home ranges during the wet season with animals widely scattered; concentrates near any water that is available during the dry season. Despite its relatively peaceful social habits, the marsh deer is reputed to become highly aggressive when wounded and has been known to charge hunters.
Rut	There is no fixed season for breeding although rutting activity peaks in October and November. Mating appears to be opportunistic as a female comes into oestrus with little aggression exhibited between stags.
Gestation and birthing	The single calf is born unspotted and similar to adults in colouration, though lighter. The gestation period is most widely considered to be around 271 days (although some observers suggest that it may last up to a year).
Antlers (typical)	A total of eight tines are typical, with a long, branched brow tine and a forked top, but 10 to 12 tines are not uncommon. Antlers are relatively heavy at between 1.6–2.5 kg (3½–5½ lb) in weight, with an average length of 61 cm (24 in).
Antler cycle	There is no fixed season for casting; mature stags with fully cleaned antlers or in velvet can be encountered at any time of year. Healthy captive stags have retained their antlers for up to 21 months before casting.
Lifespan	12–15 years
Threats	The natural predators of the marsh deer, the puma and jaguar, have largely disappeared from within this species' range.
	The main human threats to the species include the conversion of habitat, livestock-borne diseases, and over-hunting (*see main text*).

Capreolus capreolus

European roe deer

ORDER	Artiodactyla
SUBORDER	Ruminantia
INFRAORDER	Pecora
FAMILY	Cervidae
SUBFAMILY	Capreolinae

▲ A roe buck in the process of changing from winter (rump) to summer coat (neck and shoulder).

THE ROE RANKS among the most delightful of the world's deer. Small, graceful and immaculate in its foxy red summer coat, it has adapted to live not just in the deciduous woodland it prefers but habitats as diverse as the open hill, grass-covered downlands, open agricultural fields and even the urban fringe. Today, and with only a few exceptions, the chances are that in most parts of Europe ranging from Scandinavia to the Mediterranean, and as far west as Turkey and western Russia, the observer will never be far from a roe deer. It is not present only in the very north of Scandinavia, Iceland, Ireland and some of the Mediterranean islands and, although once found in some western areas of the Middle East, is now extinct in those parts. Its scientific name *capreolus* comes from the Latin meaning 'little goat'.

▶ Roe doe in full summer coat.

A number of subspecies exist, although some of these remain disputed. In general, the more widespread main race is described as *C. c. capreolus*, with *C.c. italicus* and *C. c. garganta* in more southerly regions. The slightly larger animals found to the north of the Caucasus Mountains have been provisionally described as *C. c. caucasicus*, whilst those in the Near East have been assigned *C. c. coxi*.

▲ (*left*) Italian roe *C.c. italicus* buck, pictured in Tuscany, central Italy.
Photographs: Klaus Rudloff

▲ (*right*) Italian roe doe.

By rights a woodland species, it is highly adaptable and this reflects in a rising global population, currently numbering an estimated 15 million mature individuals. This has not always been the case: over the last few centuries the roe has experienced mixed fortunes in many countries, where it has been hunted extensively and populations have declined considerably in some. The situation started to change about a century ago when the Great War of 1914–18 created a huge demand for timber across Europe, and the secondary growth that followed large-scale tree clearances created perfect roe habitat. Further replanting created yet more huge areas of new plantation which were quickly colonised. By the latter half of the twentieth century the roe was starting to reappear in places where it had long been absent, and it is now flourishing as a species. In Ireland it has never been present naturally, although there were short-lived introductions in County Sligo and other illegal ones are still rumoured today. A reintroduction programme has recently commenced in Israel.

One phenomenon that distinguishes the roe from all other deer is delayed implantation. Here, the fertilised egg does not implant into the uterus wall immediately after mating, instead floating free within the uterus for months before actual implantation takes place and the foetus starts to develop normally. This means that although the rut normally takes place around late July or early August, implantation

◄ A buck in pursuit of a doe during the rut on a misty, late July morning.

▲ Mating follows a period of prolonged chasing which is controlled by the doe.

of the fertilised egg does not occur until December or early January with kids being born towards the end of May. Roe are the only deer to do this, although other animals including stoats, badgers, bears and skunks also use this breeding strategy.

It is believed that the roe developed the ability for delayed implantation at a point in their evolution when they were at an environmental disadvantage compared to larger deer species which produced larger calves. Instead of evolving an increased body size to cope with climatic changes, it seems that the device of delayed implantation was developed instead. As a result, the roe can rut during the summer with several months of mild weather and good feeding ahead to allow the recovery of its body condition before winter sets in. This ensures that the kids are born at a favourable time of year with abundant food and a benevolent climate, and that they have plenty of time to grow to a size and strength that enhances their survival chances for the coming winter.

▶ Doe and week-old kid.

▶ A healthy roe doe will normally give birth to twin kids.

Very occasionally, individual roe deer have been found to bear tiny, vestigial canine teeth. Many of the deer species have canines, a remnant from a time when their ancestors resembled the more primitive muntjacs and before antlers had really started to evolve, but the roe is at an evolutionary stage when they have all but lost them. Some, however, still produce them as throwbacks to an earlier time.

The roe is by nature a solitary deer, normally seen alone or in small family groups. Despite their delicate appearance and shyness, roe can be highly aggressive towards each other. As spring approaches and testosterone levels rise among the bucks, the desire to establish exclusive territories means that they become increasingly intolerant

◄ Although the roe is solitary for much of the year, larger groups can be encountered during the winter.
Photograph: Klaus Rudloff

of each other. Fights between well-matched bucks are usually brief and the loser is quick to flee, but if he becomes trapped or stumbles his enraged rival will gore him savagely. It is rare to see roe, and especially bucks, in captivity. An animal that has lost its fear of man, perhaps after being hand-reared, can definitely be unpredictable and capable of inflicting very serious injuries on an unwary handler. One bottle-reared buck in a wildlife park regularly attacked both his keepers and the does confined with him; the solution was to saw off his newly grown antlers every May and to cover the stumps with sections of rubber hose.

FACT BOX – *European roe deer*

World distribution	Native to Albania, Andorra, Armenia, Austria, Azerbaijan, Belarus, Belgium, Bosnia and Herzegovina, Bulgaria, Croatia, Czechia, Denmark, Estonia, Finland, France, Georgia, Germany, Gibraltar, Greece, Greenland, Hungary, Iran, Iraq, Italy, Latvia, Liechtenstein, Lithuania, Luxembourg, Moldova, Monaco, Montenegro, Netherlands, North Macedonia, Norway, Poland, Portugal, Romania, Russian Federation, San Marino, Serbia, Slovakia, Slovenia, Spain, Sweden, Switzerland, Syria, Turkey, Ukraine and the United Kingdom. Extinct in Israel, Lebanon and Palestine.

	FACT BOX – *European roe deer*
IUCN Red List Status 2022	**Least Concern**, population increasing (last formal assessment 2015).
Sexes	*Male:* Buck *Female:* Doe *Young:* Kid
Also known as	Albanian *Kaproll ëza*; Bulgarian *Sarna*; Croatian *Srna*; Czechoslovakian *Srncia zver* or *Srnec*; Danish *Radyr*; Dutch *Ree*; Estonian *Metskits*; Finnish *Metsäkauris*; French *Chevreuil* or *Chevreuil Européen*; German *Europäisches*, *Ree*, *Reh* or *Rehwild*; Greek *Zarkardi*; Hungarian *Őz*; Iranian *Shuka*; Italian *Capriolo*; Latvian *Platradzis* or *Alnis*; Lithuanian *Stirna*; Montenegrin *Srna*; Norwegian *Radyr*; Polish *Sarna*; Portuguese *Corco*; Romanian *Caprior*; Russian *Kossula*; Serb *Srna*; Slovenian *Srnjak*; Spanish *Corzo*; Swedish *Rådjur*; Turkish *Karaca*; Yugoslavian *Srnjak*.
Recognition features	Summer coat a foxy red, grey in winter. Usually, though not always, has white spots on end of black muzzle. Erectile hair on rump patch can be puffed out when alarmed or excited. **No visible tail.** The doe in winter coat grows a pronounced anal tush – a long, downward-pointing tuft of hair at the base of the caudal patch.
Height (at shoulder)	Bucks 75 cm (29½ in), does slightly smaller.
Weight	Widely variable according to location and habitat. Bucks around 27 kg (59 lb), does around 22 kg (48½ lb). Animals from poorer habitats may be quite considerably smaller.
Food	A browsing deer which feeds selectively, mainly on buds, shoots and leaves and other high-quality fodder according to season.
Habitat	A woodland deer which adapts successfully to other habitats, including open farmland, grassland, heath and open moor. Often encountered in semi-urban areas.
Voice	Both sexes will bark when alarmed; a territorial buck will also bark as a challenge to others. The doe makes a low piping whistle when calling her young.
Annual behaviour	A solitary deer, usually encountered alone or in small family groups for much of the year. Informal groups, sometimes numbering as many as 30 animals, may form during the winter months.
Rut	From mid-July to early August; weather conditions can have a significant effect on rutting activity which tends to take place later in more northerly latitudes. The doe will encourage a buck onto her chosen rutting ground, often leading him on long and well-defined circuits or figure-of-eight paths around a prominent feature (such as a shrub or rock) before mating is allowed to take place.
Gestation and birthing	After a long gestation due to delayed implantation (*see main text*), birthing takes place in May or June. Kids are born profusely spotted. Twins are normal, occasionally triplets.
Antlers (typical)	Mature bucks produce simple antlers with three tines on each side. Does, typically in older age classes, have been known to develop pedicles or even grow small antlers.
Antler cycle	Casts November/December, clean between late February and April. Older animals tend to cast and clean first.
Lifespan	Normally around 7 or 8 years, but up to 12 years recorded in the wild.
Threats	Predated by large carnivores such as wolves and lynx across parts of its range; the young are vulnerable to foxes and domestic animals. Widely hunted by man and sensitive to displacement by introduced alien species.

Capreolus pygargus
Siberian roe deer

ORDER	Artiodactyla
SUBORDER	Ruminantia
INFRAORDER	Pecora
FAMILY	Cervidae
SUBFAMILY	Capreolinae

A MEDIUM-SIZED, GRACEFUL and attractive deer, the Siberian roe ranges across the temperate zone of eastern Europe and as far as central and east Asia. It is rather larger than its close relative the European roe, and Its scientific name *pygargus* comes from the Greek meaning 'white rumped'.

At one point the Siberian roe was considered to be a subspecies of the European roe *Capreolus capreolus* but it is now treated as a distinct species. There are currently believed to be three subspecies, *Capreolus pygargus pygargus* which occurs across the majority of its distribution; *C. p. tianschanicus* found in the southern part of its Chinese range; and *C. p. bedfordi* to the east of China. The latter two subspecies are typically smaller than the first. A comprehensive classification of the Siberian roe remains unresolved though, and it is hoped that further research into its DNA will clarify matters. The western extremes of the Siberian roe's range overlaps with the eastern one of the European roe, and hybridisation certainly occurs between the two.

Some, but not all, Siberian roe are migratory and can cover distances of well over 200 kilometres during seasonal movements. This behaviour is most pronounced in the most northerly parts of their range, where the weather has a more significant effect on feeding and prevailing conditions, and seems to be triggered by the first frosts. The deer are usually back in their summer feeding grounds by the following May. Movement between the summer and winter grounds always takes the same routes and often involves crossing large rivers and other bodies of water; although they swim well, many drownings can occur

▲ Siberian roe buck (main race) in winter coat and full velvet with antlers almost fully regrown with slight branching to the rear tines.
Photograph: Alexander F Meyer

▼ Siberian roe doe (main race).
Photograph: Alexander F Meyer

A GUIDE TO THE DEER OF THE WORLD

▶ Siberian roe buck (main race) with clean antlers and well into the spring moult, with the red summer coat showing through. Pictured in Beijing Zoo.
Photograph: Alexander F Meyer

▼ Buck and doe of the *C. p. bedfordi* race in full summer coat at the Tierpark, Berlin.
Photograph: Klaus Rudloff

amongst the exhausted animals, which can also become easy prey for wolves and other predators. At such times, huge groups numbering many hundreds of animals can form.

At one time the Siberian roe may have occurred well to the west of Moscow, but the last ones in the Ukraine were hunted to extinction during the nineteenth century. Today its western boundary appears to be the Volga River. It is possible that their range once extended even further west, a suggestion supported by the preserved skeleton of one found in a Swedish peat bog. This may be the origin of mid-European legends of the giant roebuck or *Urbock*, most examples of which have turned out to be antique antlers of more modern Siberian roe.

For a brief period during the twentieth century the Siberian roe was introduced to Woburn in England, where they were released into some woods just outside the deer park in 1910. They never thrived and disturbance by the military, who used Woburn Abbey and its surroundings during the war years, was largely blamed for much of their decline. By 1950 only three animals remained and the species disappeared soon afterwards. Beyond deliberate reintroductions in parts of Russia, where overhunting and other factors had reduced numbers to danger levels or even exterminated them altogether, there have been no other known attempts to transplant this species elsewhere in the world.

FACT BOX – *Siberian roe deer*

World distribution	Native to China, Kazakhstan, Democratic People's Republic of Korea, Republic of Korea, Mongolia and the Russian Federation.
IUCN Red List Status 2022	**Least Concern**, population decreasing (last formal assessment 2015).
Sexes	*Male:* Buck *Female:* Doe *Young:* Kid
Also known as	Asiatic deer, Altai deer, Eastern roe deer, Tartarian roe, Bedford's deer (*C. p. bedfordi*); Tian Shan roe (*C. p. tianschanicus*). Chinese *Pao* or *Paoze*; French *Chevreuil de Siberie*; German *Reh von Sibirien* or *Sibirisches Reh*; Korean *Noru*; Mongolian *Bor Göröös*; Russian *Kosulya Sibirskaya*; Siberian *Ahu*, *Illik* or *Ullich*; Spanish *Corzo Siberiano*.

FACT BOX – *Siberian roe deer*

Recognition features	A light and slender deer with colouration very similar to the European roe deer, though larger in size. The summer coat is a foxy red with a pale rump patch and no visible tail. In winter, the coat thickens and takes on a dull, light grey colouration among more northern animals; further south the winter coat is more of a greyish-brown. The white rump patch becomes more pronounced and can be flared out when the animal is alarmed.
Height (at shoulder)	71–85 cm (27½–33 in), does smaller.
Weight	Bucks average 45–50 kg (99–110 lb) but up to 59 kg (130 lb) known. Does smaller at around 35–40 kg (77–88 lb).
Food	A browser, which is more inclined to graze than the European roe; it takes a wide variety of plant material although more nutritious new growth will be chosen in preference over rougher forage. Nuts, berries, fungi and other seasonal material is also eaten when available.
Habitat	Deciduous and mixed forest, steppes, tall grass meadows and flood plains.
Voice	A hoarse bark, often repeated several times, is used to signal territorial dominance by bucks or as an alarm signal by both sexes. A doe makes a low whistle when communicating with her young. Kids make a harsh scream when threatened.
Annual behaviour	A solitary deer during the summer months, during which it is generally encountered singly or in family groups, but large groups of up to 30 animals can form in winter. Migratory parties can swell to as many as 500.
Rut	Bucks become highly territorial during the spring and leading up to the rut, which takes place between July and September. Shrubs and other vegetation are frayed with antlers and scent marked using glands on the head. Fighting between well-matched individuals can be intense and has been known to end with fatalities.
Gestation and birthing	Gestation is long, due to delayed implantation (a period during which the fertilised egg remains dormant before implanting in the uterus and developing normally). The two species of roe are the only deer to do this, and the Siberian roe appears more capable of determining implantation times than its European counterpart. Gestation can therefore last between six and ten months. Kids are generally born in May or June; two (twins) are normal, though up to four have been recorded.
Antlers (typical)	Antlers are very often 8-tined (compared to the 6 tines of the European roe), commonly ending in a fork to the rear tine. They are generally some 10 cm longer than those of the European roe, are more widely separated at the pedicles, and have been known to reach as much as 47 cm (18½ in) in length.
Antler cycle	Casting takes place from October onwards, with older animals casting first. Regrowth is generally complete by the following May.
Lifespan	Around 10 years
Threats	Significant predators include the Amur and snow leopards, wolf, lynx, and tiger, depending on their presence across its range. Weather extremes can cause periodic high mortality.
	Illegal hunting for meat and antlers can have a high impact both at local levels and along migration routes, and displacement by human activities, including resource extraction and agriculture, is also a threat.

Hippocamelus antisensis

Taruca

ORDER	Artiodactyla
SUBORDER	Ruminantia
INFRAORDER	Pecora
FAMILY	Cervidae
SUBFAMILY	Capreolinae

▲ A mature doe pictured at Huachipa Zoo, Peru, showing the stocky body and relatively short legs which are adaptations to life in mountainous regions.
Photograph: Alexander F Meyer

THE TWO SPECIES of the group collectively known as the Andean deer, the taruca and the closely related huemul *H. bisulcus* are broadly similar – with stocky, short-legged bodies covered in rather coarse hair – but there are notable differences between the two. The taruca is a slightly smaller animal, lighter in colour and with a dark underside to its tail as opposed to the white of the huemul's. The typical antlers of males are also dissimilar: while the taruca's are somewhat shorter, they also tend to take a simpler form of branching close to the base into two tines. The huemul's antlers, in contrast, branch further up the stem and may be more likely to bear extra tines. Of the two, only the taruca is likely to produce small canine teeth in its upper jaw. Both species belong to the relatively small number of deer whose newly born young do not bear spots.

The social habits of the two are also different, the taruca being a more social animal which lives in small herds while the huemul tends to be far more solitary. There is no danger of needing to differentiate between the two in the wild, though, as they cannot meet: the taruca only occurs in the northern Andes with the huemul much further to the south of the same mountain range, their natural distributions separated by over 800 miles.

▶ An illustration depicting a taruca buck with typical antlers from *The Deer of all Lands* by Richard Lydekker (1898).

The taruca is often found at much higher altitudes than its southern relative, and can share its habitat with white-tailed deer and other animals, such as alpaca and llamas, as well as domestic sheep and cattle. It prefers mountain slopes above the tree line with rocky areas and grassland vegetation interspersed with shrubs. A readily available water source is also sought. The social groups it lives in are not structurally rigid and can contain a mixture of mature adults of both sexes and grown fawns. There may be a number of adult males in any particular herd, which will have a recognisable home range of over 20 kilometres and which may also overlap with that of other herds. Animals often move between these herds on an irregular basis, and at times the more normal group size of up to nine animals has been known to swell to as many as 30. This is especially likely to happen around the time of the annual rut. Anecdotal observations by locals suggest that groups of up to 50 could be seen prior to the 1960s, but smaller modern herd sizes are very probably directly linked to the decline of the species since then. Solitary animals can also be encountered occasionally: although these are usually males, lone animals are most common in areas subject to higher human disturbance and under such circumstances solitary females are likely to be found as well.

◀ A doe with her fawn of around four months of age. Photographs: Andres Puiggros V

▼ A mixed herd of taruca in a typical northern Andes habitat, containing some older bucks which have recently cast and are in the process of regrowing their antlers, and also at least one young male with hard antler spikes.

The taruca has been recognised as endangered since the 1960s and numbers continue to decrease. While the numbers killed by sport hunters are probably small given the altitudes at which the animals live, a far higher toll is likely to be taken by indigenous people who hunt them primarily as a source of meat. Much of their population decline has been linked to poaching activity. Competition with domestic livestock has also played its part, by driving the deer out of some of their natural range, as has agricultural activity at lower altitudes. The taruca's populations are highly fragmented because of limited habitat, which is often broken up by high human densities between these areas. The overall population is currently estimated at below 21,000 animals with the greatest numbers in Peru and less than 1,000 in Chile. Of all these, though, it is possible that the total number of breeding adults may be less than 6,000.

FACT BOX – *Taruca*

World distribution	Native to Argentina, Bolivia, Chile and Peru.
IUCN Red List Status 2022	**Vulnerable**, population decreasing (last formal assessment 2016).
Sexes	*Male:* Buck *Female:* Doe *Young:* Fawn
Also known as	Guemal, Furcifer deer, North Andean deer, North Andean huemul, Peruvian huemul, Taruga, Taruka.
	Aymara *Taruja*; French *Cerf des Andes septentrionales, Guémal Péruvien, Huémuld des Andes septentrionales*; German *Andenhirsch* or *Peruanischer huemul*; Quechua *Taruka*; Spanish *Ciervo Andino septentrional, Guemal, Tarugo* or *Taruka*.

FACT BOX – *Taruca*

Recognition features	A medium sized deer with a heavy body and a stocky appearance. The coat is a speckled yellowish-grey which gives an overall sandy-brown appearance, and is made up of rather long, coarse and brittle hairs. The tail is short. There is a dark brow marking above the eyes and a paler band surrounding the muzzle. The rump patch is white and can be flared during flight. Both sexes may produce small upper canine teeth, more usually seen in the male.
Height (at shoulder)	Males 74–80 cm (29–31½ in), females smaller at around 70 cm (27½ in).
Weight	Males up to 60 kg (132 lb), female around 46 kg (101 lb).
Food	Browses on a wide variety of bushes and herbs for much of the year, supplementing their diet with grasses and sedges, especially during the rainy season. May also feed on agricultural crops such as potatoes, barley and alfalfa where these are available.
Habitat	Usually found above the mountain treeline in rocky areas of grassland with sparse vegetation, although they have also been observed in areas with more dense shrubbery. Proximity to a water source is preferred. Spends most of the year at higher elevations up to 5,000 metres above sea level, rarely descending below 3,500 metres in some parts of Bolivia and Peru, though as low as 2,000 metres elsewhere. In general, higher altitudes are sought closer to the Equator.
Voice	No specific vocalisations have been noted
Annual behaviour	A more gregarious animal than its relation the huemul *H. bisulcus*, the taruca lives in mixed sex groups of four to nine animals and sometimes considerably more. Group membership can be fluid without any particularly rigid structure, with both sexes moving between separate ones, and groups may be at their largest during the rut.
Rut	The rut takes place during the dry season in June and July. There is no territoriality; males will compete with each other for breeding rights, displaying by raising forelegs one at a time, threatening with antlers, and ultimately fighting if necessary by locking antlers and indulging in pushing trials of strength.
Gestation and birthing	Gestation lasts around 240 days, unusually long for smaller deer, and the unspotted young are born between January and March at around the peak of the wet season. A single fawn is usual, though twins have occasionally been reported. Birthing may take place later among the more southerly populations. Females move away from the main herd while fawning and stay apart with their young for about a month before rejoining it, hiding the fawn in rocky outcrops in the meantime.
Antlers (typical)	Typical antlers are branched close to the base and usually consist of a long brow tine and a longer posterior tine only, measuring around 22–27 cm (8½–10½ in).
Antler cycle	Antlers are usually cast by October. By December all adult males are in velvet and back in hard antler by May at the latest.
Lifespan	Around 10 years
Threats	The main natural predator is the puma; mountain foxes may take younger fawns.
	Human threats include destruction of habitat, displacement from preferred habitats (especially those with water sources), competition with domestic stock, trophy hunting and predation by domestic dogs. In some places the taruca is treated as an agricultural pest, and poaching for meat can often be locally severe. Antlers are sometimes used in traditional medicine to treat facial paralysis, although there is no known scientific foundation for the practice.

DEER SPECIES | CERVIDAE – CAPREOLINAE

Hippocamelus bisulcus
Patagonian huemul

ORDER	Artiodactyla
SUBORDER	Ruminantia
INFRAORDER	Pecora
FAMILY	Cervidae
SUBFAMILY	Capreolinae

Photograph: Gilbert Myers

THERE ARE JUST two members of the genus *Hippocamelus*, the Patagonian huemul and the taruca, both of which occur only in the mountainous western regions of South America. The huemul has the more southerly distribution which straddles the borders of Argentina and Chile in the Andes mountains, with an isolated subpopulation in the Nevados de Chillán region of the latter.

Alongside the Andean condor, the huemul features on the Chilean coat of arms and is the national animal. It is slightly larger than its more northern cousin and, in any case, there is unlikely to be any need to distinguish between them as they have very separate distributions. Huemul numbers are decreasing and the estimated current population is just 1,500 animals, two-thirds of which live in Chile. Quite apart from natural predation, threats ranging from habitat loss, hunting and competition from introduced wildlife and livestock are all cited as significant reasons for their decline.

▼ Along with the Andean condor, the huemal features on the Chilean coat of arms.

◄ A buck with recently cleaned antlers, with a few remnants of dried velvet still apparent, pictured among the lenga beech forests of the Torres del Paine National Park in Chile.
Photograph: Gilbert Myers

The huemul is an animal that prefers to live on higher ground for most of the year. In the summer it can be found in the rugged mountainous areas of the southern Andes, often as high as 3,000 metres above sea level. Its stocky build and relatively short legs are adaptations for this existence; huemul are poor runners and tire quickly, but they move easily over rocky ground and prefer to avoid predators by taking to cliffs where pursuit will be more difficult. They are excellent swimmers and may also seek refuge in water.

➤ A mature buck in hard horn.
Photograph: Rodrigo Silva

➤ A mature buck in hard horn, showing the short tail and rump markings.
Photograph: Sebastián Lescano

The huemul's coat is another adaptation for living at high altitudes. It is made up of two layers: a thick and woolly undercoat provides warmth, whilst the top cover – a waterproofing layer of longer, greasy guard hairs that are hollow – also provides extra insulation. With this protection the huemul can withstand temperatures of as low as -50º C. In spring the winter coat is shed and replaced by the much shorter summer pelage, which appears rather lighter in colour.

The huemul is not a highly social animal: mature males often live apart from the females, which themselves only form small groups, rarely larger than around five animals, for much of the year. Females seem to prefer higher, rockier ground where cliffs and ridge lines offer better protection to them and their young from predators, while males are more likely to be seen on flatter ground. Both sexes will move to lower ground in winter when weather conditions force them to seek more suitable pastures as, although capable of surviving considerable cold, deep snow reduces their ability to find sufficient food.

The actual timing of the rut can be extremely variable. The bucks do not appear to be strongly territorial, but seek out does as the rut approaches, often tolerating other males in the area as long as they are suitably subordinate. There is little fighting beween bucks but there may be some chasing to keep potential rivals away from a doe in oestrus, and the most dominant animal present will monopolise breeding rights.

In common with most deer, as birthing approaches the doe will seek solitude. An isolated place is usually chosen and the fawn may be moved frequently to reduce the chances of it being discovered by a predator. The new-born fawn has a thick, woolly, chocolate-coloured coat which, unlike most deer species, is not spotted. It is usually fully weaned by the time it is about five months old.

◄ A mature doe.
Photograph: Sebastián Lescano

In more remote areas the huemul can be remarkably tolerant of human presence and is easily approached, though where disturbance becomes more intense it takes only the appearance of a person or dog to put animals many hundreds of metres away to flight. The continuing decline in huemul numbers remains a major cause for concern but there has been considerable research into the species and there is hope that, with continued cooperation between Argentina and Chile, whose borders divide the animal's natural range, work will progress to improve the situation. In 2010, both countries signed a Memorandum of Understanding on Conservation, recognising the need for close collaboration to help protect the huemul from extinction. It can only be hoped that work to address the many threats to the species may yet reverse the declining trend.

FACT BOX – *Patagonian huemul*

World distribution	Argentina and Chile
IUCN Red List Status 2022	**Endangered**, population decreasing (last formal assessment 2015).
Sexes	*Male:* Buck *Female:* Doe *Young:* Fawn
Also known as	Guemal, Furcifer deer, South Andean deer, Chilean deer.
	Native *Huemul, Shoan, Tarush*; French *Cerf/Huemul des Andes méridionales* or *Hippocamelus de Chile*; German *Gabelhirsch, Südlicher Andenhirsch* or *Trughirsch*; Spanish *Ciervo Andino meridional, Huemul* or *Huemul Patagónico*.
Recognition features	Stocky build, short legs and a medium-length tail. Bucks have distinctive dark brow markings. The dark brown coat of the summer turns greyish-brown in winter. When viewed at close quarters the coat appears a mottled yellow and black. White highlights to the lower tail, inside the ears and the end of the lower jaw.
Height (at shoulder)	Males around 90 cm (34½ in), females 81 cm (32 in).
Weight	Males 65 kg (143 lb) or more, females 50 kg (110 lb).
Food	A highly selective browser, feeding largely on tender vegetation and often limited by the flora available within its habitat. In some places *gunnera* plants can be an important food item where these are available.
Habitat	Shrubland, forest, periglacial grassland and rocky areas such as inland cliffs and mountain peaks. Spends the summer in the mountains up to 3,000 metres above sea level but descends to lower ground in winter.
Voice	Generally a quiet deer. The call has been described as a laughing sound lasting 3 to 6 seconds and is largely inaudible to the human ear beyond around 30 metres. Bucks may grunt or whine softly while pursuing does during the rut. The alarm call of both sexes is a snort.
Annual behaviour	Seeks to be on higher ground until forced lower by winter snow. Lives alone or in small groups throughout the year with the sexes segregated; mature bucks tend to be solitary. Animals threatened by a predator will endeavour to hide or depart inconspicuously, resorting to flight only if necessary. It is a poor runner with low endurance and is easily caught by dogs.
Rut	Varies widely according to locality, but generally between February and May.
Gestation and birthing	Gestation is between 180 and 210 days. The single fawn (twins are rare) is usually born between September and December. Fawns are born without spots unlike many other deer. Does with new-borns are more likely to stay in the proximity of steep cliffs and are less likely to venture onto grasslands.
Antlers (typical)	Simple and forked, usually with a longer rear tine, measuring about 28 cm in length. More than 4 tines overall are rare but up to 9 have been recorded.
Antler cycle	Casts mid-July to early September, usually fully grown and clean by the following February.
Lifespan	Around 14 years
Threats	Predated by pumas and culpeo foxes, also domestic dogs. Wild cats and raptors such as condors may be a threat to the young.
	Over-hunting and poaching, along with human encroachment on traditional habitats, are major threats. The introduction of non-native Eurasian deer to Argentina and Chile during the twentieth century also resulted in some competition in which the huemul was displaced.

DEER SPECIES | CERVIDAE – CAPREOLINAE

Hydropotes inermis
Water deer

ORDER	Artiodactyla
SUBORDER	Ruminantia
INFRAORDER	Pecora
FAMILY	Cervidae
SUBFAMILY	Capreolinae

THE WATER DEER is something of an oddity among the *Cervidae* or true deer, in that the bucks never produce antlers, bearing instead very long canine tusks which it uses for both establishing dominance over other bucks and defending itself. The ancestors of our modern deer produced tusks long before they evolved antlers as weapons, although the water deer's skull structure is that of a typical deer and it may be that a failure to develop antlers does not necessarily make it primitive in ecological terms. The lack of antlers gives rise to the *inermis* of their scientific name, meaning 'unarmed', while *hydropotes* means 'water drinker', a reference to the wetland habitats that they prefer. Despite a superficially similar appearance, they are not closely related to the musk deer of the *Moschidae*.

▲ Mature buck.

▼ The skull of a mature water deer buck.

◄ A doe and fawn pictured in England.

There are two subspecies, the ranges of which once formed a continuously occupied band throughout much of eastern China and covering almost the whole of Korea some 70 years ago, but both populations are now widely separated. The Chinese water deer *H. i. inermis* is restricted to the area of the eastern Yangtze Basin, with former populations in north-eastern and south-eastern China now extinct. The Korean water deer *H. i. argyropus* is found on the western and more low-lying areas of the Republic of Korea and DPR Korea; it once also inhabited the Chinese provinces of Jilin and Liaoning bordering DPR Korea.

A creature of the coastal areas and great river valleys of its native China and Korea, the water deer will also live in other habitats and, although it does like to have some thicker cover available to retreat into, prefers more open ground with shrubs and small trees. It is a solitary animal which tends to form only loose family associations. A buck will strive to hold a territory which overlaps with the home ranges of a number of does, although when food is short a number may congregate in the better feeding areas. They will characteristically graze for a while then lie down, wherever they happen to be, to ruminate, unlike other deer which usually prefer to retreat into cover. If alarmed, they are likely to simply run a short distance and bed down even if still in the open.

During the rut, bucks fight using their tusks. These have sharp inner edges and are hinged to allow them to be brought forward as a display of aggression or to slash at an opponent's face and neck. Not usually a very vocal deer, at this time bucks will make a variety of squealing and clicking noises. Territories are defined by scraping with their feet, scent-marking with the face glands, and marking plant stems with their tusks. The water deer also possesses unusual glands located in the groin area, the inguinal glands, which are also used for scent-marking; water deer are the only deer to have these.

▶ Mature buck. Among all the true deer, the upper canine are the most highly developed.
Photograph: Brent Huffman

Although up to seven fawns have been recorded in a litter, two or three are more usual. They weigh less than a kilogram at birth and are very vulnerable to predation and spells of wet and cold weather. Mortality during the first few weeks of life can be 40 per cent or even higher under adverse conditions.

◀ A well grown fawn hidden in long grass.

The water deer has been introduced outside its natural range with varying degrees of success. The first introductions to France were made in 1954, followed by more during the 1960s, but it appears that by the year 2000 the species was no longer present there. It has been more successful in the United Kingdom, where a succession of escapes and deliberate releases since the very late nineteenth and early twentieth centuries led to its establishment, mainly in the eastern parts of England, from where it is now slowly spreading south and west. Although there are no verified figures, it has been suggested that water deer in England may now represent at least ten per cent of the world population; genetic studies suggest that these deer have their origins in a now extinct ancestral population on the Chinese mainland. The species notably suffers from a condition called post-capture myopathy, in that the stress of being captured and transported can be a common cause of fatality: as a result, it has received less human assistance in spreading than the more robust Reeves' muntjac *Muntiacus reevesi*, which has colonised much of England, as well as parts of Wales and Ireland, with far greater success.

FACT BOX – *Water deer*

World distribution	Native to China, DPR Korea and Republic of Korea. Introduced to France and the United Kingdom.
IUCN Red List Status 2022	**Vulnerable**, population decreasing (last formal assessment 2014).
Sexes	*Male:* Buck *Female:* Doe *Young:* Fawn
Also known as	Chinese water deer, Chinese river deer, Korean water deer, River deer, Korean river deer. Chinese *Zhang*; Dutch *Chinees waterhert*; French *Hydropote*, *cerf d'eau* or *cerf de marais*; German *Wassereh*; Korean *Kibanoru* or *gasha*; Spanish *Ciervo acuatico*.
Recognition features	Pelage is a uniform yellowish-red to golden brown in summer, greyer and thicker in winter, with a short, stubby tail that measures around 7 cm (3 in). There is no distinct rump patch. The hair of the winter coat is coarse, loose and easily dislodged. The rounded ears are hairy inside; these, combined with the black eyes and button nose, combine to give the impression of a 'teddy bear' face. A graceful, long-legged deer, the rump is higher than the shoulders and sits on powerful hind legs. Running is with hare-like leaps and bounds.

FACT BOX – *Water deer*

Recognition features continued	**Bucks never produce antlers** but instead have long, dagger-like upper canine tusks with sharp inner edges, averaging between 6–8 cm (2½–3 in) in length and readily visible on a mature animal. They are slightly hinged and can be held back for feeding; a buck threatening a rival 'snarls' and raises his head to bring them forward. The tusks of does are much smaller at only around 0.5 cm (¼ in).
Height (at shoulder)	Bucks 50–52 cm (19½–20½ in), does 47–49 cm (19–19½ in).
Weight	Bucks up to 19 kg (42 lb), does up to 17 kg (37½ lb).
Food	The water deer is a highly selective feeder, choosing plants including herbs, forbs and young grasses. Its digestive system is unable to process fibre efficiently so it avoids coarser material such as more mature grasses.
Habitat	Preferred habitat is coastal plains, reed beds and grassland along river estuaries, otherwise other lowland areas are also occupied. In the United Kingdom it has adapted successfully to live in parkland and farmland, but the most successful populations exist in the fenland of East Anglia which more closely resemble its natural range.
Voice	Mainly quiet. The alarm call is a harsh bark. Rutting bucks make a variety of chittering clicks and squeals.
Annual behaviour	Generally solitary throughout most of the year, forming only loose family associations. They may congregate in feeding areas, especially at less plentiful times, and are excellent swimmers, readily taking to water to swim between islets.
	Bucks will endeavour to establish territories which overlap with the home ranges of as many does as possible, marking them with scrapes made with the forefeet, depositing scent from interdigital glands and then urinating or defecating in them. They also scent-mark leaves and low branches using their preorbital and inguinal glands, as well as marking plant stems with their tusks.
Rut	The rut takes place between November and January. Among wild populations in the UK most rutting activity is during late November and December. Bucks compete aggressively during the rut, using the canine tusks to slash at an opponent's face and neck, and injuries are commonplace.
Gestation and birthing	Gestation is relatively short at around 170–180 days, after which two to three young are normally born (although up to seven have been recorded) around May or June. The water deer is accordingly the most potentially prolific of all the deer species. The fawns vary between dark brown and reddish, with two rows of faint pale spots. Mortality can be high during the first few days of life, especially when weather conditions are damp or unusually cold, and larger litters are less likely to be successful. The fawns grow fast and in many cases reach sexual maturity in time to take part in the rut during the same year of their birth – the water deer is an exceptional member of the *Cervidae* in this respect.
Lifespan	Up to 10 years, although usually rather less with 6 years considered average among animals in the United Kingdom.
Threats	Predators include leopards and feral dogs; fawns are very vulnerable to foxes and other smaller predators.
	Poaching and habitat destruction are the main threats across much of the water deer's range. In places poaching pressure is intense, often involving hunting with dogs or with snares. Apart from the market for its meat, the milk of nursing does and undigested milk in the rumens of unweaned fawns is used as a treatment for indigestion in folk medicine, and it is trapped as a perceived agricultural pest, particularly in China. The development of land for both urban development and agriculture is a significant cause of habitat loss in China and both Koreas.

Mazama americana
Red brocket

ORDER	Artiodactyla
SUBORDER	Ruminantia
INFRAORDER	Pecora
FAMILY	Cervidae
SUBFAMILY	Capreolinae

OF THE TEN species of brocket deer which are distributed across Central and South America – from Mexico in the north to as far south as northern Argentina – the red brocket is the most widespread. It can be found mostly in wet forest habitats, ranging from Colombia, across the Amazon Basin and down to the northern tip of Argentina. The species is also found on the Caribbean island of Trinidad, although it is now considered to have been eradicated by poaching activity on neighbouring Tobago. It shares much of its range with the smaller Amazonian brown brocket.

The name 'brocket' is thought to come from the Old French *broc*, meaning the tine of a deer's antler. The scientific name *mazama* is derived from an Aztec word meaning 'small deer', and *mazame* or *macame* was also a Mexican name applied to deer during the seventeenth century. It is also an obsolete term for a mountain goat.

The red brocket, in common with others of the genus *Mazama*, is one of several species of deer for which the taxonomy is uncertain. At one point it was thought to have around 14 subspecies which were mostly defined geographically, but some of these have since been reclassified as species in their own right while others remain disputed. This confusion continues, though research suggests that there are still several subspecies: clarification is much needed. Because of the taxonomic uncertainty, the IUCN has categorised the red brocket as Data Deficient and, although it remains common and widespread as a general species, does not rule out the possibility that some populations (whether species or subspecies) may actually be threatened.

Red brockets are known to play a major role within their ecosystems as an important agent of seed dispersal. Their importance may go even further, as shown by a 2015 study of

▲ Mature buck at the NUPECCE Deer Research and Conservation Centre in São Paulo, Brazil.
Photograph: Alexander F Meyer

▼ Portrait of a mature buck, showing typical antlers.
Photograph: Alexander F Meyer

A GUIDE TO THE DEER OF THE WORLD

▶ A mature doe.
Photograph: Alexander F Meyer

the role that larger ungulates, including brockets, play within the Brazilian rainforest. The conclusion was that where they were not present, the populations of some rodents grew significantly as they were faced with less competition for resources, and there was a corresponding decrease in seed survival and germination. Furthermore, the specific rodents which benefited were natural hosts for Hantavirus, which can be lethal to humans. As threats to the tropical rainforests continue unabated, the number of those large mammals that live within them may reduce still further with potential consequences for human health, as well as the overall diversity of the ecosystems themselves, that cannot be discounted.

FACT BOX – *Red brocket*

World distribution	Native to Argentina, Bolivia, Brazil, Colombia, Ecuador, French Guiana, Guyana, Paraguay, Peru, Suriname, Trinidad and Tobago, Venezuela.
IUCN Red List Status 2022	**Data Deficient**, population trend unknown (last formal assessment 2015).
Sexes	*Male:* Buck *Female:* Doe *Young:* Fawn
Also known as	Bush deer, Eye-browed deer, Large-eared deer, Pita brocket, Pricket deer.
	Argentina *Corzuela Colorado* or *Venado colorado*; Brazil *Gasucho*, *Guasú parú*, *Pita subulo*, *Veado* or *Veado pardu*; French *Brocard* or *Daguet rouge*; German *Roter mazama*; Guarini *Guasú pichta*, *Guasú pita* or *Guasúpyta*; Mexican *Coassus*, *Corzo*, *Corzuela Colorado*, *Corzuela roja*, *Temazame*, *Temazate* or *Venaditoroja*; Native *Matacanes*, *Suisizil* or *Suitsizeli*; Portuguese *Veado mateiro* or *Veado pardo*; Spanish *Temazate o corzuelaroja roja*.
Recognition features	A uniform reddish-brown, neck often slightly greyer. The underparts and lower part of the neck are paler, and the underside of the medium length tail, which measures between 8 and 15 cm (3–6 in), is white. The ears are rounded with little hair on the inside. The slender legs can sometimes appear dark in contrast to the body.
Height (at shoulder)	The largest of the brockets, measuring around 67 cm (26 in) at the shoulder.

DEER SPECIES | CERVIDAE – CAPREOLINAE

FACT BOX – *Red brocket*

Weight	Highly variable but averaging between 30–40 kg (66–88 lb) with little difference between the sexes, though exceptional males may be considerably larger.
Food	Will browse on vegetation but primarily a frugivore; in the rain forests, fruit may make up around 80% of their diet when it is available.
Habitat	A deer of dense, moist tropical forests with closed canopies, red brockets are most often found in thick cover close to water sources such as marshes and streams. Lower altitudes are preferred and it is not encountered beyond 1,000 metres above sea level.
Voice	Generally quiet but has a piecing cry; if disturbed, will snort and stamp its hooves.
Annual behaviour	The red brocket is intensely shy and retiring, as a result of which study of the species has been limited and its habits are not fully understood. It is generally diurnal and solitary, tending to maintain a small home range and remaining in cover throughout the day, though it may become more nocturnal where hunting pressure is high. Breeding pairs may be encountered but larger groupings are very rare. Scent marking is an important form of communication and is done by rubbing the forehead against a small tree, thrashing, urination and defecation. Of all the brockets, this species is the most inclined to remain within dense thicket areas. An animal will often freeze on the approach of a predator and then evade capture by leaping into the air, or by seeking water if it is close to hand. All of the brockets are confident swimmers and regularly cross rivers over 300 metres wide.
Rut	Very little is known about the breeding behaviour of the red brocket. Although the rudimentary antlers may suggest that these might not play an important role in fighting between males, aggressive behaviour including antler-to-antler contact and striking out with forefeet has been observed. Sexual maturity is reached at about a year old. There is no fixed breeding season and rutting can take place at any time of the year, although there may be local peaks in conception during the dry season with main birthing periods occurring between January to April and July to September. It is possible that some pairs may form a lasting bond, although the male plays no part in raising the young. Single males will otherwise mate more promiscuously with other females.
Gestation and birthing	After a gestation period of 200–225 days, one or two fawns are born in thick cover. Observations suggest that younger females under four years old are more likely to produce twins, only tending to produce a single fawn in later life. Fawns are light brown in colour with pale spots and may not be completely weaned until they are around six months old. They tend to remain with their mothers until sexually mature. Postpartum oestrus means that a doe can be lactating and pregnant at the same time, so producing two offspring per year.
Antlers (typical)	Only males carry antlers, which grow from a very short pedicle They are little more than simple spikes which seldom exceed 10–13 cm (4–5 in) in length. Older animals may occasionally develop a slight fork at the antler tip.
Antler cycle	There appear to be no fixed seasons for antler casting and regrowth.
Lifespan	Between 7 and 12 years
Threats	Main predators include the jaguar, puma, ocelot, tayra (a mustelid which can weigh up to 7 kg (15½ lb)), and large snakes. The red brocket is hunted for meat across much of its range, both legally and illegally. It is also threatened in places where clearance for agriculture (particularly soy bean crops) or cattle farming causes the fragmentation or loss of habitat. It is reputed to have very low stamina compared to other deer, and as such is more easily caught by dogs.

Mazama gouazoubira

Grey brocket

ORDER	Artiodactyla
SUBORDER	Ruminantia
INFRAORDER	Pecora
FAMILY	Cervidae
SUBFAMILY	Capreolinae

▲ Buck with antlers still in velvet but close to cleaning.
Photograph: Alexander F Meyer

▼ Doe and fawn, Tierpark, Berlin.
Photograph: Klaus Rudloff

ONE OF THE most widely distributed brockets, the grey brocket is an animal of the more moderately humid and dry regions typified by the more open forests, shrublands and savannahs of central South America. Its range takes over where that of the Amazonian brown brocket *M. nemorivaga*, a lover of the far denser jungle regions, ends, and overlaps with that of the larger and rather more adaptable red brocket *M. americana* – although where their ranges meet, it avoids both dense forest and open ground without cover.

One of the larger brockets, smaller only than the red brocket, it is distinguished by a greyer appearance than the other species although there can still be significant colour differences between regions and even within specific populations. Until recently both the Amazonian brown and Yucatan brown brocket *M. pandora* were treated as subspecies but these are now considered to be separate.

Densities vary considerably across its wide range; in Brazil, there is often less than one animal per square kilometre, whereas in Bolivia up to 12 individuals have been noted in a similar area. Human presence has much to do with this, and numbers decrease rapidly or even disappear completely close to human settlements. It is hunted widely for its meat. Despite some local declines it is considered to be abundant across much of its range and categorised as being of Least Concern by the IUCN.

DEER SPECIES | CERVIDAE – CAPREOLINAE

FACT BOX – *Grey brocket*

World distribution	Native to Argentina, Bolivia, Brazil, Paraguay, Uruguay.
IUCN Red List Status 2022	**Least Concern**, population decreasing (last formal assessment 2015).
Sexes	*Male:* Buck *Female:* Doe *Young:* Fawn
Also known as	Brown brocket Spanish *Cabra silvestre, Corzuela común, Corzuela parda, Guazu, Guazu virá*; Portuguese *Corça, Veado-catingueiro*.
Recognition features	Pelage is variable between greyish-brown and reddish-brown, flanks slightly paler, and a straighter back than most brockets. Lighter, browner colouration seems to prevail in grasslands while forest animals tend to be darker and greyer. There may be considerable local variations. Slightly smaller than the red brocket *M. americana*, which has more of a raised rump. Similar to the Amazonian brown brocket *M. nemorivaga* but is larger and has more rounded ears, whilst the rump and the upper surface of the tail may be tinged with orange. The preorbital glands are small.
Height (at shoulder)	Between 50–65 cm (19½–25½ in)
Weight	17–23 kg (37½–50 lb), sexes similar
Food	A selective browser of a wide variety of plant species. Although not a true frugivore, it will feed heavily on fruits according to seasonal availability. Will also eat cacti, bromeliad fruits and the leaves and roots of succulents, especially where water sources are not available.
Habitat	Found in mildly humid to dry conditions including scrub and other brushy vegetation and savannah, also found in swampland. Avoids dense forests but often found on forest edges. Will not live in open areas but will visit them to feed as long as cover is available nearby.
Annual behaviour	Solitary and territorial, active during the day but tend only to emerge into the open at night. Annual behaviour and rutting habits are believed to be broadly similar to those of the red brocket *M. americana*.
Gestation and birthing	Gestation is around 7 months, with births recorded during most of the year with the exception of May to July. Fawns are spotted and only very rarely is more than one born; for their first few days of life they are hidden in long grass or other vegetation while their mother feeds until they are strong enough to accompany her. They are weaned at around 6 months of age.
Antlers (typical)	Simple spikes between 7–10 cm (2¾–4 in)
Antler cycle	It is possible that there is no set antler cycle, and mature bucks with polished antlers might be encountered at any time of year. There are suggestions that antlers might be retained for up to 2 years before casting and regrowth.
Lifespan	Around 10 years
Threats	Predated by jaguars, pumas and ocelots as well as larger birds of prey. Very sensitive to high human density with populations declining rapidly close to settlements. Legal and illegal hunting is a serious threat in some areas; in places bans are often not enforced.

Mazama nemorivaga

Amazonian brown brocket

ORDER	Artiodactyla
SUBORDER	Ruminantia
INFRAORDER	Pecora
FAMILY	Cervidae
SUBFAMILY	Capreolinae

▲ A mature buck. All of the animals pictured are at the NUPECCE Deer Research and Conservation Centre in São Paulo, Brazil.
Photograph: Alexander F Meyer

▼ A mature doe.
Photograph: Alexander F Meyer

ONE OF THE most common and widespread of the brockets, the Amazonian brown brocket can be found across much of the northern half of South America. It lives in unflooded parts of the Amazon forest and the surrounding transitional areas of tropical deciduous forest and is very much an animal of the humid rainforest. Its range is bounded by the Andes in the west, the semi-arid stunted *caatinga* forest and scrublands of eastern Brazil, and the open grasslands and savannahs to the south. Although it probably occurs in northern Bolivia, this remains to be confirmed.

It was once treated as a form of the grey brocket *M. gouazoubira* but since 2000 has been fully recognised as an entirely separate species. Despite this, the two species may still be misidentified and misreported where their ranges overlap and much taxonomical work is needed to clarify matters.

Environmental concerns about the Amazon region are well documented. Trees continue to be cut down at an alarming rate for logging, development and human expansion, though agriculture is probably the most alarming cause of deforestation and accounts for some 80 per cent of this. Much is associated with cattle farming and the production of associated animal feed. At the time of writing (2022) it is believed that something like 25 million hectares (96,500 square miles) of the Amazon rainforest have been given over to soybean growth alone.

Habitat destruction is without doubt the Amazonian brown brocket's biggest threat. Though less abundant than the red brocket *M. americana* which also occurs across much of its range, overhunting does not appear to be a significant issue, and that which is carried out by indigenous peoples is felt to be sustainable. This brocket's secretive nature and the dense habitat that it tends to be found in, linked with a high reproductive potential, make it resistant to over-exploitation in this respect. Nevertheless, and even though the Amazonian brown brocket currently enjoys Least Concern status, the pressures on its habitat mean that it would be foolish to be complacent about the future.

DEER SPECIES | CERVIDAE – CAPREOLINAE

FACT BOX – *Amazonian brown brocket*

World distribution	Native to Brazil, Columbia, Ecuador, French Guiana, Guyana, Panama, Peru, Suriname and Venezuela. Presence uncertain in Bolivia
IUCN Red List Status 2022	**Least Concern**, population decreasing (last formal assessment 2016).
Sexes	*Male:* Buck *Female:* Doe *Young:* Fawn
Also known as	Small brown brocket. French *Cariancou*; Spanish *Matacán grisáceo, Soche gris*; Portuguese *Fuboca, Veado-branco*.
Recognition features	A uniform greyish-brown in colour, without any trace at all of a reddish tone, often with little contrast between the colour of the body and that of the neck. The rump is higher than the shoulders and may show an orange tinge with the tail measuring 6–10 cm (2½–4 in). Like most brockets, the upper surface of the tail matches the body colour while the underside is white. The ears are slightly pointed rather than rounded, and the eyes can appear disproportionately large.
Height (at shoulder)	50 cm (19½ in)
Weight	14–15.5 kg (31–34 lb)
Food	A selective browser which feeds heavily on fruits and seeds, also on leaves, flowers, and fungi. Although once thought to be an important agent for seed dispersal, it now appears that larger seeds are processed more efficiently and only smaller ones are likely to survive the digestive process.
Habitat	Lives throughout the rainforests of the Amazon region and associated areas where there is dry ground; it may be seasonally displaced by flooding in areas of lower ground (which may be avoided completely) but is also found up to 1,500 metres above sea level.
Annual behaviour	Only seen singly or in pairs and active throughout the day, this is a solitary deer that has not been widely studied and remains poorly understood. Very likely to be strongly territorial, relying heavily on scent-marking to distinguish its territory. Marking may also involve scraping the ground and depositing faeces, usually close to resting places. Tends to live in lower densities than the red brocket *M. americana*; studies have suggested 0.5 animals per km^2 compared to double that for the red brocket.
Rut, gestation and birthing	Rutting can take place at any time of year. Observation of animals in captivity indicate that gestation is approximately 210 days. Though it appears to breed all year round, in the Peruvian Amazon there appear to be peaks with most births occurring in January, March and April, and again between July and October. The timing seems to be associated with the rainy season. Like other brockets, the single fawn is spotted. Twins have not been recorded.
Antlers (typical)	Up to 11 cm (4½ in) but often much shorter. Antlers are straight or slightly curved spikes on slender pedicles.
Antler cycle	Not studied, but casting and regrowth does not appear to be seasonal.
Lifespan	Around 10–12 years
Threats	Natural predators include jaguar, ocelot and large raptors. The main human threat comes from habitat destruction; most hunting by indigenous people is felt to be sympathetic with availability and fully sustainable. May also be susceptible to diseases spread by cattle.

Mazama bororo, M. bricenii, M. chunyi, M. nana, M. pandora, M. rufina and *M. temama*

Small red, Mérida, Peruvian dwarf, Brazilian dwarf, Yucatan brown, dwarf red and Central American red brockets

FEW OF THE brocket species have been subjected to any great depth of study, and much remains to be learned about them. They occupy a similar ecological niche to that filled by the muntjacs in Asia, and by the small duiker antelopes in Africa. Like these, the brockets are also shy and retiring, exhibit very limited sexual dimorphism, live a more solitary lifestyle, and tend to be only encountered singly or in pairs. Brocket taxonomy is confusing and will almost inevitably be subject to change as we come to understand more about the genus. Evidence is increasingly emerging to suggest closer links with the mule and white-tailed deer of the genus *Odocoileus* and may well trigger far wider taxonomic revisions.

As they are similar in appearance and habits, seven of them are dealt with here, though more complete information is provided separately for the more widespread red brocket *M. americana* (the largest of the brockets), grey brocket *M. gouazoubira*, and Amazonian brown brocket *M. nemorivaga*. The remaining seven species are small deer standing between 35–61 cm (14–24 in) at the shoulder and with broadly similar habits. All of the brockets are found from Mexico and throughout Central and South America down to as far as northern Argentina. Most brockets tend to prefer to live in dense thickets, from which they may emerge to feed in more open, cultivated areas. Many of them have a very limited distribution. The sexes are generally known as buck and doe, and the young is a fawn.

All have a uniformly coloured coat in varying shades of a reddish or greyish brown, with short tails between 7.5–13 cm (3–5 in) in length, and the rump is carried higher than the shoulders. There often appears to be no set season for breeding, although there may be peaks in birthing in some areas: nor does there seem to be one for antler casting and regrowth. Gestation lasts in the region of seven to eight months and the single fawn (twins occur occasionally) is born spotted. The antlers of males are typically no more than simple spikes and seldom exceed much beyond 10 cm (4 in); only very rarely, those of an older animal in some species may form a slight fork at the tips. Hard antlers can be retained for over a year and might be cast at any time.

Life expectancy is likely to be between 10 and 15 years at most. Most of the following species are categorised as Vulnerable with a decreasing population trend. Common threats include habitat loss or degradation, legal and illegal hunting, and predation by domestic or feral dogs. Natural predators can include pumas, jaguars, ocelots, foxes, constricting snakes and larger birds of prey depending on their presence.

Until as recently as the 1990s, there were thought to be just four distinct brocket species, with some 26 subspecies between them; present thinking, though, places the brockets into ten distinct species recognised by the IUCN. In addition to the red, grey and Amazonian brown brockets, covered in separate entries, these are *Mazama bororo, M. bricenii, M. chunyi, M. nana, M. pandora, M. rufina* and *M. temama*.

Mazama bororo

Small red brocket

ORDER	Artiodactyla
SUBORDER	Ruminantia
INFRAORDER	Pecora
FAMILY	Cervidae
SUBFAMILY	Capreolinae

The **Small red brocket** *M. bororo* was first suggested as a distinct species only in 1992, having been once thought a hybrid of the red and Brazilian dwarf brockets. It is very restricted in its range, which lies within the Atlantic Forest biome of southern Brazil where it occupies the humid tropical and subtropical forests. It is reddish brown in colour, similar to the red brocket, but much smaller at around 38 cm (15 in) at the shoulder and weighing 15–20 kg (33–44 lb). It is considered to be seriously endangered, mainly as a result of habitat loss or fragmentation.

▲ Small red brocket buck.
Photograph: Roland Wirth

Distribution	Brazil
IUCN Red List Status 2022	**Vulnerable**, decreasing (last formal assessment 2015)
Also known as	Portuguese *Veado-mateiro-pequeno*

◄ Small red brocket. The photograph is of a captive animal at the NUPECCE Deer Research and Conservation Centre in São Paulo, Brazil, one of the world's leading centres for research and conservation of neotropical deer species.
Photograph: JMB Duarte

Mazama bricenii

Mérida brocket

ORDER	Artiodactyla
SUBORDER	Ruminantia
INFRAORDER	Pecora
FAMILY	Cervidae
SUBFAMILY	Capreolinae

▲ Mérida brocket, pictured at the Jaime Duque Park, Bogotá, Colombia.
Photograph: Alexander F Meyer

▼ Portrait of Mérida brocket (with irregular growth of right antler).
Photograph: Alexander F Meyer

Another highly vulnerable species, currently described as the **Mérida brocket** *M. bricenii* but once treated as a subspecies of the dwarf red brocket, now appears likely to lose its status as a distinct species. Recent research has indicated that it is no more than a junior synonym of the dwarf red brocket *M. rufina*. It too has a very limited and patchy distribution, this time in the Andes mountains of northern Colombia and western Venezuela. Here, though, it inhabits higher ground and is found between 1,000 and 3,200 metres above sea level, where it occupies montane forests and the páramos (the high, treeless tropical plateaus of South America). In these places small-scale agricultural activities degrade the habitat and there is an added issue of illegal coca and opium plantations in some parts of Colombia, as well as land exploitation for mining, road building and settlements. It is one of the medium-sized *Mazama* deer, standing 45–50 cm (17½–19½ in) at the shoulder and weighing 8–13 kg (17½–28½ lb). The glossy dark brown coat has a strong reddish tinge, and the throat is distinctly orange and the head darkish. The antlers of males seldom exceed 5 cm (2 in) in length.

Distribution	Colombia and Venezuela
IUCN Red List Status 2022	**Vulnerable**, decreasing (last formal assessment 2016)
Also known as	Meroia or rufous brocket Spanish *Candelillo, Locha, Soche de Páramo, Venado Matacán Andino*

DEER SPECIES | CERVIDAE – CAPREOLINAE

Mazama chunyi

Peruvian dwarf brocket

ORDER	Artiodactyla
SUBORDER	Ruminantia
INFRAORDER	Pecora
FAMILY	Cervidae
SUBFAMILY	Capreolinae

The **Peruvian dwarf brocket** *M. chunyi* is found to the east of the Andes mountains in Bolivia and Peru, where it occupies forests and highlands over 1,000 metres above sea level to as high as 4,000 metres. It has been described as being coloured a cinnamon to rufous brown with greyer legs and neck. It is probably the smallest of the brockets, being only 35–38 cm (14–15 in) at the shoulder and weighs 8–12 kg (17½–26½ lb). Some animals may have a darker neck and head, which might be a contributing factor along with the small size to it once being confused, like the dwarf red brocket, with the northern pudu *Pudu mephistophiles*. Very little is known about its ecology. Populations are severely fragmented and continue to decrease in range, while numbers are thought to be declining by around 40 per cent over three successive generations. Habitat degradation is considered to be the main cause.

▲ Peruvian dwarf brocket in typical high altitude habitat.
Photograph: Carlos Otávio Gussoni

◀ Colouration of the Peruvian dwarf brocket can vary. This one has the dark face that might cause confusion with the northern pudu *Pudu mephistophiles*. The picture was taken at 3,000 metres above sea level in a private conservation area near Cusco, southern Peru.
Photograph: Oscar Mujica/Peru Verde

◀ A Peruvian dwarf brocket buck, captured for treatment after injuries sustained in forest fires, at a sanctuary in Machu Picchu, Peru; it was later released successfully. Illustrates the small size and typical antlers of the species.
Photograph: Daniel Blanco/Peru Verde

Distribution	Bolivia and Peru
IUCN Red List Status 2022	**Vulnerable**, decreasing (last formal assessment 2016)
Also known as	Chunyi or dwarf brocket Spanish *Cabrito, Chuñi, Chuñitaruka, Cuñi, Venadillo*

Mazama nana
Brazilian dwarf brocket

ORDER	Artiodactyla
SUBORDER	Ruminantia
INFRAORDER	Pecora
FAMILY	Cervidae
SUBFAMILY	Capreolinae

▲ Brazilian dwarf brocket at the NUPECCE Deer Research and Conservation Centre in São Paulo, Brazil.
Photograph: Alexander F Meyer

▼ Portrait of a Brazilian dwarf brocket doe.
Photograph: Fabrício Vilela

Another dwarf brocket is the **Brazilian dwarf brocket** *M. nana*. Its range is far more uncertain; although it is believed to be found across much of southern Brazil, extending over the border into eastern Paraguay and just into north-east Argentina, records are scarce. As forests are increasingly broken up to make way for agriculture, scattered populations may remain in what pockets are left to them though it is considered to be the most threatened deer of its region. Some observers are divided regarding its habitat preferences; while some maintain that it may prefer more mountainous habitats, others see it as more a creature of the moist lowland forests of the lower hills where it is more regularly seen. Another of the smaller brockets, it has a shiny, dark chestnut-red pelage, measures some 45 cm (17½ in) at the shoulder and seldom weighs much more than 15 kg (33 lb). Compared to other brockets it is relatively short-legged and has large preorbital glands.

Distribution	Argentina, Brazil and Paraguay
IUCN Red List Status 2022	**Vulnerable**, trend unknown (last formal assessment 2015
Also known as	Pygmy brocket or lesser brocket Spanish *Corzuela enana*; Portuguese *Veado-mão-curta*

DEER SPECIES | CERVIDAE – CAPREOLINAE

Mazama pandora

Yucatán brown brocket

ORDER	Artiodactyla
SUBORDER	Ruminantia
INFRAORDER	Pecora
FAMILY	Cervidae
SUBFAMILY	Capreolinae

One of the larger brockets is the **Yucatán brown brocket** *M. pandora* which, as its name implies, is found only on the Yucatán Peninsula of south-eastern Mexico, its range extending slightly over the neighbouring borders with Belize and Guatemala. Here the climate is humid, the terrain is largely flat and a mixture of tall and short jungles provide its preferred habitat. It is more of an adaptable generalist than some of the other brockets and will also range across more open vegetation types including shrubland. Research now suggests that it may actually be far more closely related to the genus *Odocoileus* than to *Mazama*, a discovery that has the potential to drive far wider reclassifications.

The Yucatán brown brocket is a uniform brown to grey brown in colour, with large ears compared to others of the genus and has a patch of bristly hair on the wide forehead between the eyes. The antlers of males are distinctive, being set well apart on wide pedicles, and can measure around 15 cm (6 in). Average weight is around 15 kg (33 lb) and shoulder height some 50 cm (19½ in).

▲ Yucatán brown brocket buck, pictured at Xcaret Park, Playa del Carmen, Mexico.
Photograph: Alexander F Meyer

◄ Yucatán brown brocket doe.
Photographs: Alexander F Meyer

◄ Portrait of Yucatán brown brocket buck in velvet.

Distribution	Belize, Guatemala and Mexico
IUCN Red List Status 2022	**Vulnerable**, decreasing (last formal assessment 2015)
Also known as	Spanish *Temazate café*

Mazama rufina

Dwarf red brocket

▶ Dwarf red brocket pictured at Quito Zoo, Ecuador.
Photograph: Alexander F Meyer

ORDER	Artiodactyla
SUBORDER	Ruminantia
INFRAORDER	Pecora
FAMILY	Cervidae
SUBFAMILY	Capreolinae

Distribution

Colombia, Ecuador and Peru

IUCN Red List Status 2022

Vulnerable, decreasing
(last formal assessment 2015)

Also known as

Little red brocket

Spanish *Venado chonta*, *Venado de páramo*

The **dwarf red brocket** *M. rufina* is a small mountain form of the genus. It is restricted to higher ground between 1,500 and 3,500 metres above sea level in the northern Andes of Colombia, Ecuador and Peru where it inhabits the cooler, wet cloud forests. Being largely nocturnal, it is seldom seen and lives in small territories either alone or in pairs. It is one of the smaller brockets, standing around 45 cm (17½ in) at the shoulder and weighing 10–15 kg. The body is rounded and robust on short legs with a reddish pelage and a dark head and legs which appear almost black in some individuals – this colouration sometimes leads to it being confused with the northern pudu *Pudu mephistophiles*, although it is a notably larger animal. Antlers are simple spikes measuring up to 8 cm (3 in) in length.

Mazama temama

Central American red brocket

▶ Central American red brocket pair (buck on right).
Photograph: Brent Huffman

ORDER	Artiodactyla
SUBORDER	Ruminantia
INFRAORDER	Pecora
FAMILY	Cervidae
SUBFAMILY	Capreolinae

Distribution

Belize, Colombia, Costa Rica, El Salvador, Guatemala, Honduras, Mexico, Nicaragua, Panama

IUCN Red List Status 2022

Data Deficient, decreasing
(last formal assessment 2015)

Also known as

Northern brocket

Spanish *Temazate, Venado cabrito, Venado de montaña, Venado temazate*;
Portuguese *Veado-mateiro*

The final species is the **Central American red brocket** *M. temama*. Distributed across much of Central America in primary and secondary tropical forest up to 2,800 metres above sea level, it tends to avoid more open areas. It has a reddish-brown pelage while the head and neck contrast as a dark grey or even black. A larger brocket, it stands around 61cm (24 in) at the shoulder and might weigh up to 20 kg (44 lb). The antlers of the buck seldom exceed 8 cm (3 in). It is one of the least studied of the South American deer and very little is known about its precise range and overall numbers. Until its distribution and ecology are better understood, it remains categorised as Data Deficient by the IUCN although it is considered to be threatened. Systematic hunting may be one reason, and it is also controlled locally in the course of crop protection, particularly among bean croplands.

DEER SPECIES | CERVIDAE – CAPREOLINAE

Odocoileus hemionus

Mule deer

ORDER	Artiodactyla
SUBORDER	Ruminantia
INFRAORDER	Pecora
FAMILY	Cervidae
SUBFAMILY	Capreolinae

ALONG WITH THE closely related white-tailed deer *O. virginianus*, the mule deer is considered to be one of the key species among the New World deer. The ranges of the two overlap, that of the white-tailed deer effectively covering much of North America whilst the mule deer is confined to more westerly parts. The two have certainly been known to interbreed and produce hybrids, but this is surprisingly uncommon outside captivity, and the survival rates of any progeny are said to be extremely low. Compared to white-tailed deer, most mule deer are larger and are better adapted to thriving in more extreme climates. Furthermore, their ability to 'stott', that curious bouncing gait (also known as 'pronking') in which all four feet leave and return to the ground at the same time, enables them to ascend slopes quickly or negotiate obstacles in places where running is a less efficient means of escape from predators.

▲ A mature buck in Yellowstone National Park.
Photograph: David Mark

▼ (*left*) A yearling Rocky Mountain mule deer buck with rudimentary pedicles from which his antlers will eventually grow, pictured in Arches National Park, Utah.
Photograph: Alexander F Meyer

▼ (*right*) A mature Rocky Mountain mule deer buck.
Photograph: Coke Smith

A GUIDE TO THE DEER OF THE WORLD

▲ (*left*) A mature doe in mid-bound.
Photograph: Brent Huffman

▲ (*right*) Fawns retain their spots until they are around four months old.
Photograph: Pixabay

The black-tailed deer was once treated as a separate species, but now they and the mule deer are considered to be one and the same. Nevertheless, the Sitka and Columbian subspecies are held to be a distinct group within the species, with closer links to the white-tailed deer. A significant feature distinguishing them from the typical mule deer subspecies is the black upper surface to the tail compared to the largely white, black-tipped tail of the latter.

There are currently considered to be at least nine, and potentially ten, subspecies:

Common name	Scientific name	Range (*entirely insular and isolated)
California mule deer	*O. h. californicus*	Mid-California
Cedros Island deer	*O. h. cerrosensis*	Cedros Island, Baja California, Mexico*: a dwarf form. The population is small, heavily threatened by poaching, dogs and human presence, and is classified as **Vulnerable**.
Columbian black-tailed deer	*O. h. columbianus*	British Columbia to northern California
Desert mule deer	*O. h. crooki*	North Mexico
Southern mule deer	*O. h. fuliginatus*	California
Rocky Mountain mule deer	*O. h. hemionus*	West and Central North America: the largest of the subspecies.
Inyo mule deer	*O. h. inyoensis*	California (NB: the validity of this as a separate subspecies has been questioned).
Peninsula mule deer	*O. h. peninsulae*	Baja California, Mexico: the smallest and lightest in colour of all the subspecies.
Tiburon Island mule deer	*O. h. sheldoni*	Tiburon Island, Mexico*: a very small subspecies.
Sitka black-tailed deer	*O. h. sitkensis*	Coastal area and islands off British Columbia and Alaska: smaller on average than many of the more southerly races.

◀ California mule deer sparring.
Photograph: David Boston

The mule deer has been introduced outside its natural range to Hawaii and Argentina. In the early 1960s, 40 Columbian black-tailed deer were released on Kauai Island, Hawaii; today they represent a modest but carefully managed renewable resource, which is tolerated with limited hunting permitted. This provides a stark contrast to the issues associated with the introduced and invasive axis deer *Axis axis* on some other Hawaiian islands. Around the 1980s mule deer were stocked on a number of ranches in the foothills of the Argentinian Andes for hunting; although there were concerns that they might escape into the adjacent national parks, seemingly these fears have not been realised. Several attempts to introduce the mule deer onto both the North and South Islands of New Zealand around the turn of the last century all failed.

Within North America, Sitka black-tailed deer were introduced to the Queen Charlotte (now Haida Gwaii) Islands off the British Columbia coast in the 1890s. Around the Gulf of Alaska, they were introduced to Prince William Sound between 1917 and 1923, the Kodiak Island Archipelago between 1924 and 1930, Yakutat in

▼ (*left*) Columbian mule deer doe.

▼ (*right*) A Sitka mule deer buck with antlers half-grown.
Photographs: Coke Smith

1924, and the Skagway and Haines area during the 1950s, further extending their northerly ranges on the west coast.

Across most of its range the mule deer is abundant with stable populations. This is thanks to effective levels of management at provincial, federal and state levels as appropriate, to monitor abundance, determine management objectives and regulate hunting. In some parts of Canada and the USA, however, there is some unease about slight declines in populations, while there have been local extinctions suggested in the Chihuahuan desert region of Mexico. Most of the subspecies are not considered to be threatened, although the small numbers of Cedros Island deer are subject to poaching and dog attacks and are singled out as being Vulnerable.

FACT BOX – *Mule deer*

World distribution	Native to Canada (Alberta, British Columbia, Manitoba, Northwest Territories and Yukon), Mexico (Baja California, Chihuahua, Coahuila, Nuevo León, Sonora and Tamaulipas) and the United States (Alaska, Arizona, California, Colorado, Idaho, Iowa, Kansas, New Mexico, Montana, Nebraska, Nevada, North Dakota, Oklahoma, Oregon, South Dakota, Texas, Utah, Washington and Wyoming). Introduced to Argentina and the United States (Hawaii).
IUCN Red List Status 2022	**Least Concern**, population stable (last formal assessment 2015).
Sexes	*Male:* Buck *Female:* Doe *Young:* Fawn
Also known as	Black-tailed deer, bounding deer, brush deer, burro deer, cactus buck, desert buck, donkey deer, grey buck, great-eared buck, hill deer, jumping deer, plains deer (*also see subspecies above*). French *Cerf mulet, cerf mulet à queue noire* or *daim fauve à queue noire*; German *Maultierhirsch* or *shwartzwedel-hirsch*; Mexican *Venado cola negra* or *venado mula*; Spanish *Ciervo mula*. Native American: Chipewayan *Yatúé*; Cree *Ah-pe-tchi-mu-sis, apsecmoosis, ap-is-chich-i-koosh* or *yatúé*; Dogrib *Tohdzi*; Ogallala Sioux *Tah-heen chála*; Yankton Sioux *Tah-char*; Taos *Pahna*.
Recognition features	A medium-sized deer with a rusty red or tan-coloured coat in summer, becoming brownish-grey in winter. There are regional variations with various shades of red, grey and brown, desert forms being generally paler than woodland ones. The insides of the legs and belly are white, the rump patch white or yellowish. The tail is slightly shorter than that of the white-tailed deer; that of the mule deer is white with a black tip, though black almost covers the upper surface on the black-tailed deer group (Columbian and Sitka). The mule deer has distinctively long ears, which give rise to its common name. The face has a V-shaped mark above the eyes, often extending into a dark patch – more distinctive on bucks – and a pale band above the nose.
Height (at shoulder)	Average 84–106 cm (33–42 in) for males, 80–100 cm (31–39 in) for females.
Weight	Average 114–136 kg (250–300 lb). An exceptional Rocky Mountain mule deer buck might reach 213 kg (470 lb). Sitka black-tailed deer are notably smaller than most races, averaging far less at between 48 kg (106 lb) and 90 kg (198 lb). The smallest of all the subspecies is the Peninsula mule deer, sometimes weighing as little as 45 kg (99 lb) for males and 42 kg (92 lb) for females, followed closely by the Cedros and Tiburon subspecies.

DEER SPECIES | CERVIDAE – CAPREOLINAE

FACT BOX – *Mule deer*

Food	An intermediate feeder which primarily browses new growth on shrubs and trees; also takes forbs and grazes on grasses. Acorns, seeds and fleshy fruits are also eaten according to season. It avoids highly fibrous material which is less easily digested.
Habitat	This highly adaptable deer uses habitats ranging widely between desert, semi-desert, shrub woodland, the Great Plains, and temperate forest as well as the tropical deciduous region of Baja California. It can often be found at elevations of around 2,300 metres, and up to 3,000 metres, above sea level during the summer months.
Voice	During the rut bucks make low, repeated bleats, increasing in intensity to a bellow, and bark at rivals. Does will also bellow, and both sexes bark in response to threats.
Annual behaviour	A migratory animal, especially in mountainous areas, the mule deer prefers to spend the summer months on higher ground and winters in lower valleys where food is more plentiful. The same discrete home ranges tend to be used year on year. Social groupings of females are formed of 'clans' based on maternal descent; these clans can combine during the winter to form larger herds which contain both bucks and does. Bucks segregate themselves in the spring when they disperse to their summer ranges and live a more solitary lifestyle, although they can form groups of unrelated animals. Mule deer have excellent eyesight and hearing. Predator avoidance strategies can involve hiding, stealthily manoeuvring, or bounding away uphill to disadvantage pursuers. Although they swim well they seldom take to water. If a predator is identified some way off, mule deer may immediately move away for several miles to a safer location.
Rut	The rut mostly takes place between late September and mid-November. Though bucks compete fiercely, there is a great deal of bluffing without physical conflict and many confrontations end with a lesser buck simply backing off. Both bucks and does range widely when in search of a partner; the bucks lose condition during the breeding season.
Gestation and birthing	Gestation is around 204 days and most birthing occurs in June, although it may take place as early as April or as late as July. Twins are common and triplets are occasionally recorded. The fawns are spotted and can weigh between 2 and 5 kg (4½–11 lb); the spots fade by the time they are about 4 months old.
Antlers (typical)	Mule deer antlers are bifurcated, typically being an arrangement of even forks rather than a main beam with single tines leaving it. A normal format consist of short, upright brows with double forks on each side, making a total of 10 points; deer in the black-tailed group often do not have a third main tine and only produce 8 points. The most impressive antlers are said to be produced by Rocky Mountain mule deer in Colorado and Wyoming.
Antler cycle	Casting is between January and March, the older bucks generally shedding their antlers first. Regrowth is not immediately apparent and is usually complete and clean among older bucks by early September.
Lifespan	Typically around 9–11 years
Threats	The primary predators are coyotes, cougars and wolves. Bears (black and grizzly), bobcats, Canadian lynx and wolverines are also a threat, although mainly to fawns or infirm adults. The most pressing current threat is Chronic Wasting Disease, a transmissible spongiform encephalopathy, which is almost invariably fatal and has been diagnosed in the Rocky Mountains and other mid-western regions of the USA. Others include competition with domestic grazing, feral dogs, habitat changes and other impacts of human presence.

Odocoileus virginianus

White-tailed deer

ORDER	Artiodactyla
SUBORDER	Ruminantia
INFRAORDER	Pecora
FAMILY	Cervidae
SUBFAMILY	Capreolinae

▲ A typical North American buck.
Photograph: David Mark

► Twin fawns are common.
Photograph: David Ranck

▼ The antlers of the mature buck are characteristically swept forward.
Photograph: Pexels

THE WHITE-TAILED DEER is the most widely distributed and numerous wild ungulate found in the Americas; population estimates can vary wildly, but it has been suggested that there may be as many as 15 million in the USA alone. Some 38 subspecies are listed by the IUCN and some sources claim that there may yet be more, though the situation has been complicated by transplantations and interbreeding. Although the species is considered to be of Least Concern overall, some of the subspecies are less numerous, with the Columbian and the Florida Key white-tailed deer in particular classified as 'seriously threatened' under the US Endangered Species Act. Elsewhere some populations have proven difficult to assess, mainly due to accessibility, over-hunting or a lack of protection.

DEER SPECIES | CERVIDAE – CAPREOLINAE

Subspecies of the white-tailed deer

Common name (– white-tailed deer)	Scientific name	Range (*entirely insular and isolated)
Acapulco –	O. v. acapulcensis	Southern Mexico
Northern woodland –	O. v. borealis	South-east Canada and north-east USA
Venado –	O. v. cariacou	French Guiana and extreme northern Brazil
Carmen Mountain –	O. v. carminis	Northern Mexico
Chiriqui –	O. v. chiriquensis	Panama
Florida Key –	O. v. clavium	Florida Keys (Florida, USA)*
Coues –	O. v. couesi	Arizona, USA and northern Mexico
Curaçao -	O. v. curassavicus	Curaçao
Dakota -	O. v. dacotensis	North Dakota, USA
Venado	O. v. goudotii	Colombia and west Venezuela
South American -	O. v. gymnotis	Venezuela and the Guianas
Hilton Head Island -	O. v. hiltonensis	Hilton Head Island (South Carolina, USA)*
Columbian -	O. v. leucurus	Oregon, USA and western coastal area
Kansas -	O. v. macrourus	Kansas, USA and surrounding states
Avery Island -	O. v. mcilhennyi	Avery Island (Louisiana, USA)
Margarita Island -	O. v. margaritae	Margarita Island, Venezuela
Mexican -	O. v. mexicanus	Central Mexico
Miquilhuan -	O. v. miquihuanensis	Northern and central Mexico
Chiapas -	O. v. nelsoni	Southern Mexico to Nicaragua
Blackbeard Island -	O. v. nigribarbis	Blackbeard Island (Georgia, USA)*
Oaxaca -	O. v. oaxacensis	Southern Mexico
Northwestern or Rocky Mountain -	O. v. ochrourus	North-west USA and Canada
Florida coastal -	O. v. osceola	North-west Florida, USA
Andean -	O. v. peruvianus	Peru, extreme north-western Bolivia
Coiba Island -	O. v. rothschildi	Coiba Island, Panama*
Florida -	O. v. seminolus	Florida, USA
Sinaloa -	O. v. sinaloae	Mid-western and southern Mexico
Bulls Island -	O. v. taurinsulae	Bulls Island (South Carolina, USA)*
Texas -	O. v. texanus	Texas, USA
Mexican lowland -	O. v. thomasi	Southern Mexico
Rain forest -	O. v. toltecus	Southern Mexico to El Salvador
Venado	O. v. tropicalis	Ecuador and Peru, possibly also Colombia
Nicaraguan -	O. v. nemoralis	Central America
Venado	O. v. ustus	Ecuador, possibly also southern Colombia and northern Peru
Hunting Island -	O. v. venatorius	Hunting Island (South Carolina, USA)*
Northern Veracruz -	O. v. veraecrucis	Coastal eastern Mexico
Virginia -	O. v. virginiana	Virginia, USA and adjoining states
Yucatan -	O. v. yucatanensis	Yucatan, Mexico and Honduras

A GUIDE TO THE DEER OF THE WORLD

1. Portrait of a northern woodland white-tailed buck *O. v. borealis*. **Photograph:** Brent Huffman

2. A buck of the Nicaraguan subspecies *O. v. nemoralis* photographed in Costa Rica. **Photograph:** Alexander F Meyer

3. Coue's white-tailed deer doe, Arizona. **Photograph:** Alexander F Meyer

4. A mixed group of venados *O. v. goudotii* with the bucks in velvet, in Parque Jaime Duque, Bogotá, Colombia. **Photograph:** Alexander F Meyer

5. A young venado *O. v. cariacou* buck with new antler growth just starting to appear, pictured at the NUPECCE Deer Research and Conservation Centre in São Paulo, Brazil. **Photograph:** Alexander F Meyer

6. South American white-tailed doe *O. v. gymnotis* at the Tierpark, Berlin. **Photograph:** Klaus Rudloff

7. The rare Florida Key white-tailed deer *O. v. clavium*. **Photograph:** Donald Hastings

Unrestricted hunting was almost the undoing of the white-tailed deer. Before the arrival of European settlers, native Americans lived in balance with the wildlife that they relied upon to support their largely nomadic lifestyles, but colonial farming saw the widespread clearance of habitat and increasing numbers of domestic stock. Meat hunting with guns, traps, snares and dogs proliferated: deer populations started to dwindle and disappear entirely in some places, very probably along with some subspecies. The extent of the slaughter cannot be overstated and for example, in December 1872 alone, no less than six tons of prepared venison was shipped from Litchfield, Minnesota, to the markets of the East. By 1880 significant concern was beginning to be expressed about the future of the white-tailed deer and finally game laws started to be enacted to impose strict bag limits on hunters.

A major turning point came in 1937, when the US Congress passed its Federal Aid in Wildlife Restoration Act: this obliged all individual states to institute wildlife agencies, using the revenues raised from taxes on sporting arms and ammunition and hunting licences. Despite some local resistance and continued poaching, the deer returned, assisted by transplantations: it was not until much later that some states, such as Kansas in 1965, felt that enough deer were present to justify a hunting season. Recoveries since have been so successful that in some places high deer populations are having a serious effect on cash crops, semi-urban areas are seeing more and more animal encroachment, and collisions with motor vehicles are increasing. Paradoxically, the same forces which almost wiped out the white-tailed deer also radically reduced the large predators – such as wolves, cougars and bears – which might now assist in regulating their numbers.

The rarest of the subspecies, and one of the six entirely confined to islands, is the Florida Key white-tailed deer *O. v. clavium*, the smallest of the North American native deer. Its size is attributed to a condition called insular dwarfism, which occurs when a species has evolved to have a smaller body-size as a result of being limited to reduced environments. Confined to just a few of the islands that comprise the Florida Keys, it is largely restricted to those that provide fresh water supplies during the dry months, and it is also under pressure from human encroachment and hurricane damage to its habitat. Numbers may have reduced to just 25 during the 1950s, and in 2016 a screw-worm infestation may have killed as many as one-eighth of the total population. Today there are estimated to be only between 700 and 800 animals.

▲ (*top*) Bucks sparring.
Photograph: Bryan Hansen

▲ (*middle*) Twin fawns of the northern woodland species.
Photograph: Brent Huffman

▲ (*bottom*) Fawns are left hidden alone for their first few weeks.
Photograph: Robert Woegner

The most successful introduction of white-tailed deer outside their native range has undoubtedly been in Finland. Of an original eight animals originally shipped from Minnesota, only one buck and four does survived the sea journey to eventually escape from their enclosure in 1938. They were supplemented by a further four animals in 1949. Today there are believed to be more than 100,000 white-tails living wild in Finland, and the Finnish Natural Resources Agency issues around 40,000 hunting permits each year in an effort to control population growth. Elsewhere, the deer have been less successful; although efforts to introduce them to Bulgaria failed, a small free-living population remains in the Czech Republic, some 50 kilometres to the south of Prague. Viable but very localised populations also exist in New Zealand.

The Finnish success is probably due to a lack of competition in a country where the native deer, which include roe, reindeer and Eurasian elk, only existed in low numbers at the time of the introductions. White-tailed deer are considered to be poor competitors when faced with the European deer species, hence their limited success in New Zealand where the introductions of other species have enjoyed greater success; in parts of the USA where sika and axis deer have been released, the white-tailed has been found to be at a local disadvantage.

FACT BOX – *White-tailed deer*

World distribution	Native to most of southern Canada and much of the USA (though absent from some western states of the USA, and from Mexico to the west of the Gulf of California), Central America, and south as far as northern Colombia, much of Venezuela, Guyana, Suriname and French Guiana. Further populations in Peru on the west and east sides of the Andes reaching as far as the extreme west of Bolivia. Introduced to Prince Edward Island (Canada), the Czech Republic, Finland, New Zealand and Slovakia.
IUCN Red List Status 2022	**Least Concern**, population stable (last formal assessment 2015).
Sexes	*Male:* Buck *Female:* Doe *Young:* Fawn
Also known as	Bannertail deer, Bush deer, Key deer, Long-tailed deer, Meadow buck, Plains deer, Swamp deer, Towhead deer, Toy deer (Key deer), Willow deer (among many more local variations). Aztec *Iztek maza*; Brazilian *Veado valheiro do mato*; Czechoslovakian *Jelenec virzinsky*; Cree *Apeese-mongoos*; French *Cerf à queue blanche*; German *Virginiahirsh* or *weisswedel*; Mexican *Aculliame*; Spanish *Cariacú* or *Venado cola blanca*; Sioux *Squinator*, *Tah-chah-seentay-skah* or *Tah-heenchalah*; Taos *Pah-hu-mana*.
Recognition features	The summer coat is generally a reddish-brown with a white patch on the throat and pale inner ears. Typically, there is a band of white hair above the nose and also around the eyes. The eponymous tail is between 10 and 37 cm (3.9 to 14.6 in) long, white on the underside and held erect and flagged when the animal is alarmed. The coat turns to a dull grey/brown in winter.
Height (at shoulder)	Usually 80–100 cm (31–39 in) for a buck, does somewhat smaller, but widely variable between subspecies. In general, larger forms are found to the north of the species' range, decreasing in size further south. A Florida Key buck will average only 76 cm (30 in) tall at the shoulder, while the smallest subspecies on Margarita Island may be as small as 60 cm (23½ in). Animals from the Andes are larger than those from more tropical habitats.

FACT BOX – White-tailed deer

Weight	Weights also vary considerably. Averages for bucks range between 68 and 136 kg (150 to 300 lb) although bucks weighing up to 180 kg (400 lb) are regularly recorded in northern parts of the range. Does are lighter and average 45 to 90 kg (100 to 200 lb). White-tailed deer from more tropical southern areas may average closer to 35 to 50 kg (77 to 110 lb), while a Margarita Island buck may weigh as little as 30 kg (66 lb).
Food	A predominantly browsing deer which takes a wide variety of vegetation according to local availability. This can include legumes, grasses, buds, twigs and new growth, as well as seasonal fruits and nuts. Yucca, cacti and hardy shrubs are eaten in desert areas, and conifers may be heavily browsed in winter when other foods are scarce.
Habitat	An adaptable deer which inhabits a wide variety of habitats, from woodland, farmland and swamp to cactus and thornbush deserts. Ideal habitat would include dense cover for movement and lying up, with food sources around the edges.
Voice	Normally quiet but may snort or whistle, especially when disturbed. A buck pursuing a doe in oestrus makes a characteristic grunting sound. Fawns may bleat.
Annual behaviour	The white-tailed deer is naturally shy and cautious, especially in areas where it is hunted heavily by humans. It is largely solitary, especially during the summer when it is usually only seen singly or in family units. Bucks may occasionally form small groups but these disband before the rut. Female fawns may stay with their mothers for up to 2 years, but a buck fawn will only do so for a year. Large herds, mainly comprising of does and fawns, may be seen during the winter but the sexes may mix. They often congregate in 'yarding' areas, where heavy cover offers both food and protection from the elements.
Rut	In North America rutting can start as early as September but peaks in late October or early November. Bucks will spar between themselves to achieve dominance and gain access to individual does, afterwards accompanying them for 1 or 2 days before seeking another. Further south, rutting may take place much later and depends on the locality; in Peru, for example, it can take place as late as March.
Gestation and birthing	After a gestation period of around 7 months, between 1 and 3 spotted fawns are born, usually in May or June. They are left hidden for their first 3 to 4 weeks, during which time their mother returns to feed them 4 or 5 times a day. After this time they accompany her on foraging trips and are weaned by 10 weeks of age.
Antlers (typical)	The antlers of a mature buck curve forwards and inwards in a characteristic sweeping formation. The number of tines produced can vary considerably: 7 or 8 is average although there may be many more. The antlers of deer in Central and South America tend to bear fewer tines compared to animals further north.
Antler cycle	Most bucks in northern America shed their antlers in January or February, although immature animals may cast considerably later. Most regrowth is complete with antlers clean of velvet by September. In southern America, antler shedding may be more irregular, and bucks with antlers in velvet may be encountered at any time of the year.
Lifespan	Around 10 years in the wild with up to 20 years recorded, though frequently considerably less.
Threats	White-tailed deer are an important prey item for a wide variety of large predators which can include wolves, cougar, bears, bobcats, lynx, coyotes and jaguars. More specifically in southern America, human threats can include over-hunting, poaching (which has been known to cause local population extinction), habitat loss and feral dogs.

Ozotoceros bezoarticus

Pampas deer

ORDER	Artiodactyla
SUBORDER	Ruminantia
INFRAORDER	Pecora
FAMILY	Cervidae
SUBFAMILY	Capreolinae

▲ A buck of the main race *O. b. bezoarticus*, Bioparque M'Bopicuá, Uruguay.
Photograph: Alexander F Meyer

▼ Doe (main race).
Photograph: Alexander F Meyer

ONCE ABUNDANT AND widespread across the grasslands of South America, the range of the pampas deer has now shrunk to the point that its remaining populations are highly isolated in very reduced pockets. The world population may number as few as 20,000 animals but could be higher. Five subspecies are recognised, all being broadly similar in appearance and habits, but with some variations in coat shade. *Ozotoceros bezoarticus bezoarticus* is found in eastern and central Brazil, while *O. b. leucogaster* inhabits south-western Brazil, south-eastern Bolivia, Paraguay and northern Argentina. *O. b. celer* is distributed across the Argentinian pampas. *O. b. arerunguaensis* and *O. b. uruguayensis* are found only in Uruguay.

The alternative name of 'Stinking deer' comes from the well-developed interdigital glands on the rear hooves that produce a pungent odour, which has been likened to that of onions. It is particularly noticeable around bedding areas and well-used pathways and may even be detected from as far as a mile away. It has been suggested that this smell could be associated with an alarm signal, and that these deer may even be able to express increased amounts deliberately when stressed.

The scientific name of the pampas deer refers to a bezoar: this is an object that can form in the stomachs of several animal species, including deer, when something indigestible becomes stuck inside the digestive tract and over time is coated with minerals until it becomes smooth and hard. In many ways, bezoars are a sort of mammalian pearl, having parallels with what happens when a foreign object becomes trapped inside a mollusc. Such stones have been reputed to have medicinal qualities, and one local belief was that a hunted pampas deer would reputedly spit out the stone to distract the hunter and thus save its life.

DEER SPECIES | CERVIDAE – CAPREOLINAE

◂ (left) A buck of the subspecies *O. b. leucogaster* in the Iberá National Park, Argentina.

◂ (right) A pampas subspecies *O.b. celer* doe with her short tail raised, pictured in Campos del Tuyú National Park, Argentina.
Photographs: Francisco González Táboas

It is ironic that the pampas deer has few natural predators yet has reached a point where it is classified as Near Threatened. In the past, exploitation for its hides and bezoars played an important part in its decline – records covering a 10-year period in the late nineteenth century show that some 2 million hides were exported to Europe from Buenos Aires alone. Over-hunting still occurs and is not helped by the fact that the pampas deer is naturally curious and less likely to flee at the sight of humans. Human encroachment is, however, the main concern today. Farming has taken over the specialised pampas habitat that this deer relies upon, while farm stocks have introduced diseases. All are contributing to a continuing decline to the point where remaining populations are increasingly fragmented, although some more enlightened ranchers are beginning to set aside conservation areas to support the deer.

For this fragile species, more research to increase our understanding of it and urgent conservation measures are needed if it is not to be allowed to diminish even further.

▾ *O. b. leucogaster* buck.
Photograph: Karl Rudloff

FACT BOX – *Pampas deer*

World distribution	Native to Argentina, Bolivia, Brazil, Paraguay and Uruguay.
IUCN Red List Status 2022	**Near Threatened**, population decreasing (last formal assessment 2015).
Sexes	*Male:* Buck *Female:* Doe *Young:* Fawn
Also known as	American roe, Stinking deer, Camping or Field deer (Brazil), White deer.
	Argentina *Venado* or *gamo* (female); Brazil *Veado brancho, veado compeiro* or *veado campiero*; French *Cerf des Pampas*; German *Pampshirsch*; Guarani *Guazu-ti* or *guazu-vira*; Mapuchi *Chuli* or *chruli*; Spanish *Ciervo de la Pampa*; Paraguay *Venadillo*; Puelche Indian *Joam shesie*; Tupi *Veado*, Uruguay *Venado de Campo*.

FACT BOX – *Pampas deer*

Recognition features	A medium sized, lightly built deer. The colour of the upper body ranges from a light yellowish-grey to a reddish-brown with lighter underparts according to subspecies and geographical location. The short, wide tail is darker on the top and can be raised when alarmed or running to show the white underside. Females can have whorls of hair on their foreheads which resemble antler stubs. There is no significant difference between summer and winter coats.
Height (at shoulder)	70–75 cm (27–30 in)
Weight	30–40 kg (66–88 lb), males slightly larger than females.
Food	Little studied, but it appears that the pampas deer browses selectively on new green growth as well as feeding more generally on shrubs and grass seed-heads.
Habitat	A deer of the open grasslands that prefers to avoid woodland or mountainous country.
Voice	Generally silent. Both sexes bleat and utter an alarm whistle.
Annual behaviour	A sedentary deer which exhibits no marked daily or seasonal movement. More solitary in winter, moving singly or in pairs. They start to collect together during the spring and by summer herds – which can hold as many as 50 animals – may be encountered. This is an incautious deer that can be overly curious and investigate the unusual rather than flee. Females with fawns may feign a limp as part of a distraction display, and have been known to attack potential predators (including humans). Flight is a series of long, flat jumps with poor endurance.
Rut	Mainly a seasonal breeder with most rutting taking part during the early months of the year; in Argentina and Uruguay rutting is mostly in February. However, rutting and subsequent births have been recorded at all times of the year. Several males may compete for a female and fighting is frequent, in which antlers are used for thrusting and forefeet are flailed at opponents. There is no attempt to defend a harem or territoriality, nor is there any pair bonding after mating.
Gestation and birthing	Most fawns are born between September and November after a gestation period lasting 7–7½ months. Fawns are spotted and only a single one is born.
Antlers (typical)	Males typically carry light and simple 6-point antlers with a brow and rear tine on each side. An average head will measure around 34 cm (13 in) in length.
Antler cycle	Casting occurs in August or September, and the new antlers are fully grown by the following December.
Lifespan	Around 12 years
Threats	There are few natural predators in its pampas habitat but animals may sometimes be taken by pumas and maned wolves. Loss of habitat to agricultural clearance and cattle farming is the most significant issue, with available habitat reduced to less than 1 per cent of what it was a century ago. Habitat fragmentation remains the most serious threat to the species. Uncontrolled hunting and feral dogs are also responsible for declines.

DEER SPECIES | CERVIDAE – CAPREOLINAE

Pudu mephistophiles
Northern pudu

ORDER	Artiodactyla
SUBORDER	Ruminantia
INFRAORDER	Pecora
FAMILY	Cervidae
SUBFAMILY	Capreolinae

▲ A rare photograph of the elusive northern pudu taken in Pichincha Province, Ecuador. Photograph: R Ahlman, www.pbase.com/ahlman

STANDING ONLY A little more than a foot high at the shoulder, the northern pudu is distinguished by being the smallest member of the *Cervidae* or true deer and can be found only in a fragmented number of sub-populations across the northern Andes of Colombia, Ecuador and northern Peru. Its close relative the southern pudu is only slightly larger, though at no point do the ranges of the two overlap. Not only do their habitat preferences vary considerably, but their distribution is separated by some 2,000 miles of the central Andes.

Unlike the southern, the northern pudu is a creature of the uplands, living in mountain forests and humid grasslands at elevations above 2,000 metres, where its small size makes it extremely difficult to detect. It is well adapted for these damp habitats, having a thick coat comprised of long, stiff hairs, usually carried pressed flat against the body. An angry animal is said to bristle its fur and shiver.

It is only very seldom seen, living a largely solitary existence and only likely to be glimpsed with others of its kind when rutting or in mother and fawn pairs. At other times it is intolerant of and highly aggressive towards others. Such behaviour might be responsible for British zoologist William Edward de Winton choosing to give it the scientific name *mephistophiles* in 1896 after the demon of German folklore and the Faust legend, though the reason may simply be no more than a perceived demonic appearance caused by the sharply contrasting dark face against a paler neck and brown body.

The pudu runs in a series of leaps and bounds, driven by its powerful haunches, and in a style described as saltatorial (a term derived from that used to describe the limbs of grasshoppers and other

◀ An early illustration from *The Deer of all Lands* by Richard Lydekker (1898), which highlights the distinctive facial markings. The picture is based on an immature female, the only specimen available to naturalists at the time.

▲ A northern pudu pictured in typical habitat, captured on a trail camera in Ecuador.
Photographs: Wildlife Conservation Society – Ecuador Program

invertebrates which are modified for jumping). An animal pursued by a predator has little endurance, though, and if chased by dogs may quickly tire and succumb if it does not reach the sanctuary of cover quickly. There is a local belief that extreme fear can cause these deer to die from heart failure, though this has not been substantiated.

The northern pudu appears to be a more primitive deer than its southern cousin *Pudu puda*, as evidenced by the fact that it has not completely evolved to the point of entirely losing the canine tusks carried by its ancestors. The teeth of immature animals often include an upper milk canine, and a permanent upper canine may also be present in the teeth of some adults (albeit in a very vestigial form). Milk canines are only very rarely found in the immature southern pudu and almost never in adults, and the latter also has more pronounced preorbital scent glands and wider feet, though neither species has tarsal or metatarsal glands and only small interdigital glands.

The IUCN categorises the northern pudu as Data Deficient. Although there seems to be a strong ongoing decline with a long history of over-exploitation, of greater concern are habitat loss and predation by dogs associated with human encroachment. However, there remains much to be learned about its true distribution and the status of local populations. One of these, on the eastern slopes of the Andes in Peru, may even be a new species or subspecies, and is currently under investigation. Once more information becomes available, the species will be re-assessed.

FACT BOX – *Northern pudu*

World distribution	Native to Colombia, Ecuador and Peru.
IUCN Red List Status 2022	**Data Deficient**, population decreasing (last formal assessment 2018).
Sexes	*Male:* Buck *Female:* Doe *Young:* Fawn
Also known as	Ecuador pudu, rabbit deer. French *Pudu de l'Equateur, Poudou de nord, Pudu de nord* or *Pudella*; German *Nördlicher pudu*; Spanish *Ciervo enano, Pudú norteño, Sachacabra, Venadito de los Páramos, Venado conejo*.

FACT BOX – *Northern pudu*

Recognition features	A very small, stocky deer with a rounded body, carried on short, slender legs. The dense coat is largely a dark reddish-brown with a paler neck, with almost black head and feet which contrast sharply against the main body. The preorbital glands are small compared to those of *Pudu puda*. It has large haunches, rounded ears and a short snout; the overall appearance can be pig-like though it is only the size of a small dog. The tail is hard to distinguish and about 3 cm (1 in) in length.
Height (at shoulder)	32–35 cm (12½–13¾ in)
Weight	Up to around 9 kg (20 lb); there is very little size or weight dimorphism between the sexes.
Food	A selective browser, living primarily on the shoots, leaves and buds of herbaceous plants, grasses and fruit according to seasonal availability.
Habitat	Lives at higher elevations than the southern pudu and can be found between 1,700 and 4,000 metres above sea level in habitats ranging from montane forest to humid grasslands and scrublands.
Annual behaviour	Very little is understood about the behaviour of the northern pudu. It is shy and highly secretive, and probably largely nocturnal though research has been limited due to the inaccessible places it inhabits. If pursued, it will often try to gain sanctuary in water. It is believed that both sexes are highly territorial and aggressive towards others of their species, and that it is less likely to tolerate living in small groups as the southern pudu can do. Daily movement is often along established trails which are marked with scent from the suborbital glands, urine and faeces. Fighting between individuals is intense and includes butting and thrashing at an opponent with forelegs; females will bite when fighting other females, and a victorious male will bite another he is pursuing. A submissive animal may duck its head or lie flat on the ground.
Rut, gestation and birthing	Mating takes place around April and May and is followed by a 7-month gestation period. Only one young is born although twins have been very rarely recorded. The fawn weighs only about 400g (14 oz) and is a plain brown colour without any spots. It grows quickly and weighs 6 kg (13 lb) by the time it is 6 months old, remaining with its mother for up to a year. Sexual maturity may be reached between 6 months and a year old.
Antlers (typical)	Simple unforked spikes, usually curving backwards and around 6 cm (2¼ in) in length.
Antler cycle	Unconfirmed but assumed to be similar to that of the southern pudu, with antlers cast around July and then regrown and clean of velvet by early November.
Lifespan	8–10 years
Threats	Natural predators include puma, smaller cats, foxes and owls.
	Heavily exploited for its meat in the past; habitat loss associated with encroaching human settlements and predation by domestic dogs are now felt to be the prevalent threats.

Pudu puda
Southern pudu

ORDER	Artiodactyla
SUBORDER	Ruminantia
INFRAORDER	Pecora
FAMILY	Cervidae
SUBFAMILY	Capreolinae

▲ A typical mature buck.
Photograph: Klaus Rudloff

THOUGH THE SOUTHERN pudu cannot claim to be the smallest of the world's true deer – that distinction belongs to its northern cousin *P. mephistophiles* – it is a close-run thing. It is a truly diminutive animal, the males of which carry only rudimentary spike antlers, and is found only in the forests of southern Chile and south-western Argentina. There, amongst other challenges, it faces decreasing habitat through the depletion of forests, poaching can be intensive, and it is heavily predated by domestic dogs. Its name has its origins in *Mapudungun*, the language of the indigenous Mapuche people of southern Chile and south-western Argentina. Both the breeding and antler cycles seem to be regulated by daylight conditions; this is borne out by the rapid adaptation of animals kept in captivity in the Northern Hemisphere.

▶ A mature doe.
Photograph: Brent Huffman

▲ An adult buck (rear) courting a doe.
Photographs: Brent Huffman

▼ A mature buck with particularly well-developed antlers.

The IUCN currently classifies the southern pudu as Near Threatened but unless the existing trends change there is every likelihood that it will be moved into the Vulnerable category. Until recently the overall population was thought to number around 10,000 animals although there are indications that the actual figure may be higher. Nevertheless, numbers are still considered to be decreasing.

There is hope that the species can recover. Some 98 per cent of its recorded presence within Argentina is in national parks where it receives improved levels of protection, while in Chile there are also both public and privately owned protected areas. Furthermore, the southern pudu is widely kept in zoos and other captive collections and a stud book is maintained for individual animals; much of what we know about the biology of the species actually comes from the study of these.

In the wild, illegal hunting for subsistence or more commercial purposes is an important concern. On the 8,394 square kilometres (3,241 square miles) of Chiloé Island, off the west coast of Chile, more than 600 pudus were known to be captured during the 1980s, many of which were perhaps intended for private collections. Chiloé is a major stronghold of the pudu, which may actually exist there as a distinct subspecies, although this theory has not yet been proven. It is, significantly, a place where pumas and foxes do not currently exist. An ongoing major project to construct a bridge to connect the island with the mainland is a current concern, in that it might offer an opportunity for predators to access the island; in addition, it would enable mainland and island deer to mix genetically, with unknown consequences. Completion of the bridge is planned for 2023. It is a good example of how road developments may create threats beyond the more obvious prospect of animals being killed in collisions with motor vehicles.

The IUCN remains concerned by the gaps in our knowledge regarding the southern pudu, listing areas which need to be addressed so that its conservation needs can be better understood. These include the effect that numbers of introduced invasive species, such as the European hare, have on the abundance of the pumas that prey on them, and in turn on the pudu too. Another invasive species of concern is the wild boar, which may have a significant effect on fawn mortality: and it is also quite possible that pudu may be vulnerable to diseases carried by domestic cattle. Finally, consideration needs to be given as to how the species might be able to exist in deforested areas given over to plantation. Hence there are multiple threats: all of these factors, and more, need to be carefully weighed up before appropriate steps can be taken to reverse the pudu's decline.

➤ Fawns are born spotted.
Photograph: Klaus Rudloff

FACT BOX – *Southern pudu*

World distribution	Native to Argentina and Chile.
IUCN Red List Status 2022	**Near Threatened**, population decreasing (last formal assessment 2016).
Sexes	*Male:* Buck *Female:* Doe *Young:* Fawn
Also known as	Chilean pudu, Southern pudu. French *Poudou de sud*, *Pudu de sud* or *Pudella*; German *Südlicher pudu*; Spanish *Ciervo enano*, *Pudú*, *Pudú meridional*, *Venadito* or *Venado*.
Recognition features	A very small deer of stocky build with short, slender legs. Pelage colour may show wide variations according to sex, age, location and time of year but is generally a reddish-brown with slightly lighter underparts. The ears and the area surrounding the lips is more orangey. The snout is short, ears are rounded and the tail, which is usually not readily visible, is 3–4 cm (1–1½ in) long. The preorbital gland is noticeable (though not to the degree seen in other deer such as the muntjacs) and less pronounced in females.

FACT BOX – Southern pudu

Height (at shoulder)	37–41 cm (14½–16 in). Males only very slightly larger than females.
Weight	9–13 kg (20–28½ lb)
Food	A very selective browser which takes a variety of leaves, seeds, buds, fruits, and herbs. Although not usually found far from water sources, pudu can go for long periods without drinking as they get most of the moisture they need from their food sources.
Habitat	Uses both mature and disturbed forests, preferring areas with a well-developed understorey. Most feeding tends to take place in clearings and on the forest edge where food is more abundant. Shade is important, as the pudu appears to be intolerant of excessive heat. Not found at altitudes above 1,700 metres.
Voice	May bark if disturbed or alarmed; also said to make a hiss-like whistle.
Annual behaviour	Not strictly solitary, but rarely encountered in groups of more than 3 or 4 animals with a strict hierarchy and led by a dominant buck. They can be highly territorial within these groups. Fighting is common between animals of a similar size, after a threatening display which involves a number of stances, including broadside display in which the back is arched with the weight on the hind limbs and the tail held horizontal. Males have been known to kill rivals intruding on their territory: they may be chased to exhaustion, then bitten and struck with the forefeet. Active throughout both day and night, tending to rest during the middle part of the day. Scent-marking is important and is done by rubbing the antlers and forehead against vegetation, urination, and defecation. Much of their movement seems to be along established trails. They are very agile and will climb onto fallen logs and stand on their hind legs to reach food sources. When threatened by a predator, flight is in a zig-zag pattern and animals may hide in tunnels in the undergrowth or available burrows. Pudus tire quickly and are very vulnerable to sustained chasing.
Rut	The rut takes place between April and June (the autumn period in the Southern Hemisphere) with repeated mating taking place over a 3-day period.
Gestation and birthing	A single fawn, occasionally twins, is born between November and January after a gestation period lasting about 7 months (various researchers have put it between 197 and 223 days). This is a long time for such a small deer, and it has been suggested (though it remains to be proven) that there may be a degree of delayed implantation involved. Fawns have a reddish coat, with rows of pale spots along the upper part of the body. They weigh 890 g (13 oz) at birth and grow rapidly, are weaned at 2 months, and become sexually mature by 6 months (females) or 8 months (males).
Antlers (typical)	Simple spikes, usually of no more than 6–9 cm (2½–3½ in) in length, often curving backwards.
Antler cycle	Antlers are cast around July and are regrown and clean of velvet by early November.
Lifespan	Probably 8–10 years; up to 17 years recorded in captivity.
Threats	Natural predators include the puma (for which it is an important prey species), smaller cats, foxes, and eagle owls. Human threats come from habitat destruction for reasons including agriculture, logging and cattle-ranching. The establishment of exotic tree plantations with reduced understorey can remove much previously available habitat. Pudu are also over-hunted in places and killed by domestic dogs. Road development is a cause of concern because of the associated habitat clearance, further introductions of dogs (domestic or feral), or enabling the movement of predators.

Rangifer tarandus
Reindeer *or* caribou

Photograph: Isaac Bursey

ORDER	Artiodactyla
SUBORDER	Ruminantia
INFRAORDER	Pecora
FAMILY	Cervidae
SUBFAMILY	Capreolinae

The reindeer is a unique member of the deer family, in that it thrives in the more inhospitable and frequently frozen parts of the far Northern Hemisphere where other species would struggle and fail. Although a number of subspecies exist, they can in general terms be divided into the larger woodland and smaller tundra forms. The name comes from the Old Norse *hreindyri* – *hrein* is the specific name for the species, whilst *dyri* is a more general term for any type of animal. In North America the animals are called caribou, a word derived from the name *yalipu* given to them by the indigenous Micmac people of Canada, meaning 'the scratcher' or 'the shoveller'. This refers to their habit of digging in the snow for food, in particular for reindeer moss, a lichen which covers immense areas of northern tundra and taiga ecosystems and which forms a major part of their winter diet.

Although there are wide differences between the subspecies, a typical male reindeer might measure around 114 cm (45 in) high at the shoulders, while a full grown North American bull caribou might reach as high as 127 (50 in) and weigh up to 272 kg (600 lb). Body forms can

▶ The antlers of cows are smaller and lighter than those of bulls.
Photograph: Francesco Ungaro

vary considerably though; in general terms, the more southerly, woodland-dwelling animals can tend to be as much as a third larger than their northern, open-ground cousins. The size, weight and complexity of antlers show similar variations, and coat colours usually become lighter in northern habitats to reflect Arctic conditions. Some island forms, such as the reindeer of Spitzbergen and the Queen Charlotte Islands, became progressively smaller and shorter legged as a result of not having to deal with predation by wolves. On Newfoundland, though, where there were once wolves as well as large bears, the caribou grew much larger.

Reindeer are well adapted to living in colder habitats. Their fur has two layers: a soft, woolly undercoat which insulates them, and a longer-haired overcoat which consists of air-filled hairs. This not only repels water and provides insulation but also adds buoyancy when they swim; they ride noticeably higher in the water than other deer when they take to it. The hooves are large, to assist with travelling on snow and also with swimming (reindeer can run at up to 50 mph and have been recorded swimming at up to 4 mph). In addition, the feet adapt to the seasons, with pads becoming sponge-like in spring to give increased traction when the tundra is wet and soft. In winter they

▲ The colouration of calves is variable.
Photograph: Pixabay

◄ Reindeer feet are large and splay widely, an adaptation for walking and running on soft ground.

harden off: this exposes the rim of the hoof, which prevents slipping in ice and snow, while also enabling the deer to dig for food at a time when it may be buried under a frozen surface.

Breathing in sub-zero temperatures could cause the animals a serious problem, but another reindeer adaptation is a specialised and enlarged nasal passage; here the incoming air is warmed before it is passed into the lungs. Meanwhile, warm blood being pumped into the legs exchanges heat with the cooler blood circulating back into the torso, a highly efficient way of reducing heat loss. Reindeer foot bones are also adapted to produce a clicking sound as tendons rub across bones when the animal is walking or running, a noise which can be heard several metres away. The volume of the click has a direct relationship with the size of the animal and is therefore an important way of communicating social standing, as well as maintaining contact within the herd during the long Arctic nights.

Reindeer are notably unique among deer species in that both sexes habitually grow antlers. Those of the bulls tend to be larger and more complex, but in most cases these start to be cast shortly after the October rut, whilst the cows may keep theirs until they give birth in May or June. By retaining antlers during the harder months when competition for food is keenest, the cows possess an advantage despite their smaller body size.

Potentially there are 15 subspecies, although some of the taxonomy is considered to be outdated by various authorities:

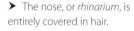

▶ The nose, or *rhinarium*, is entirely covered in hair.

▼ Woodland caribou cow starting to grow new antlers, with her young calf.
Photograph: Brent Huffman

DEER SPECIES | CERVIDAE – CAPREOLINAE

Species		Distribution	Primary habitat
Busk reindeer	*R. t. buskensis*	Russia and neighbouring regions	Woodland
Labrador caribou	*R. t. caboti*	Canada (Labrador and Quebec).	Tundra
Woodland, boreal woodland or mountain woodland caribou	*R. t. caribou*	South-west Canada and the north-west mainland USA. The most widely distributed of the subspecies. Spends much of the year in proximity to woodland and is less migratory.	Boreal forest
Grants or porcupine caribou	*R. t. granti*	Canada (Yukon) and the USA (Alaska). Migratory.	Tundra
Finnish forest reindeer	*R. t. finnicus*	Finland and north-western Russia	Woodland
Barren ground caribou	*R. t. groenlandicus*	Canada (Nunavut and the Northwest Territories) and western Greenland. Highly migratory.	Tundra
Osborn's caribou	*R. t. osborni*	Canada (British Columbia).	Woodland
Novaya Zemlya reindeer	*R. t. pearsoni*	Russia (Novaya Zemlya archipelago).	Island subspecies
Peary caribou	*R. t. pearyi*	Canada (Nunavut and Northwest Territories). The smallest of the North American subspecies.	Island subspecies
Kamchatkan or Okhotsk reindeer	*R. t. phylarchus*	Russia (Kamchatka Peninsula and regions around the Sea of Okhotsk). The largest of the European subspecies.	Woodland
Svalbard or Spitzbergen reindeer	*R. t. platyrhynchus*	Norway (Svalbard archipelago). The smallest subspecies.	Island subspecies
Siberian tundra reindeer	*R. t. sibiricus*	Russia and Siberia	Tundra
Mountain or Norwegian reindeer	*R. t. tarandus*	Norway (Fennoscandian Peninsula) and Eastern Iceland.	Mountain and tundra
Newfoundland caribou	*R. t. terraenovae*	Canada (Newfoundland).	Woodland
Siberian forest reindeer	*R. t. valentinae*	Mongolia (Altai Mountains) and Russia (Ural Mountains).	Boreal forest

There are two further named subspecies, both of which are now considered to be extinct. The diminutive Queen Charlotte Islands or Dawson's caribou *R. t. dawsoni* was specific to Graham Island, part of the Queen Charlotte Islands archipelago off the coast of British Columbia, Canada, but was last recorded in 1935; while the last of the East Greenland caribou *R. t. eogroenlandicus* probably disappeared around 1900. The causes have been variously attributed to over-hunting, habitat loss and introduced diseases.

▲ Mountain reindeer. **Photograph:** Brent Huffman

▲ A woodland caribou, almost completely moulted into summer coat and with antlers in velvet. **Photograph:** Alexander F Meyer

▲ Finnish forest reindeer. **Photograph:** Klaus Rudloff

▲ Siberian tundra reindeer at San Diego Zoo. **Photograph:** Klaus Rudloff

▲ Herds normally consist of a few dozen animals, but these can join up to become many thousands on migration. **Photograph:** Natalia Kollegova

Although some of the subspecies are largely sedentary, others represent some of the very few deer species which migrate, often covering thousands of miles every year as they move between their feeding grounds. Water is no barrier and large lakes, rivers and coastal inlets are crossed without hesitation. For the spring migration, small herds of just a few dozen animals can band together to form huge herds of many thousands, and even the newly born calves are able to travel with their mothers within days of their birth.

Although other deer species, most notably the moose or elk *Alces alces,* have also been occasionally trained as pack animals or to pull sleds or carriages, only the reindeer can be considered to have been truly domesticated by man. To many indigenous people, reindeer are a vital part of their culture, providing milk, meat and skins and forming an integral part of day-to-day life. Some actually live with the herds, tending them and moving with them on migration. These domesticated herds are found from northern Sweden, Finland and much of northern Russia and Siberia, and across to Mongolia and northern China, as well as in some parts of North America. There are estimated to be as many as three million herded animals in northern Europe alone.

Reindeer have been introduced to places where other deer would fail to establish themselves, in most cases as a source of meat and for sport. The earliest example is Iceland where, by royal decree, animals were taken from Norway to Eastern Iceland to be farmed under captive conditions in the late eighteenth century. When the experiment failed, the surviving animals were released and established themselves in the wild. There are estimated to be around 7,000 wild reindeer in Iceland today, and the species is so successful that between 1,200 and 1,300 permits to hunt them are issued every year in order to keep numbers in check.

Elsewhere, Norwegian whalers introduced reindeer to South Georgia in the South Atlantic from 1911 onwards, once again as a source of meat and also for hunting. Here again they were successful, to the point that the authorities eventually decided on a total cull because of the damage that they were doing to the natural environment. This was completed in 2017 and it is believed that none now remain. Reindeer from South Georgia were shipped to the Falkland Islands in 2001 to establish a deer-farming programme to diversify agriculture there, a project which continues today.

The only other reindeer population that exists in the Southern Hemisphere is on the Kerguelen (or Desolation) Islands in the southern Indian Ocean, where animals from Sweden were released in the early years of the twentieth century. There they now number some 3,000 to 5,000 but, as they are causing similar levels of ecological damage as those on South Georgia did, it is possible that they may also suffer a similar fate.

Another story of reindeer introductions is a frequently quoted example of 'boom and bust', in which conditions permit the population of one or more species to expand unnaturally and out of keeping with the wider environment. St Matthew Island is a remote area of about 357 km² (137 ml²) located in the Bering Sea off the coast of Alaska. Originally the only mammals inhabiting the island were arctic foxes and the voles that they preyed upon, with perhaps an occasional visit from a polar bear from across the pack ice. In 1944 the US Coastguard introduced 29 reindeer to act as a food source and for recreational hunting by their personnel. When the coastguard station was abandoned soon afterwards, the reindeer population exploded due to a lack of predators, and by 1963 had reached 6,000 animals – the 'boom'. At this point, the lichen that the reindeer depended on as a food source ran out and over the course of a single winter there was a massive die-off – the 'bust'.

When researchers reached St Matthew Island in 1966, they found that only 42 animals, all but one of them cows, were still alive. This imbalance between the sexes is probably attributable to the fact that, during the final crucial months when available food was almost non-existent, only the cows carried antlers and were thus able to assert themselves in competition for the dwindling resources. The single bull remaining was infertile. Unable to reproduce, the reindeer population on the island had disappeared by the 1980s.

St Matthew Island is frequently held up as a classic case study of over-population and sustainability. Scientists later attributed the population crash to a combination of factors: the limited food supply coinciding with unfavourable climatic factors, as the winter of 1963–64 was particularly severe.

▲ Domesticated reindeer can demonstrate wide varieties of colouration.
Photograph: Klaus Rudloff

▼ Reindeer once occurred well to the south of their modern distribution but were driven northwards by hunting pressure and a warming climate. This is one of a domesticated herd of around 150 reindeer reintroduced to the Cairngorms of Scotland from Sweden in 1952 (wild reindeer lived in Scotland until about the thirteenth century).

On a more cheerful note, reindeer inevitably feature in the images associated with Christmas and are often pictured pulling a sled filled with presents. While Santa Claus in various forms has been part of the western Christmas tradition for a very long time, probably as far back as the fourth century, his association with reindeer is comparatively recent. They first appeared pulling his sled in the poem *A Visit from Santa Claus* written by Clement Clark Moore in 1823, in which they were called Dasher, Dancer, Prancer, Vixen, Comet, Cupid, Dunder and Blixem (later changed to Donner and Blitzen). Rudolf the Red-nosed Reindeer did not appear until 1939 when another American, a copywriter called Robert May, was tasked with producing a promotional booklet for the US retail giant Montgomery Ward. He toyed with the names Reginald, Rollo, Rodney and Romeo before finally deciding on the name that would become synonymous with overcoming and embracing physical differences and realising your true potential.

It is difficult not to wonder, though, if Rudolf had a nasty skin condition, since another special reindeer adaptation for living in cold environments means that their noses are completely covered in hair to protect against frostbite.

FACT BOX – *Reindeer*

World distribution	Native to Canada, Finland, Greenland, Mongolia, Norway, Russia and the United States. Introduced to the Falkland Islands, Iceland, Kerguelen Islands and South Georgia.
IUCN Red List Status 2022	**Vulnerable**, population decreasing (last formal assessment 2015).
Sexes	*Male:* Bull *Female:* Cow *Young:* Calf
Also known as	There are numerous variations on reindeer or caribou which describe specific locations or habitats. Chinese *Yün-lu* or *xun-lu*; Danish *Rensdyr*; Dutch *Rendier*; Finnish *Metsäpeura* or *poro*; French *Renne*; German *Ren, rentiere, wildren* or *karibou*; Greenland *Tuttu*; Iceland *Hreidyr*; Mongolian *Tsaa buga*; Norwegian *Rein, reinsdyr* or *villreingevir*; Russian *Severni olen* or *sewernij olen*; Sami *Boazo*; Spanish *Reno*; Swedish *Ren, renar* or *vildren*; Yugoslavia *Evropski severni jelen*. Native American: Algonquin *Adik* or *wishak*; Chipewyan *Et-then*; Cree *Ah-tik, ateke, attehik* or *awask-ses*; Dogrib *Ek-wo weski*; Inuktitut *Tuktu*; Loucheux *Vadzaih* or *vuth-zi*; Micmac *Xalibu* or *yalipu*; Slavey *Maccarib, medzihnodii* or *no-ti*; Sioux *Pohano* or *see-hah tang-kah*.
Recognition features	Colours can vary according to subspecies, region, sex and season; woodland caribou bulls in summer are a dark brown, while animals in Greenland and the high Arctic can be almost white, and a greyish-brown can predominate elsewhere. Colouration seems most variable among some of the European subspecies. The underparts are white and there is a short tail. The head has a broad muzzle and short ears, and the neck is maned. The hooves are broad and flat, and concave underneath. Southern forms are generally larger, while domesticated animals tend to be smaller than wild ones.
Height (at shoulder)	Typical heights for most European subspecies range between 112–119 cm (44–47 in) and those of North American subspecies average 107–127 cm (42–50 in). Sexual dimorphism is marked with males considerably larger than females, especially among the larger subspecies.

FACT BOX – Reindeer

Weight	Widely variable, typically between 90–272 kg (200–600 lb).
	Peary caribou, the smallest of the North American caribou, typically weigh just 110 kg (240 lb) for males and 60 kg (130 lb) for females.
	In Europe, the smallest subspecies is the Svalbard reindeer where bulls average just 65–90 kg (143–198 lb) and cows 53–70 kg (117–154 lb).
Food	A generalist feeder which takes shrubs, forbs, fungi, sedges, grasses and others according to season and availability. Lichens are an important food source in winter.
Habitat	Occupies habitats including coastal plains, mountainous regions, forest and Arctic tundra according to distribution.
Voice	Generally silent; both sexes may snort or grunt.
Annual behaviour	Highly gregarious; lives in herds which can vary from just a few animals to several thousands during migration. Herds tend to be at their largest during the summer months, and some subspecies can travel up to 5,000 km (not far short of 3,000 miles) every year. When feeding in snow, deep craters can be dug with the forefeet to reach food material underneath; dominant animals may often usurp subordinate ones to take theirs.
Rut	The rut takes place around September and October, when dominant bulls compete for access to cows and will attempt to hold small harems of up to 15 females. Fighting between bulls can be intense, with serious injuries or even deaths sometimes occurring. Bulls stop feeding during the rut and lose condition rapidly.
Gestation and birthing	Gestation averages 225–235 days and the single calf, which may weigh anything between 3–8 kg (6½–17½ lb) is born unspotted around late May or early June. Synchronised birthing often occurs in herds as a defence against piecemeal predation.
Antlers (typical)	Barren-ground and mountain caribou grow the most impressive antlers; a good set will feature a wide 'shovel' brow tine on at least one side and measure some 135 cm (53 in) in length with a span of 100 cm (39 in). Those of the northernmost subspecies tend to be smaller and spindlier.
	The antlers of females are considerably smaller and lighter than those of bulls. Some cows do not develop antlers at all.
	Among the bulls of the larger subspecies, the ratio of antler size to body size is the greatest of all deer.
Antler cycle	Casting dates can be highly variable; in general terms, older bulls start casting about a month after the rut while younger ones may retain their antlers until as late as April.
	The antler cycle of cows is some 5 to 6 months out of synchronisation with the bulls, and pregnant cows may retain theirs until calving in May or June. This ensures that they remain able to defend their feeding craters against competitors, which might include younger bulls.
Lifespan	12–16 years; bulls typically have shorter lifespans than cows.
Threats	Major natural predators include wolves and bears where they occur across the reindeer's range. New-born calves are especially vulnerable to predation.
	Human threats largely come from landscape changes related to energy production, other industrial projects and road development. Unregulated hunting can also present a threat, and competition with domesticated reindeer herds has been noted in northern Europe. The potential effects of climate change, with its influence on weather patterns, food availability and parasitic infestations, cannot be discounted.

Axis axis
Chital *or* Axis deer

ORDER	Artiodactyla
SUBORDER	Ruminantia
INFRAORDER	Pecora
FAMILY	Cervidae
SUBFAMILY	Cervinae

▲ Mature stag and hind.
Photograph: Bishnu Sarangi

ONE OF THE foremost deer of the Indian subcontinent must be the chital or axis deer, which is widely distributed and common across much of the area with the exception of the extreme northwest. An elegant, medium-sized deer, most usually seen in large herds, its almost golden upper body is strikingly patterned with a profusion of white spots. Indeed the word 'chital' comes from the Hindu *cītal* meaning 'spotted' or 'variegated', a name origin shared with the cheetah. The antlers of the stag are long and sweeping though uncomplicated, usually consisting of no more than a long brow tine and a rear dorsal tine towards the top.

▶ Calves join the main herd once they are mobile enough to accompany it.
Photograph: Alexander F Meyer

Some sources have suggested that there may in fact be two separate subspecies, namely the Indian chital *Axis axis axis* and the Ceylon axis *A. a. ceylonensis* which occurs only in Sri Lanka (where the name chital is not used). Although the animals found in Sri Lanka tend to be slightly smaller than those occurring on the mainland, any distinction between the two remains a subject of dispute and it is generally accepted that there are no subspecies of chital.

◄ The hotter parts of the day are spent laid up.
Photographs: Bishnu Sarangi

Chital tend to be active throughout the day, pausing only to rest in the shade of the open forest habitats they prefer when the sun's rays are strongest and temperatures are at their highest. Once the midday glare has passed, activity picks up again and hits a peak by the approach of dusk. The deer wander widely as part of their feeding pattern. Their main food source consists of grasses, but as the seasons progress and these dry out, losing much of their nutritional content, the deer will turn to other

▼ Feeding activity is heaviest at dawn and dusk, tailing off around midday.

material. They will often choose to feed near trees containing langur monkeys, which not only drop fruits that the deer can take advantage of but also provide early warning of the approach of a predator from their higher vantage points. In return, the monkeys benefit from the protection provided by the keener sense of smell possessed by the deer. Chital will drink at least once a day, and often more during the hotter months, so a guaranteed source of water is important to them and if it is not present, even if only as small, scattered pools, they are likely to seek an alternative habitat.

▲ A langur monkey watches over a grazing herd of chital.
Photograph: Pixabay

Social groups consisting of mothers and their offspring form the basis of larger herds, although the herd structure is not rigid and family parties can drift away to rejoin the herd later. Adult stags will often join these groups to take part in the rut before leaving again. Bachelor herds may also be encountered, often consisting mainly of younger stags who are not sexually active. Any herd threatened by a predator will usually flee as a group rather than split up, an alternative defensive measure employed by some other species too. Chital are quite tolerant of human presence and have been known to gather near forest camps and even more permanent forms of habitation, quite possibly as a defence against the predators that tend to avoid such places. This species is an important prey item for many large predators, such as tigers, leopards, and dhole amongst others; mortality can be highest among female and juvenile animals. Older stags also seem to be more susceptible than young ones, possibly because of a tendency to become distracted and less vigilant during the rut, or their greater tendency to live separately from the larger groups.

Stags engage heavily in marking activity, depositing scent from the sub-orbital glands on their faces onto vegetation and often standing on their hind legs to reach higher branches. They also use urine for the same purpose. Fights are not as intense as those seen in some of the other deer species; a display involving the head held horizontally with ears held low, the upper lip curled up and fur bristling, often precedes a pushing match with antlers locked. Such a fight's conclusion does not usually result in the determined pursuit of a defeated rival: more often the protagonists simply break off and depart quietly.

Stags do not maintain a harem or demonstrate lekking behaviour, but instead jealously guard a chosen hind in oestrus against rival suitors. The fawns can be born at any time of year and, like their parents, are spotted but with a shaggy coat that makes the markings less conspicuous than those of adults. This helps them to hide more easily on the forest floor where they are cached by their mother for the first one or two weeks of their lives, being returned to only for feeding. By the time they are a month old they are completely mobile and fully able to keep up with their mothers and the rest of the herd.

The chital has been the subject of many artificial introductions, with varying degrees of success, to several parts of the world. It is of particular concern on some of the Hawaiian islands, where no deer species previously existed until the first group of chital arrived as a gift to King Kamehameha V in 1968: initially they were welcomed as a source of protein for the islanders. Since then, though, numbers have grown alarmingly and may currently be as high as 150,000. A number of factors, including a lack of natural predators, the fact that the species can breed at any time of the year, plus the tendency of hunters to focus on the antlers of stags, leaving a disproportionately high breeding population of females, have all combined to encourage this growth. Environmentalists have become deeply concerned by increasing land erosion and the associated sedimentation which damages coral reefs. The annual economic damage caused by the deer is estimated in millions of dollars and hunters are now encouraged to pursue them without seasons or bag limits in an attempt to contain the problem. At the time of writing (2022), recent droughts have exacerbated these issues, with starving deer increasingly raiding crops and dying in high numbers.

◄ A mature stag with antlers fully grown but still in velvet. Photograph: Brent Huffman

FACT BOX – *Chital*

World distribution	Native to Bangladesh, Bhutan, across the Indian mainland, Nepal, and Sri Lanka.
	Also introduced to Argentina, Armenia, Australia, Brazil, Croatia, India (Andaman Islands), Moldova, Pakistan, Papua New Guinea, Ukraine, various parts of the United States (including the Hawaiian Islands, Texas, Florida and California) and Uruguay.
IUCN Red List Status 2022	**Least Concern**, population trend currently unknown (last formal assessment 2014).
Sexes	*Male:* Stag *Female:* Hind *Young:* Calf/fawn

FACT BOX – Chital

Also known as	Spotted deer, Indian spotted deer, Ceylon deer, Ganges stag.
	Bengali *Buro khotiya*; French *Cerf axis*; German *Axishirsch*; Hawaiian *Kia*; Hindi *Chitra* or *Jhank*; Kannada *Saranga jinke*; Korku *Darkar*; Malayalam *Pulli maan*; Nepalese *Chittal*; Sinhalese *Tic huha* or *Tic muwa*; Tamil *Pali-man* or Pullimal; Telegu *Dupi*.
Recognition features	The coat is a bright golden/rufous brown completely covered with white spots, with a dark dorsal stripe which runs from the neck to the tail. Underparts, throat, rump and the insides of the tail, ears and legs are a creamy white. Both sexes have well developed sub-orbital glands in front of the eyes.
Height (at shoulder)	Stags 86–92 cm (33½–36 in), hinds smaller at around 70 cm (28 in).
Weight	A mature stag can weigh as much as 110 kg (243 lbs) but many average 81kg (180 lb). Hinds range between 25 and 45 kg (55–99 lbs).
Food	A grazing deer that prefers to feed heavily on grasses but will also browse on herbs, foliage, and fruits when grasses are less nutritious during dry seasons.
Habitat	Will occupy a variety of habitats, especially deciduous forest with light undergrowth (which offers poor concealment to predators) as well as light thorn scrub and grassland. Dense cover is avoided. Well shaded cover to lay up in during the day and the proximity of water sources are both important.
Voice	A variety of bellows, barks, and growls. Dominant males make a high-pitched growl or moan when facing off rivals, or scream in challenge. Both sexes will utter a shrill bark, often persistently, when alarmed or if a predator is detected.
Annual behaviour	A gregarious deer which typically lives in family units led by an adult female, her previous year's offspring, and her current fawn(s). Herds consist of two or more of these social units and have been known to number as many as 100 animals, though around 40 is more usual; groups are often joined by individual animals of varying sex and age classes.
Rut	Rutting can take place at any time of year, though activity peaks around April and May. The stag will guard a hind in oestrus against rivals; fighting tends to involve pushing matches with locked antlers and likely to be discontinued before injuries occur.
Gestation and birthing	Gestation lasts some 225–230 days and birthing peaks during the winter months, though there can be geographical variations. Twin calves are common and triplets not unusual. Females can return to oestrus within a few weeks of giving birth.
Antlers (typical)	Six tines, three on each side, are typical with a brow tine and a simple fork at the end of the main beam. Length averages around 76 cm (30 in), though often longer.
Antler cycle	Most stags cast their antlers around August or September and are back in hard horn by March. The season is not fixed, however, and stags in velvet can be encountered at any time.
Lifespan	Between 5 and 10 years (up to 22 years in captivity)
Threats	Predation is the greatest cause of chital mortality. Common predators include tigers, leopards, wolves, dhole dogs, Indian rock pythons and mugger crocodiles. Poaching can be an important local issue, as can competition from domestic stock and human encroachments on habitat.

Axis calamianensis
Calamian deer

ORDER	Artiodactyla
SUBORDER	Ruminantia
INFRAORDER	Pecora
FAMILY	Cervidae
SUBFAMILY	Cervinae

▲ Calamian deer stag.
Photograph: Brent Huffman

THE CALAMIAN DEER is one of just three deer species found in the Philippines, the others being the Visayan spotted deer *Rusa alfredi* and the Philippine sambar *Rusa marianna*, although none of their ranges are known to coincide. It is closely related to the much more widely distributed hog deer *A. porcinus* and the Critically Endangered Bawean deer *A. kuhlii* with which it shares many similar physical features and aspects of behaviour. Current research currently suggests that all three species could yet be moved from *Axis* and into the genus *Hyelaphus*. Like the hog deer, the Calamian prefers to dash through cover with its head held low in the manner of a wild pig, rather than bound away, if disturbed.

◄ Calamian deer hind, San Diego Zoo.
Photograph: Alexander F Meyer

The Calamian deer's Endangered status is largely due to its very limited distribution. It is only found on three of the larger Calamian Islands in the Philippines (Busuanga, Calauit and Culion) but is absent from the fourth, Coron. It is also believed to have once been present on a number of smaller islands but, despite more recent introductions to some of them, is currently only known to survive on two, Marily and Dimaquiat.

The establishment of a wildlife sanctuary and game preserve on the 3,700 hectare Calauit Island in 1977 was initially very beneficial to the Calamian deer, which probably numbered little more than 30 or 40 animals on the island at the time, most of these having been introduced earlier. There, by order of then-President Ferdinand Marcos, all of the indigenous human residents were compulsorily relocated to another island before a variety of ungulates from Kenya including giraffes, zebras and various antelopes were introduced. Large areas of bamboo forest were cleared to create a more beneficial habitat for the introduced animals which, combined with the climatic conditions, was considered to closely resemble their African environment. The conditions and subsequent protection certainly benefited the native deer, which were said to have multiplied to around 1,300 by 2005; however, human recolonisation gradually restarted during the late 1980s and culminated in full reinstatement of the dispossessed Tabanwa people's lands in 2010. Deer numbers have steadily reduced since then, standing at around 1,000 by 2013, although their exact current status is not known. Meanwhile the African antelope have largely died out, but numbers of giraffe and zebra still remain. Poaching pressure has, unfortunately, now returned to concerning levels but the Calauit Safari Park is still one of the most popular tourist attractions in the Philippines and Calauit Island remains an important stronghold for the species.

The Calamian deer is widely hunted for its meat; its hide is used for making drums, and its antlers for decoration. An increase in human settlement is encroaching on much of the available habitat and, although there is strong legislative protection for the species, this is inadequately enforced. Even where there is less of a human presence, there are no meaningful reserves over much of its range. There are still hopes, though, that reintroductions to the much larger island of Palawan, where it is thought to have once existed before becoming extinct in fairly recent times, may take place. A breeding unit already exists there run by the Philippines' conservation organisation, the Katala Foundation. Its aim is to establish suitable numbers of deer for planned releases; if the project is successful, it may be an important move in helping to reverse the declines elsewhere.

▼ (*top*) Calves are born unspotted.
Photograph: Brent Huffman

▼ (*bottom*) Portrait of a mature stag in velvet shortly before cleaning his antlers, Phoenix Zoo.
Photograph: Klaus Rudloff

DEER SPECIES | CERVIDAE – CERVINAE

FACT BOX – *Calamian deer*

World distribution	Native to the Philippines (Calamian Islands)
IUCN Red List Status 2022	**Endangered**, population decreasing (last formal assessment 2014).
Sexes	*Male:* Stag *Female:* Hind *Young:* Calf
Also known as	Calamian hog deer, Philippine deer French *Cerf-cochon Calamien, Cerf de Calamiane* or *Cerf de Culion*; German *Calamian-Hirsch* or *Calamian-Schweinshirsch*; Filipino *Pilandoc*; Spanish *Ciervo Porquerizo de los Calamianes* or *Ciervo de los Calamianes.*
Recognition features	A heavy bodied deer with slightly raised hindquarters, similar to the hog deer *Axis porcinus* but distinguished by a shorter face, shorter, more rounded ears, and slightly longer and darker legs. The overall pelage is a uniform golden-brown with paler underparts and dark brown to almost black legs. The ears have very pale inner surfaces. A white underside to the lower jaw extends backwards to the throat. The tail is short and bushy, around 15 cm (6 in) long with a pale underside.
Height (at shoulder)	Stags 60–65 cm (24–25½ in), hinds smaller.
Weight	Stags 40–42 kg (88–92½ lb), hinds 23–29 kg (51–64 lb).
Food	Herbs, grasses, leaves, and other new growth.
Habitat	Grassland and open forest
Voice	The call is soft, high-pitched and has a nasal tone.
Annual behaviour	Mostly diurnal, with activity peaking during the morning and late afternoon. May become more nocturnal during periods of extreme heat. Unlike the more solitary hog deer, Calamian deer can form herds of up to 30 animals, although around 12 are more usual (especially where they are more heavily persecuted).
Rut	There is no fixed season for the rut although most activity peaks around November. Rutting behaviour is very similar to that of the hog deer; stags attempt to court and mate with one hind at a time rather than attempt to gather harems. At such times fighting between stags is commonplace.
Gestation and birthing	Gestation is around 220–225 days, after which a single calf is born; twins are rare. Most birthings tend to take place around June, though young can be born at any time of the year. The calf is unspotted, unlike that of the hog deer, with an average weight of 1.5 kg (3¼ lb) for a stag calf and 1 kg (2¼ lb) for a hind.
Antlers (typical)	Typical antlers are 6-pointed, with well-developed brow and back tines. They have an average length of around 24 cm (9½ in) although up to 39 cm (15½ in) has been recorded.
Antler cycle	There is no seasonality for casting and regrowth, each cycle lasting between 9 and 10 months, and stags can be encountered at various stages of antler development at any time of year. Stag calves start to develop their first antlers from around 8 months old.
Lifespan	12–14 years; up to 18 years recorded in captivity.
Threats	Adults have no significant natural predators; calves may be vulnerable to pythons and larger birds of prey. The main human threat is uncontrolled hunting, coupled with habitat loss resulting from new settlements and agricultural clearances.

Axis kuhlii

Bawean deer

ORDER	Artiodactyla
SUBORDER	Ruminantia
INFRAORDER	Pecora
FAMILY	Cervidae
SUBFAMILY	Cervinae

▲ Mature stag in velvet with antler growth almost complete, Taman Safari Indonesia.
Photograph: Alexander F Meyer

▼ Mature hind, San Diego Zoo.
Photograph: Alexander F Meyer

THE BAWEAN DEER has the most limited range of any of the deer species, being entirely confined to Bawean Island in Indonesia's Java Sea. The island has a land mass of just 197 square kilometres (76 square miles). Here the animals live mainly in the central and south-western regions, away from the more cultivated parts of the island which comprise at least 60 per cent of the land mass. The species was once also found on Java but has long been extinct there, the causes being variously attributed to natural predation, over-hunting by humans, or competition with the more dominant rusa deer *Rusa timorensis* and southern red muntjac *Muntiacus muntjak*.

The Bawean is very similar in appearance and habits to the hog deer *A. porcinus* and the Calamian deer *A. calamianensis* to which it is closely related; recent analysis has suggested that the three species form their own genus *Hyelaphus*, quite distinct from the chital *A. axis*. In common with some other deer species which have evolved on islands without naturally occurring large land predators, it is notably short-legged in comparison to its relatives; it is also very vocal in the day-to-day communications which might otherwise betray its presence. It remains highly secretive, though, and tends to hide itself away; this is believed to be related to a heightened awareness of other predators such as pythons and the larger birds of prey.

The Bawean deer was first described by German naturalist Salomon Müller in 1836, though not on its island of origin but in the small town of Tuban on the north coast of Java, where the local governor kept a small herd in his garden. Müller named his discovery in honour of another prolific German naturalist, Heinrich Kuhl, who

DEER SPECIES | CERVIDAE – CERVINAE

▲ (*left*) Portrait of a mature stag with exceptional but otherwise typically formed antlers, Jakarta Zoological Garden.
Photographs: Klaus Rudloff

▲ (*right*) Young stag, showing tail length.

had died 15 years earlier aged just 23: he had spent a year in Java before succumbing to a liver infection brought on by a combination of the climate and over-exertion. During his short time there, Kuhl had described many new species and despatched a large number of specimens including some 200 skeletons, 200 mammal skins, 2,000 bird skins, 1,400 fish and many insects and crustaceans to the Leiden Natural History Museum in the Netherlands.

An isolated island some 150 kilometres (93 miles) north of Java, the largely hilly landscape of Bawean was once covered with rainforest but human activities have caused this to shrink to a fraction of its former extent. Teak plantations alone now account for around 15 per cent of the land area. Very shy of humans, the Bawean deer has retreated to the vicinity of dense forests around the steeper, less accessible slopes, emerging mostly at night to feed. It was once considered plentiful and subjected to uncontrolled hunting, but hunting ceased altogether when new laws came into effect in 1977. Poaching does not appear to be an issue, although occasional animals are accidentally killed by dogs during pig hunts.

Estimates of the number of remaining Bawean deer vary but they may be lower than 250 mature animals and certainly no higher than 500 overall. This is considered to be on the edge of a population that is unviable in the longer term despite numbers appearing to be stable. As a result the Bawean deer is categorised as Critically Endangered and faces a high risk of extinction in the wild.

FACT BOX – *Bawean deer*

World distribution	Native to Indonesia (Bawean Island).
IUCN Red List Status 2022	**Critically Endangered**, population stable (last formal assessment 2014).
Sexes	*Male:* Stag *Female:* Hind *Young:* Calf
Also known as	Bawean hog deer, Kuhl's deer, Kuhl's hog deer.
	Bahasa Sunda *Uncal Bawean*; Bahasa Java *Menjangan Bawean*; French *Cerf-cochon de Bawean*; German *Bawean-Schweinshirsch* or *Kuhlhirsch*; Indonesian *Rusa Bawean*; Spanish *Ciervo Porquerizo de Kuhl* or *Ciervo de Kuhl*.

FACT BOX – *Bawean deer*

Recognition features	Similar in appearance to the hog deer *A. porcinus* but with a shorter face and legs. The pelage is a uniform brown with a grizzled appearance when viewed at closer quarters. There may be a pale throat patch and most animals have obvious white eye rings, though there is usually no distinct dorsal line along the line of the back. The body is heavy, and the rump is held higher than the shoulders. The tail is bushy, around 20 cm (7½ in) long and has a white underside.
Height (at shoulder)	Stags around 68–70 cm (26½–27½ in), hinds smaller.
Weight	40–60 kg (88–132 lb)
Food	Predominantly a grazer which feeds mainly on forbs and grasses, it will also take young leaves, twigs and fruits. It visits agricultural fields to feed on the young leaves of cassava and corn plants.
Habitat	Primary and secondary forest, also visiting burnt clearings during the dry season.
Voice	Highly vocal, both sexes communicating with short, sharp repeated barks. That of the hind is slightly higher pitched. Alarmed animals will also bark. A hind separated from her calf will issue a high-pitched, quiet squeak to re-establish contact.
Annual behaviour	A largely solitary deer which may occasionally be encountered in small groups. It is largely nocturnal: much of the day is spent lying up in dense undergrowth from which the deer will emerge as night falls to feed and interact with others in more open clearings. Individual animals may have regular resting places, and often create well-trodden trails between these sites and feeding areas. Freezing or creeping away unobtrusively is preferred to flight, but a disturbed animal may dash away with head held low in typical hog deer fashion, before settling to hide after a short distance and then moving off quietly.
Rut	Rutting activity peaks during September and October, although breeding may take place at any time of the year. In captivity, breeding has been noted as taking place year-round with a 9-month interval between births. Stags will court an individual receptive hind and challenge rivals by barking and snorting, often repeated over long periods and accompanied by foot stamping. Opponents will reply with a similar bark while approaching. Fighting with antlers may then take place.
Gestation and birthing	Most calves are born between April and June after a gestation period of between 225–230 days. Twins are rare. The newly born calf bears only very faint spots which disappear quickly.
Antlers (typical)	Typical antlers are grown on prominent pedicles and carry 3 tines on each side, comprising a main beam with well-defined brow and back tines. They tend to be shorter than those of the hog deer and rarely exceed around 30 cm (12 in) in length although one exceptional set measured 47 cm (18½ in).
Antler cycle	Antlers start to develop when the stag calf reaches around a year in age. There does not appear to be a set antler cycle, and stags may be found in hard antler throughout the year.
Lifespan	Probably up to 15 years
Threats	No natural predators other than pythons and larger birds of prey; newly born calves may fall victim to wild pigs and macaque monkeys. Human-related habitat loss, largely from teak plantations and agricultural clearance, is an important threat, as is predation by feral dogs. There are also fears that an increasing prevalence of invasive plants may degrade habitat quality. Hunting is no longer considered to be a threat.

DEER SPECIES | CERVIDAE – CERVINAE

Axis porcinus

Hog deer

ORDER	Artiodactyla
SUBORDER	Ruminantia
INFRAORDER	Pecora
FAMILY	Cervidae
SUBFAMILY	Cervinae

THE HOG DEER was once extremely common across parts of Pakistan, northern India and much of Southeast Asia, but has declined alarmingly since the middle of the twentieth century. It is a medium-sized deer with a heavy build but comparatively short legs and face; its general appearance, coupled with a habit of rushing through low vegetation with head held low much in the manner of a wild pig rather than bounding, led to its common name. Despite its relatively small size, stags can produce comparatively long antlers.

Although previously categorised as one of the *Cervus* deer, current thinking groups the hog deer with the others of the *Axis* genus (although research suggests that it, along with the Calamian deer *A. calamianensis* and Bawean deer *A. kuhli*,

▲ Mature stag in winter coat. Whipsnade Zoo, UK.

◀ A captive stag in velvet with hinds, all in summer coat, at Shadow Nursery, USA.
Photograph: Alexander F Meyer

▼ The face of the hog deer is relatively short and the preorbital gland small but readily visible.

▲ Adult hind in summer coat with faint spots visible.
Photograph: Brent Huffman

▶ Apart from those of Cambodian animals, the calves are born spotted (Tierpark, Berlin).
Photograph: Klaus Rudloff

may yet be moved into a separate permanent genus *Hyelaphus*). There are believed to be two subspecies: the more widespread *A. p. porcinus*, and the slightly larger *A.p. annamiticus* which now appears to be extinct in Vietnam but may still be represented by the small Cambodia population. Certainly there are notable differences and, while the species gives birth to spotted young across most of its range, the young of those in Cambodia appear to be born without spots. More research into their separate genetic markers is needed before we can be more certain of their status.

Only 50 years or so ago, the range of the hog deer extended in a continuous strip from southern Pakistan, across northern India, and then down to the very south of Myanmar. At the same time a large separate population, commonly described as the *annamiticus* subspecies, ranged across eastern Thailand, Cambodia and onto the borders of Vietnam. Today, though, it is reduced to isolated sub-populations in the western parts of its range and has disappeared completely in much of Myanmar. The once widespread eastern subspecies is now only considered to exist in mainland Thailand, where it has been reintroduced in the Phu Khiao Wildlife Sanctuary in the centre of the country. It has also been introduced to the Mu Ko Chang National Park, an island off the southern extremity of the country. Another tiny remnant exists in the Kratie Province of Cambodia.

Being so far removed from its traditional ranges, there is a belief that hog deer might have been introduced to Sri Lanka by either the Dutch or the Portuguese; whatever the case, although once widespread across the island, it has now retreated into a small coastal area in the south-east. Elsewhere, there have certainly been introductions to Australia, the first arriving in Victoria during the 1860s. They are also found in New South Wales and their range is said to be expanding. In the USA they are established in Florida, Hawaii and Texas.

The decline of the hog deer has been most rapid in Southeast Asia, where numbers are estimated to have fallen by some 90 per cent between 1991 and 2012.

▼ An adult female hog deer in its natural habitat, Manas National Park, Assam.
Photograph: Alolika Sinha

Over-hunting, alongside habitat destruction and fragmentation are considered to be the main reasons for this. In most, if not all, of its range it is protected but heavy levels of poaching continue and it is declining even within some National Parks and other protected areas. At one point it was seriously persecuted in the name of crop protection, having a fondness for eating rice, but although this is no longer considered to be a major issue it still brings the hog deer into close contact with human activity and makes it more vulnerable. In Southeast Asia animals are still killed to supply the market for bushmeat and traditional medicine; compared to some other deer, it is apparently considered relatively easy to hunt. Flooding may also be an issue; in addition to drowning animals, it can also concentrate them on isolated pockets of higher ground where they become easier targets.

▼ Gatherings often occur in areas offering good feeding. This group is in the Kaziranga National Park, Assam, India.
Photograph: Brent Huffman

FACT BOX – *Hog deer*

World distribution	Native to Bangladesh, Bhutan, Cambodia, India, Nepal and Pakistan. Reintroduced to Thailand Possibly extinct in China, Laos, Myanmar and Vietnam. Introduced to Australia, Sri Lanka and the USA.
IUCN Red List Status 2022	**Endangered**, population decreasing (last formal assessment 2014).
Sexes	*Male:* Stag *Female:* Hind *Young:* Calf
Also known as	Brown porcine deer, Dwarf axis deer, Paddyfield deer, Para, Spotted porcine deer, Swamp deer (Sri Lanka). Assamese *Con Huu*; Bengali *Nutri I harin* or *Wiil-munha*; Burmese *Darai, Dasai, Dayai, Dayai-nyo, Dayai–pyauk, Day ay* or *Da-ye*; Cambodia *Kandank tuôt*; Chinese *Tun lu*; French *Cerf cochon* or *Cerf cochon d'Indochine*; German *Schweinhirsch*; Gond *Bher-samur*; Kachin *Zau-nyi*; Nepalese *Khar laguna* or *Sugoria*; Rohilkhand *Dodar*; Shan *Sat Hkai*; Sinhalese *Gona Muwa, Varkenshort* or *Wil-muha*; Spanish *Ciervo porcino* or *Ciervo porquerizo de Indochina*; Sri Lanka *Mann*; Tamil *Para-kulman*; Thai *Nua-Sai*; Tibetan *Shawa*.

FACT BOX – Hog deer

Recognition features	Stoutly built, with relatively short legs and slightly raised hindquarters. Pelage is generally a uniform brown or yellowish-brown; older stags may be a darker brown. Underparts are dark in all cases. In the summer coat faint spots may line either side of the dark dorsal stripe or be scattered on the body. Older animals may develop more lightly coloured faces and necks. Preorbital glands are small but visible. The tail is of medium length and brown with a white underside and often has a visible white tip. The rump hair can be flared when the animal is alarmed.
Height (at shoulder)	Stags between 66–74 cm (26–29 in), hinds smaller at around 61 cm (24 in).
Weight	Stags 36–45 kg (80–110 lb), hinds around 30–32 kg (66–70 lb).
Food	Grasses, leaves, new growth, flowers and fruits.
Habitat	Prefers floodplains and swampy grasslands including paddy fields. Long grass is sought as a source of cover. Tends not to venture onto higher ground and avoids closed canopy forests but may be displaced from regular habitats where seasonal flooding occurs.
Voice	Utters a warning bark; also whistles when alarmed. It is generally accepted that there is no specific rutting call.
Annual behaviour	Daily movement is minimal and may not exceed 400 metres within their small home ranges, which may overlap with those of other animals. Stags can be aggressive towards each other and, particularly where densities are low, may become more territorial. Most movement is early and late in the day, with hotter periods spent lying up. Where regularly disturbed or subjected to hunting pressure, habits can become increasingly nocturnal. Largely solitary and generally only seen alone or in hind/calf pairs, though gatherings of over 40 animals are not uncommon in areas of good feeding with sprouting grasses. There is no social cohesion, though, and a disturbed group will scatter in all directions, heads held low and tails raised to display the white underside, to seek dense cover.
Rut	Variously between September and December depending on location (peaks in September and October in Nepal and India but may be later elsewhere). Stags do not attempt to hold a harem but just court and defend one hind at a time. As well as fighting with their antlers, aggressive biting between stags is commonplace.
Gestation and birthing	Gestation lasts between 220 and 230 days, after which 1 or 2 calves are born. With the exception of Cambodian animals, the calves are spotted. They spend their first weeks hidden in cover, start to accompany their mothers after about a month, are weaned by 6 months and become sexually mature at 8 to 12 months old.
Antlers (typical)	Antlers usually carry a total of 6 points with long brow and back tines on each side. They are relatively large in comparison to the body size, averaging 39 cm (15½ in). *A. p. annamiticus* antlers tend to be larger and can reach up to 46 cm (18 in). The largest on record measured 61 cm (24 in) and came from Myanmar.
Antler cycle	Casting takes place between March and early May
Lifespan	Around 15 years; up to 20 years recorded.
Threats	Predators include tigers, leopards, clouded leopards, dhole and python and others where they occur across their range. Human threats are predominantly hunting and habitat degradation.

Cervus albirostris

White-lipped deer

ORDER	Artiodactyla
SUBORDER	Ruminantia
INFRAORDER	Pecora
FAMILY	Cervidae
SUBFAMILY	Cervinae

▲ A mature stag.
Photograph: Brent Huffman

AT ONE TIME, the white-lipped deer ranged widely across the eastern Tibetan Plateau, but its distribution has shrunk to just some 10 per cent of what it once was. The species now occurs in only fragmented populations in more limited areas within the Chinese provinces of Gansu, Qinghai, Sichuan and Yunnan as well as eastern Tibet. The largest populations appear to be in eastern Sichuan. While there are currently no available estimates of overall numbers, the population in 1998 was only thought to be around 7,000 animals and it has probably declined further since. Individual herds might once have numbered several hundreds of animals, though today the numbers are so decreased that such densities would be unusual.

➤ (left) Stag in hard horn at the Tierpark, Berlin, showing the typically flattened antler beams and wide spacing between the first and second tines.
Photograph: Klaus Rudloff

➤ (right) Portrait of mature hind, showing the white muzzle markings that give rise to the common name of white-lipped deer.
Photograph: Brent Huffman

Living at altitudes of between 3,500 to 5,100 metres above sea level, and often in remote and largely inaccessible areas, but descending to lower ground in winter, the white-lipped deer is well adapted to its habitat. The combination of relatively short legs, powerful haunches and wide hooves enables it to be an agile climber in the mountainous terrain that it inhabits, and its nasal cavities are enlarged to enable it to breathe more easily in the rarefied air. A higher than usual count of red blood cells further assists with oxygen uptake. The depth of the long and coarse winter coat is 33.5 mm (over 1¼ in) thick, more so than that of the much larger elk *Alces alces*, and this effectively protects it against the frequently extreme climate.

◄ Relatively short legs, wide hooves and powerful haunches are all adaptations for living in mountainous regions. A hind in San Diego Zoo.
Photograph: Alexander F Meyer

▼ Hind and well-grown calf.
Photograph: Klaus Rudloff

Commonly also known as Thorold's deer, the white-lipped deer was first noted when a member of an expedition to what was then known as Chinese Turkestan, led by Nikolai Mikhailovich Przewalski, the foremost Russian explorer of the day, obtained the skin and skull of an old stag. Przewalski formally described the species some years later in 1883 and the deer was initially placed in its own genus *Przewalskium* but later consideration moved it to the wider *Cervus* genus. It was Dr W. G. Thorold who procured two more specimens from Tibet in 1891 and for a while the species was indeed known as *Cervus tholdi*. The *albirostris* of the present scientific name is derived from the Latin *albus* meaning white and *rostrum* meaning snout.

In places where they are hunted, white-lipped deer are very wary of humans and will observe them intently at long ranges, running quickly and easily over rough ground at speeds of up to 35 miles per hour when disturbed. Hinds are almost invariably found close to rockier terrain offering ready escape routes, while stags seem more prepared to tolerate flatter, more open ground. Where they are not persecuted, wild white-lipped deer are relatively relaxed about human presence and quickly become tame in captivity. They have been widely farmed in China for their meat, velvet and other by-products and are considered hardier than other livestock under demanding winter conditions. Despite the fact that they are adapted to living at higher altitudes, they adjust readily to conditions on lower ground and are kept and bred in a number of zoos and other collections worldwide.

The extremely fragmented nature of the present white-lipped deer populations and the decline in their numbers is a major cause for concern, though it is hoped that active measures to curb poaching have helped to stabilise these. The widespread breeding that was carried out on Chinese government farms during the 1970s and 1980s – partly in an attempt to prevent poaching but also to produce venison for the domestic market – has since fallen off, as a result of over-production, overseas competition from New Zealand deer farms, and falling prices. It is hoped, though, that a reassessment of the species will see its Vulnerable status improved to a relatively safer category.

FACT BOX – *White-lipped deer*

World distribution	Native to China
IUCN Red List Status 2022	**Vulnerable**, population trend unknown (last formal assessment 2014).
Sexes	*Male:* Stag *Female:* Hind *Young:* Calf
Also known as	Dybowski deer, Lhasa stag, Przewalski deer, Thorold's deer, white-faced Tibetan deer. Chinese *Bai-chun-lu*; French *Cerf de Thorold*; German *Weisslippenhirsch*; Spanish *Ciervo de labios blancos*.
Recognition features	A large deer, the summer coat is a greyish-brown with lighter underparts and a distinct ginger rump patch, and a short tail of about 12 cm (5 in) in length. The head is slightly darker than the rest of the body with white markings around the nose and lips and below the chin, and the muzzle is broad. The ears are long, spear-shaped and white on the inside. In winter the coat becomes paler and very much thicker. The hooves are short, wide and bovine, and the dew claws are very pronounced. The preorbital glands are large, and the metatarsal glands are defined with lighter, tufted hair. A special feature of this deer is that the lie of the hairs on the withers (the portion of the back between the shoulder blades) reverses, which can give a ridged appearance.
Height (at shoulder)	120–140 cm (47–55 in), stags being notably larger than hinds.
Weight	Stags 180 to 230 kg (400 to 510 lb), hinds 90 to 160 kg (200 to 350 lb).
Food	Predominantly a grazer of grasses, herbs, alpine forbs and lichens, it will also eat the leaves and bark of bushes and small trees. Sedges can be an important food source in summer.
Habitat	Although it variously inhabits conifer forests, willow scrub, rhododendron and alpine grasslands, it is often most likely to be encountered in more open ground and above the tree line.

FACT BOX – *White-lipped deer*

Voice	Rutting stags make high-pitched bellows, starting with a moan and then rising in pitch, repeated up to 5 times; challenging stags make lower-pitched growls and grunts which are also uttered when pursuing hinds. Both sexes make a loud alarm call, and hinds and calves utter a variety of grunts and mews. Additionally, the carpal bones produce a cracking sound when walking; the function of this is not fully understood but may be related to communication within the herd.
Annual behaviour	A highly gregarious and crepuscular deer, usually found in single sex herds which can be large if local densities of animals permit. It favours higher ground during the summer but moves to lower altitudes in winter, often to the vicinity of lakes and rivers where food is more abundant. At such times mixed herds are more common. Stags create and roll in wallows, which may also be subsequently used by hinds.
Rut	The rut takes place between late September and November, sometimes extending to late December. At this time the male and female herds come together, and stags compete for the right to breed with visual and vocal displays; parallel walking is frequently followed by fighting with antlers but fights tend to be short. Stags may defend a few hinds but do not gather large harems in the manner of red deer *C. elaphus*. Once the rut has finished, older stags often become reclusive while younger ones may stay with the hinds.
Gestation and birthing	Birthing takes place between late May and early July following a gestation period estimated as around 246 days. The single calf bears spots and is large with an average birth weight of 8.6 kg (19 lb). It is born in a hidden location well away from the main herd but will later join a nursery group, which might comprise up to 40 hinds and their calves; until this time its mother may locate itself on rocky areas above where the calf is hidden, returning to it only to suckle. The calf's spots fade by the time that it is about 6 weeks old. Calves do not become sexually mature until they have reached their second year, but stag calves may not actually breed until they have achieved the body weights needed to assert dominance, at around 5 years.
Antlers (typical)	The long antlers usually have 5 tines on each side and display a tendency to flattened beams with a wide space between the first and second tines. A typical set might measure around 100–110 cm (39–43 in) in length.
Antler cycle	Antlers are shed in March and start to regrow immediately, with growth complete and velvet shed by the end of August.
Lifespan	Around 12 years; up to 21 years recorded in captivity.
Threats	Occasional natural predators are wolves and snow leopards. Hunting for meat, antlers and organs for use in traditional medicine has been the main cause of this species' decline, although stricter gun control in China and a decline in poaching, along with extensive deer farming to reduce the demand for poached animals, appears to have reduced the pressures. Competition with livestock and the associated degradation of habitat remains a serious issue.

Cervus canadensis

Wapiti

ORDER	Artiodactyla
SUBORDER	Ruminantia
INFRAORDER	Pecora
FAMILY	Cervidae
SUBFAMILY	Cervinae

▲ A bull wapiti bugling during the rut.
Photograph: Pixabay

▼ Cows grazing in Banff National Park, Canada, showing the distinctive rump patch.
Photograph: Jon Bowes

ONE OF NORTH America's most iconic deer species, it may come as a surprise to some Westerners to discover that the wapiti also occurs in northern Asia. It is the second largest species of deer in terms of body size, only being smaller than the moose *Alces alces*. Once considered to be a subspecies of the red deer *C. elaphus* it is now held to be distinct, with some very marked structural and behavioural differences. Whilst numbers in general may be increasing on a global scale, there is still cause for concern over some of the subspecies, especially in parts of Asia.

The popular alternative name of elk, widely used in the USA and Canada, is often a source of confusion as it is the same as that used for the entirely unrelated *Alces alces* in northern Europe (the latter species is called a moose in North America). It has its origins in English-speaking settlers, coming from more southerly parts of Europe and unfamiliar with *A. alces*, vaguely applying the name to what they saw as a larger version of the red deer. The use of 'wapiti' reduces any danger of misidentification and comes from the Native American Shawnee, meaning 'white rumped'.

The species can be very relaxed around humans where it is not persecuted and has a reputation for adjusting more quickly to captivity than some other deer. In the Banff National Park in Alberta, Canada, wild wapiti regularly visit the town from which the park takes its name to give birth to their calves, despite high numbers of tourists; for the deer, this is a preferable alternative to doing so in localities frequented by wolves. Bulls will also rut in the town, deliberately blocking humans from approaching their harems of cows. Although they can become dangerous at such times, wapiti are less likely to be as aggressive as red deer habituated to human presence in parks or farms.

The past taxonomy of the wapiti has been confusing, especially as it was once grouped as a subspecies of the red deer, with additional uncertainty over the exact status of the Tarim red deer *C. hanglu*. Furthermore the North American animals were split into a number of subspecies, some of which are no longer recognised, by various observers. Modern analysis currently suggests that there are eight subspecies (although further revision cannot be discounted):

▲ A bull North American elk displaying while a cow grazes in the background.
Photograph: Brent Huffman

Species		Distribution	Remarks
North American elk	*C. c. canadensis*	North America. Declared extinct by the US Fish & Wildlife Service in 1880 but recent IUCN reclassifications have re-established it as an extant subspecies.	Medium sized: males 320–475 kg (705–1,047 lb) and females 275–375 kg (606–827 lb). Shoulder height 1.7–2.1 m (5 ft 7–6 ft 11 in).
Alashan wapiti	*C. c. alashanicus*	North China	A small, more lightly-coloured wapiti.
Tule elk, Dwarf elk or Valley elk	*C. c. nannodes*	California	The smallest of the North American wapiti, though the term 'Dwarf elk' is deceptive and their reduced size is reflective of habitat; this subspecies is the most tolerant of living in marginal habitats and desert conditions. Bulls average 180–240 kg (397–529 lb) in weight and stand around 127 cm (50 in) at the shoulder.
Roosevelt's elk, Canadian wapiti or West American wapiti	*C. c. roosevelti*	Vancouver Island, Washington State and Oregon.	The largest of the wapiti, it stands up to 150 cm (59 in) at the shoulder. A good bull can weigh as much as 600 kg (1,300 lb).
Altai wapiti, Sayansk, Tian Shan wapiti, boach or bogi	*C. c. sibiricus*	North-east Kazakhstan, north Xinjiang to south Siberia and northern Mongolia.	The largest of the Asian wapiti, a bull standing around 140cm (55 in) at the shoulder.
Manchurian wapiti, Isubra/ Izubra or Bedford's deer	*C. c. xanthopygus*	South-east Siberia, the far east of Russia, Ussuriland and Manchuria.	Bulls weigh 170–350 kg (370–770 lb), cows 140–215 kg (309–474 lb).
Sichuan deer, Kansu deer or MacNeill's deer	*C. c. macneilli*	Central and south-west China (north Qinghai, Gansu, Shaanxi, west Sichuan and east Xizang provinces).	A bull will weigh around 204 kg (450 lb) and stand 122–127 cm (48–50 in) at the shoulder.
Shou or Tibetan red deer	*C. c. wallichii*	South-west China (south-east Xizang province and Bhutan).	The winter pelage is a sandier colour than the other subspecies with a greyer face.

▶ A captive Roosevelt's elk bull.
Photograph: Alexander F Meyer

▼ (left) Altai wapiti bull, Ostrava Zoo, Czech Republic.
Photograph: Klaus Rudloff

▼ (right) Altai wapiti cow and calf at the Tierpark, Berlin.
Photograph: Klaus Rudloff

Wapiti distribution can be more fragmented than the continuous ranges suggested by the distribution map, particularly some of those within Asia, though the species has been successfully reintroduced to some south-western regions of its former Asian range. Similar reintroductions have also taken place within the USA. Wapiti hybridise readily with the similar but rather smaller red deer *C. elaphus* when conditions are right, and nowhere is this more apparent than in New Zealand where both species have been introduced, and where it is suggested that there are actually no longer any pure wapiti left as a result of interbreeding. Hybridisation is often marked by an increased tendency for antlers to terminate in a 'cup' of three points, an occurrence more regularly seen among red deer.

Wapiti blood has occasionally been deliberately introduced to some wild red deer populations in an attempt to increase average body size but seldom with any success, subsequent generations quickly reverting to a size that their environment will support. The practice is more successful under the comparatively artificial conditions of deer farms, where wapiti genes are often introduced to red deer stock through artificial insemination. Wapiti themselves are widely farmed, primarily for their venison, but the Altai wapiti is also farmed in Russia for its velvet which commands a high price for use in Chinese, Korean and Japanese traditional medicine.

Apart from the successful New Zealand introductions, those on a smaller scale in Italy have met with more limited success in the enclosed La Mandria Regional Park near Turin, though similar attempts that took place around 1890 in the Po Delta region were unsuccessful.

There were thought to be in excess of 10 million wapiti in North America before the arrival of European settlers but over-hunting during the nineteenth century reduced the populations dramatically and extirpated them completely in some states. Animals were slaughtered in huge numbers for their hides and meat, with some bulls killed purely for their vestigial canine teeth. Often referred to as 'ivories', they were once in high demand for the jewellery market. By the time the wanton killing was stopped, the wapiti had disappeared from some 90 per cent of its original range: this had once stretched from the Pacific Ocean in the west to almost as far as the Atlantic in the east.

Once common in central California until the mid-nineteenth century, the Tule elk was reduced to a mere handful of animals by 1875 by gold miners in the area; protection and transplants since then enabled numbers to grow to an estimated 3,900 by 2010. Elsewhere in the USA, conservation measures and the strict regulation of hunting has assisted recovery to the point that wapiti are felt to be over-abundant in some places, most especially those which lack natural predators to regulate population growth, and recreational hunting is the only controlling factor. The annual harvest in the USA is now around 200,000.

▲ (*left*) Tule elk bull.
Photograph: Klaus Rudloff

▲ (*right*) Tule elk bull, pictured in mid-moult and in the process of growing new antlers.
Photograph: Klaus Rudloff

◄ Tule elk cow, pictured at the Tierpark, Berlin.
Photograph: Alexander F Meyer

Numbers of some of the Asian subspecies are considered to be largely stable, though illegal hunting remains a significant threat to some of them. The Altai wapiti is felt to be steady at around 35,000 animals, and the Manchurian wapiti has probably increased three-fold from its 1980s status to as many as 150,000. The status of the Sichuan deer is, however, unknown, and the Shou was until fairly recently considered to be extinct until a few animals were rediscovered in Tibet (Xizang province, China) and Bhutan. It is very probable that both of these subspecies suffer from a considerable degree of illegal hunting.

While the overall picture is encouraging, there is certainly no justification for complacency as far as some of the lesser-known subspecies of wapiti are concerned. In addition, the increasing prevalence of Chronic Wasting Disease among North American deer is becoming a major worry.

FACT BOX – *Wapiti*

World distribution	Native to Bhutan, Canada, China, Kazakhstan, Kyrgyzstan, Mongolia, Russian Federation and the United States. Extinct in Mexico. Introduced to Italy and New Zealand.
IUCN Red List Status 2022	**Least Concern**, population increasing (last formal assessment 2015).
Sexes	*Male:* Bull *Female:* Cow *Young:* Calf
Also known as	Elk. There are many local variations; also *see subspecies above*. Chinese *Loo, Ma Lu, Ala-shan-ma-lu, Bai-tun-lu, Shan-ma-lu* or *Tian*; French *Cerf wapiti, Le Cerf* (French Canadian), *Wapiti d'Amérique, Wapitie d'Asie* or *Wapiti de Sibérie*; German *Wapiti, Wapiti Asiatischer* or *Ussuri hirsch*; Russian *Altajsskij Maral*; Spanish *Wapiti* or *Uapiti*; Mongolian *Maral Buga*. Native American: Cree *Awaskees, Moostoosh, Mus-koose, Wawaskeeshoo* or *Wawaskisa*; Dogrib *Molakwo*; Guarani *Guazu-ti*; Hopi *Chyze-ze-scha*; Ojibwa *Mush-koose*; Shawnee *Wapiti*; Sioux *Hay-hah-kah*; Slavey *Jedhi*; Taos *Tu una*; Yankton Sioux *Eh-kahg-tchick-kah*.
Recognition features	A very large deer, similar in appearance to the red deer *Cervus elaphus* but notably bigger, with thick bodies, slender legs and short tails. North American wapiti are generally a tawny brown in summer, becoming greyer in winter, slightly darker on the head and legs, with a yellowish-brown rump patch. The darker neck can contrast sharply with the body, and both sexes can produce manes (more usually among hinds in the US subspecies). The summer coat of the Manchurian wapiti is more distinctly red with a rump patch that more closely resembles the main coat; the contrast is greater with the darker winter coat. Some other Asian wapiti are lighter in colour (*see subspecies above*). Subspecies living in arid climates tend to have lighter coats than those of woodland animals, with less of a contrast between neck and body shading.
Height (at shoulder)	Bulls between 75–150 cm (29½–59 in) according to subspecies, cows notably smaller.
Weight	Bulls between 180–500 kg (396–1,102 lb), cows 170–295 kg (375–650 lb): in most populations bulls average around 25 per cent heavier than cows.
Food	Shrub and tree shoots, grasses, sedges and shrubs.

DEER SPECIES | CERVIDAE – CERVINAE

FACT BOX – *Wapiti*

Habitat	Open deciduous woodland, mountainous and wooded ground, upland moors, grassland.
Voice	A highly vocal deer. The call most associated with the wapiti is the bugling of a rutting stag, a high-pitched whistle that can carry for very long distances. Cows also make a variation of the bugle, most often during May and June as birthing approaches. Alarmed adults of both sexes make a hoarse bark, while distressed calves utter an extended scream. Calves also bleat to their mothers.
Annual behaviour	Lives in single sex herds for most of the year. One of the most gregarious deer species, summer herds tend to comprise smaller groupings but in winter herds of hinds and young bulls might number several hundred animals. Mature bulls tend to form smaller parties and are often encountered alone. Most daily activity is crepuscular. Some populations, especially those in mountainous regions more seriously affected by seasonal snowfall, migrate considerable distances of up to 140 km between summer and winter grounds. Lower valleys are sought in winter, but wapiti have been found up to 5,000 metres above sea level in summer. The Tule elk of California is the most sedentary of the subspecies.
Rut	Male and female herds start to congregate in August, and the rut generally reaches its height by late September. Bulls vocalise heavily and display with their antlers, wallowing frequently, and endeavour to gather harems of hinds, defending them from competing bulls to maintain exclusive breeding rights. Fighting is commonplace between equally matched bulls. Cows breaking away are herded back, often violently using antlers, although courtship is less aggressive. In California the Tule elk rut can start much earlier, generally in mid-July.
Gestation and birthing	Gestation lasts around 247 days. In common with most herding deer, the single spotted calf is born away from the main herd, not joining it until it is around 2 weeks old, and weighs about 15 kg (33 lb) at birth. Twins are relatively uncommon at less than 1 per cent of all births.
Antlers (typical)	Typical antlers carry 6 tines on each side with the top 2 forming a fork. Sometimes more tines are produced, and occasionally a 'cup' of 3 tines at the top of the antler is formed (although this is often indicative of hybridisation with red deer). In relation to the body, wapiti antlers are comparatively longer than those of the red deer. The largest recorded in North America measured 154.1 and 141.3 cm (60½ and 55½ in) on either side; their Asian equivalents were 152.4 cm (60 in). Weight and thickness may vary between subspecies. The Altai wapiti and the American subspecies are reputed to grow the largest antlers; a set grown by a large Roosevelt's elk might weigh as much as 18 kg (40 lb).
Antler cycle	Antlers are shed between January and March and regrown throughout the summer. There is only a short gap between velvet shedding and the commencement of rutting.
Lifespan	Around 15 years on average; up to 20 years recorded.
Threats	Natural predators can include wolves, coyotes, Siberian tigers, and bears where they occur within the wapiti's range. Smaller predators, such as coyote packs, can be a threat to calves. Chronic Wasting Disease is a growing threat in North America. There is also concern about the potential for inbreeding and a limited gene flow among smaller Tule elk populations. In parts of Russia and Asia, illegal or unregulated hunting for meat, hides, velvet and other body parts for traditional medicines is responsible for significant local population declines. Human disturbance from logging, industrialisation, mining and other causes can result in habitat loss or fragmentation.

Cervus elaphus

Red deer

ORDER	Artiodactyla
SUBORDER	Ruminantia
INFRAORDER	Pecora
FAMILY	Cervidae
SUBFAMILY	Cervinae

▲ A main race *C. e. elaphus* stag roars out a challenge in Richmond Park, London.

▼ (*left*) Red deer have long been maintained in parks and other enclosures both for decoration and as a food source. These stags are grazing in London's Richmond Park, once a Royal hunting park.

▼ (*right*) Considered to be an especially manageable species in captivity, red deer are commonly farmed for their venison.

THE RED DEER is one of the more well-known and iconic of the deer species. It has always been important to humans and is depicted in European cave art dating from some 40,000 years ago; archaeologists have revealed it to be a major source of food, skins and tools to early man. Much later it became a prized object of the chase among the early medieval European nobility; laws, many of them harsh, were enforced to preserve the right to hunt it. Many of the terms we still use to describe deer come from the formal language of hunting that developed during this period (*see Chapter 1*). It is more amenable than some other species to being kept in captivity, and even today is widely maintained in parks as well as farmed for its venison.

The red deer is distinguished by being the only deer species native to the continent of Africa, where the seriously threatened Barbary red deer can be found in the Atlas Mountains of Algeria, Morocco and Tunisia. Although abundant and widespread across much of its range and categorised overall as being of Least Concern, most of the subspecies are in fact anything but. Over-hunting has caused serious declines within the Barbary, Crimean, Caspian and Corsican red deer populations, leading to

a total extinction of the latter in Corsica by 1969. It is hoped that reintroductions since 1985 will successfully re-establish the subspecies. Likewise in Italy, the Mesola red deer is considered to be highly threatened; although competition from the more successful fallow deer within their range has been reduced, there remains a serious threat of inbreeding and a National Conservation Plan has been in place since 2010.

Recognition of the various subspecies has been subject to much change, but seven are currently listed by the IUCN (although the list could yet be subject to further revision):

▲ A mixed herd of Barbary red deer with the stag in velvet.
Photograph: Brent Huffman

Species		Distribution	Remarks
Red deer	Cervus. e. elaphus	Continental Europe, United Kingdom and Ireland Abundant and widespread	Size varies considerably depending on geographical location and available habitat: stags 116–125 cm (45½–49 in) high at the shoulder, weighing around 120–250 kg (264–551 lb), hinds 107–115 cm (42–45 in) and 80–120 kg (176–264 lb).
Barbary red deer, Barbary stag or Atlas deer	C. e. barbarus	Algeria, Morocco (reintroduced 1989) and Tunisia Rare	Stags typically 102–112 cm (40–44 in) high at the shoulder, weighing around 90–100 kg (200–220 lb).
Corsican red deer	C. e. corsicanus	Corsica (extinct and reintroduced in 1985) and Sardinia Rare	Stags typically 99–107 cm (39–42 in) high at the shoulder, weighing around 76–90 kg (168–184 lb).
Caspian red deer or maral	C. e. maral	Anatolia Seriously threatened	A larger subspecies – stags average 137 cm (52 in) at the shoulder and weigh around 230–320 kg (500–700 lb).
Mesola red deer	C. e. italicus	Italy Highly threatened and liable to inbreeding	Stags average 107cm (42 in) at the shoulder, hinds 95 cm (37 in). Stags average 108 kg (238 lb), hinds 76 kg (168 lb). Relatively simple antlers with narrow spread and usually just forked tops. Only recently recognised as a new subspecies.
Crimean red deer	C. e. brauneri	Crimea Although there is no data available for this species it is thought to be very rare.	Similar in size to the lower height and weight ranges of C. e. elaphus.
Carpathian red deer	C. e. montanus	Carpathian mountains of eastern Europe	Very large bodied but tends to have disproportionately small antlers compared to stags of C. e. elaphus in the same region; stags can weigh over 300 kg (661 lb) and as much as 340 kg (750 lb).

▲ (*top left*) A Barbary red deer stag in the Tierpark, Berlin.
Photograph: Alexander F Meyer

▲ (*top right*) A leucistic Caspian red deer stag in Zleby Game Park, Czechia.
Photograph: Klaus Rudloff

▲ (*bottom left*) A stag of the Spanish form of the main race.
Photograph: Klaus Rudloff

▲ (*bottom right*) A Scandinavian main race stag.
Photograph: Klaus Rudloff

Hybridisation remains an important worry. The red deer hybridises readily, both between subspecies and with other *Cervus* species, especially where populations are imbalanced, and the offspring are generally fertile. Many populations can already be considered to be hybrid. Releases and translocations, both deliberate and accidental, have occurred and have mainly involved sika *Cervus nippon* and wapiti *Cervus canadensis*. In many cases wapiti have been used in an attempt to increase the size of native stock, though in most cases any initial success in this respect has seen subsequent generations reverting to a size that the natural environment is able to support. It is notable that, in deer parks where red deer and sika exist side by side and rut at around the same time, as long as there is an appropriate balance with sufficient dominant stags the two species tend to ignore each other. Attempts to hybridise red deer with deer outside the *Cervus* genus have been largely unsuccessful, although there have been suggestions of successful matings with Père David's deer *Elaphurus davidianus* and sambar *Rusa unicolor*.

A stag roars in defence of his harem of hinds during the rut.

Hummelism, a condition particularly associated with red deer in which the adult stag grows no antlers, is almost certainly linked to poor initial development in the red deer calf and is usually observed where poorer habitats offer low levels of nutrition. Normally a male calf will start to grow his first set of antlers at around eight months old. This is reliant on the calf having already developed pedicles, the bony projections on the skull from which the antlers grow. Production of pedicles is linked to the calf reaching a threshold body weight of around 56 kilograms on average. If this weight is not reached by the time the calf is about six months old, subsequent antler development is affected even if the deer grows normally thereafter. Hummels are usually fertile, frequently holding hinds and breeding successfully, although they will be at a serious disadvantage if physically challenged by an antlered rival. Their offspring are usually normal antlered animals. Hummelism is not considered to be linked to genetic factors. It has also been seen in other species, including white-tailed deer *Odocoileus virginianus*, mule deer *Odocoileus hemionus*, and woodland caribou *Rangifer tarandus*. In Germany a hummel red stag is known as a *plattkopf*, literally 'flat head'.

The red deer is one of the species most widely associated with non-native introductions. The most successful was in New Zealand where the first arrivals in 1851 were supplemented by many more. By the 1920s it was seen as a serious pest, as a result of agricultural depredations and increasing damage to an ecosystem which had previously

A hind with her well grown calf in early autumn.

held no large ungulates and is now subject to severe control measures. Because they live in such a beneficial habitat, though, New Zealand red deer are considered to produce some of the most impressive antlers of their species. In Argentina and Chile the red deer is considered invasive and held responsible for the displacement of native species, including the huemul *Hippocamelus bisulcus*. In Australia, its range covers Queensland, New South Wales, Victoria and South Australia where its impact, although still unwelcome in places, is less severe.

FACT BOX – *Red deer*

World distribution	Native to Algeria, Armenia, Austria, Azerbaijan, Belarus, Belgium, Bosnia and Herzegovina, Bulgaria, Croatia, Czechia, Denmark, Estonia, France, Georgia, Germany, Hungary, Iran, Ireland, Italy, Latvia, Lithuania, Luxembourg, Moldova, Montenegro, Netherlands, North Macedonia, Norway, Poland, Romania, Russian Federation, Serbia, Slovakia, Slovenia, Sweden, Switzerland, Tunisia, Turkey, Ukraine and United Kingdom.
	Reintroduced to Greece and Morocco.
	Introduced to Argentina, Australia, Chile and New Zealand.
	Extinct in Albania, Israel, Jordan, Lebanon and Syria.
IUCN Red List Status 2022	**Least Concern**, population increasing (*though see main text*) (Last formal assessment 2015).
Sexes	*Male:* Stag *Female:* Hind *Young:* Calf
Also known as	Western red deer (*see also subspecies above*)
	Argentina *Ciervo Colorado, Europeo* or *Noble*; Bulgaria *Blagoroden elen*; Chile *Ciervo Colorado*; Chinese *Ma-lu*; Croatian *Jelen*; Czechoslovakian *Jelen evropsky* or *Jelenia zver*; Danish *Krondyr*; Dutch *Edelhert*; Estonian *Hirv*; Finnish *Saksan hirvi*; French *Cerf élaphe* or *Cerf rouge*; German *Rothirsch* or *Berber-edelhirsch* (*Barbary*); Greek *Elafi*; Hungarian *Gimszarvas*; Iranian *Gavazn*; Irish *Fia (rua)*; Italian *Cervo*; Latvia *Staltradzis*; Lithuanian *Taurusis elnias*; Montenegrin *Elen*; Norwegian *Hjort*; Polish *Jelen*; Portuguese *Veado*; Romanian *Cerb*; Russian *Blagorodnij olen*; Serb *Jelen*; Slovenia *Jelenjad*; Spanish *Ciervo, Ciervo común, Venado* or *Venado de Europa occidental*; Swedish *Krönhjort*; Turkish *Geyik* or *Ulu geyik*.
Recognition features	A medium to large deer, though size is variable according to subspecies (*see above*), geographical location, and natural resources. Pelage is generally a reddish-brown in summer, becoming greyish-brown in winter, with some slight variations between subspecies. The colour of the rump patch can range from a dirty white to a dark yellow or pale tan and extends above the base of the short tail. A dark dorsal stripe often extends down the neck and along the ridge of the back to the tail; traces of spots may be visible along either side in some adult animals.
	As the rut approaches, the neck of the stag will swell and he develops a pronounced mane.
Height (at shoulder)	Males typically 105 to 130 cm (41 to 51 in), females 100 to 114 cm (39 to 45 in). *See subspecies.*
Weight	Males typically 120 to 250 kg (264 to 551 lb), females 80 to 120 kg (176 to 264 lb). *See subspecies.*
Food	Shrub and tree shoots, grasses, sedges, herbs, ivy, heathers, and seasonal fruits and fungi according to availability. Will strip bark from trees, especially in winter, and can cause serious damage to agricultural crops.

FACT BOX – Red deer

Habitat	A forest deer by nature, preferring deciduous woodland interspersed with open meadows, the red deer is highly adaptable and may voluntarily occupy scrub or open ground above the wood line. In some places, such as Scotland, it has been forced by clearances to live on open moorland: in such places a smaller body size and shorter antlers reflect the adaptation to a more exposed habitat with reduced resources.
Voice	Generally silent for much of the year, the stag creates a loud, lion-like roar during the rut which he uses to advertise his dominance and challenge rivals. At this time hinds will make quieter nasal grunts. At other times both sexes bark when alarmed.
Annual behaviour	Lives in single sex herds for much of the year, with male offspring staying with their mothers for around a year, coming together only at the time of the rut. During the hotter months the deer will seek higher ground to avoid the heat and biting insects. Both sexes will wallow in regularly used boggy areas as a form of further relief; stags also wallow during the rut to enhance their appearance. Where appropriate, winter is often spent at lower altitudes as a refuge from weather conditions and where feeding is better. Throughout summer some herds can be small, especially those inhabiting woodland, but larger ones sometimes numbering over 100 animals can form during the winter. Red deer swim strongly and frequently cross large bodies of water as part of their daily movements or to escape predators.
Rut	The rut takes place between late September and the end of October in western Europe, slightly earlier further east where it peaks in late September. Stags compete for the attentions of hinds by roaring: the volume and frequency of roars determine their attractiveness. They then endeavour to defend their harems, which can number around 20 hinds, from rivals; roaring now demonstrates size and dominance, and is followed by parallel walking if a challenge is made. This may result in a lesser stag breaking off, but if the two assess each other to be well-matched, fighting will occur which consists of pushing contests with locked antlers. A defeated stag is pursued aggressively and serious injuries can be sustained. A dominant stag defending a harem barely feeds during this time and can lose up to 20 per cent of his body weight.
Gestation and birthing	Gestation lasts around 235 days, after which a single calf weighing around 15 kg (33 lb) is born. Twins are rare. Calves are spotted at birth but these markings fade and are barely visible by 2 months of age. In some poorer upland habitats, mature hinds may miss a year in breeding to allow them to recover condition; these animals are known as 'yeld'.
Antlers (typical)	Antler length and weight can vary widely across both subspecies and habitats. A typical set would have brow, bey and tray tines, and a further 2 or 3 forming a cup or crown at the tips. They might weigh anything between 1 kg (2 lb 3 oz) and 5 kg (11 lb) and measure between 70 cm (27½ in) and 120 cm (47 in). The most impressive antlers tend to be borne by stags from Eastern Europe and may carry as many as 20 or more tines, whereas an above-average animal in Scotland might only have a total of 12 tines.
Antler cycle	Antlers are shed between February and the end of March, to be fully regrown by late August or early September.
Lifespan	Around 5 years
Threats	Preyed on by grey wolves and brown bears where they occur; Eurasian lynx and wild boar will also take calves. Poaching, over-hunting and habitat loss can all be significant local concerns. Hybridisation is a major issue, especially with the closely related wapiti *Cervus canadensis* and sika *Cervus nippon* which have been introduced from the USA in parts of its range; introductions have also brought with them diseases and parasites previously unencountered.

Cervus hanglu

Tarim red deer

ORDER	Artiodactyla
SUBORDER	Ruminantia
INFRAORDER	Pecora
FAMILY	Cervidae
SUBFAMILY	Cervinae

▲ Bactrian deer stag.
Photograph: Brent Huffman

THE TARIM RED deer is notable for its extremely scattered and isolated distribution across limited parts of northern Asia. It is also a taxonomically confusing species. At one time most of the various *Cervus* species, including the Tarim red deer and the North American wapiti, were considered to be no more than subspecies of the red deer *Cervus elaphus*, and indeed the Kashmir stag was even once thought to be an isolated subspecies of the wapiti, but re-evaluations based on genetics have separated them.

The Tarim red deer was elevated to species level by the IUCN in 2016 but, although that distinction is recognised here, it must be accepted that further revisions may yet take place and some sources still do not recognise it. There are three provisional subspecies, themselves all subject to clarification, and all of which are widely separated geographically in discrete, seriously fragmented populations. The photographs of Bactrian deer accompanying these pages can be considered illustrative of all three, and slightly varying physical features and behaviours may be attributable to regional isolation:

▼ A Kashmir stag depicted in *The Deer of all Lands* by Richard Lydekker (1898).

Kashmir stag *Cervus hanglu hanglu*. Once widespread throughout the valleys and mountains of Kashmir, this is the rarest of the provisional subspecies, with its only viable population considered to be in the Dachigam National Park near Srinagar. There are a few other populations, all of them very small, elsewhere. Prior to 1947, the Kashmir stag enjoyed the strictly protected status of being 'royal game' but declined rapidly once this protection was removed. There may still have been as many as 5,000 animals in the 1940s, but a 2019 census suggested that this had reduced to just 237. Stags are more vulnerable to poaching, especially during the rut, and a 2016 survey in Dachigam National Park determined a stag-to-hind ratio of 1:11.

Bactrian deer *C. h. bactrianus*. The smallest of the subspecies and found in west Turkestan, Kazakhstan, Uzbekistan, Tajikistan and northern Afghanistan. It once had a wide range but by the 1960s this was much reduced. By 1999, largely as a result of military conflict and other sources of disturbance across its range, the population had fallen to around 400: but meaningful conservation efforts since have enabled numbers to rise to 1,430 and they continue to increase. Although a number of successful reintroductions have occurred, one – in the Ajar Valley of Afghanistan – was subsequently hunted to extinction.

◄ A Bactrian deer stag showing the rump pattern.
Photographs: Brent Huffman

◄ Bactrian deer adult hinds, their lower legs muddy from wading.

Yarkand deer *C. h. yarkandensis*. The largest of the three subspecies. Found in the deciduous forests and steppe of the Tarim Basin in the autonomous East Turkestan region of north-west China, from which this group of deer derive their generic name. Separated from the Bactrian deer by the Tien Shan mountains on the border with Kazakhstan.

The IUCN Red List categorisation of Least Concern may be somewhat misleading, as it reflects the fact that the numbers of the Bactrian deer subspecies are looking increasingly healthy, thanks to intensive conservation efforts; they probably comprise something like 75 per cent of the overall species population. However, the Yarkand deer of the Tarim Basin declined from an estimate 10,000 animals in the 1950s to no more than 5,000 in 1991. The current population appears to be concentrated in three separate locations; precise numbers are unknown but the decline may be continuing.

It is the Kashmir stag, though, that is the most worrying in terms of its future. Quite apart from the gender imbalances already alluded to, breeding success is consistently low with only 7.5 calves recorded for every 100 females in 2019; during the 15 years prior to that, the ratio never exceeded 27 calves to 100 females, and was often considerably less. The situation is not helped by their main breeding area in the Dachigam National Park being shared with flocks of sheep during the summer, along with their shepherds and guard dogs, with resulting levels of disturbance and calves occasionally being killed by the latter. Although efforts are being made to improve matters, including the encouragement of community awareness and a more enlightened attitude towards wildlife management, there is little sign of success to date and the level of local engagement is disappointing.

FACT BOX – *Tarim red deer*

World distribution	Native to Afghanistan, China, India, Kazakhstan, Tajikistan, Turkmenistan and Uzbekistan (*see main text*). Possibly extinct in Pakistan.
IUCN Red List Status 2022	**Least Concern**, population increasing (*but see main text*) (last formal assessment 2017).
Sexes	*Male:* Stag *Female:* Hind *Young:* Calf
Also known as	Central Asian red deer **Bactrian**: Bactrian red deer, Bukhara red deer **Kashmir stag**: Hangul, Kashmir deer, Kashmir red deer. Chinese *Ma-lu*; French *Cerf Rouge du Turkestan, Cerf de Bactriane, Cerf du Turkestan, Cerf rouge du Turkestan, Cerf élaphe du Cachemire, Cerf de Yarkand*; German *Buchara-hirsch, Yarkand-hirsch*; Kashmiri *Hangal* or *Honglu*; Spanish *Ciervo Asiático, Ciervo Bactriano, Ciervo de Cachemira*; Tibetan *Yi* or *Rithak churin*.
Recognition features	**Kashmir stag**: brown/liver in winter, lighter and reddish in summer, rump patch white, narrow and does not extend above the tail base. Hinds sometimes carry light spots on their summer coat. **Bactrian deer**: a smaller deer, lighter ash-grey in colour with a dirty white rump patch. Adults may carry a few spots on the upper parts of their summer coats. The dorsal stripe is only faint. **Yarkand deer**: the most lightly coloured of the subspecies. A uniform pale red or sandy colouration with a light rump patch and darker legs; dorsal stripe more pronounced on the neck than the rest of the back. All have a short tail. Stags develop a pronounced mane and thickened neck as the rut approaches.
Height (at shoulder)	**Kashmir stag** (male): 122–127 cm (48–50 in) **Bactrian deer** (male): 120 cm (47 in) **Yarkand deer** (male): 135–140 cm (53–55 in) Sexual dimorphism is marked, females being smaller than males though not by as much as in the red deer *C. elaphus*.

DEER SPECIES | CERVIDAE – CERVINAE

FACT BOX – *Tarim red deer*

Weight	**Kashmir stag** (male): 204 kg (450 lb) **Bactrian deer** (male): 130 kg (286 lb) **Yarkand deer** (stag): 250 kg (551 lb)
Food	Predominantly tree shoots, grasses, sedges and shrubs.
Habitat	The Kashmir stag will use habitats including deciduous woodland, upland moorland, natural grasslands and pastures, often moving between them according to food availability. Both the Bactrian and Yarkand deer tend to inhabit forested corridors surrounded by more open, often desert areas. Some Bactrian populations may live almost exclusively in reed and scrub areas with little tree cover.
Voice	Stags make a bull-like roar while challenging rivals during the rut. Kashmir stags may also end their roars with a bugling call similar to that of the wapiti *C. canadensis*. Otherwise largely silent, but both sexes may bark when alarmed.
Annual behaviour	A herding species which lives in small groups for much of the year. Mature males form their own herds apart from those consisting of females and juveniles, coming together only for the rut. Kashmir stags living in more mountainous areas may spend the summer on high ground between 2,700 and 3,600 metres above sea level and descend to lower altitudes in winter. Bactrian and Yarkand deer are less migratory in their habits but may move into desert areas at night or when the weather is cooler. All are strong swimmers and have been known to cross fast-flowing rivers regularly.
Rut	Generally late September to early November for the Bactrian and Yarkand deer; the Kashmir stag ruts mainly in October. In all subspecies the stags will endeavour to collect parcels of hinds together and then defend them against rivals to secure breeding rights.
Gestation and birthing	After a gestation period of 230–238 days, calves are born from late May through to July (Kashmir stags late April or May). They are spotted at birth and twins are extremely rare.
Antlers (typical)	**Kashmir stag**: usually 10 tines, consisting of a brow, bey, trey and a terminal fork. A good set measure around 95 cm (37½ in); the largest recorded were 112 cm (44 in). **Bactrian deer**: similar to the Kashmir stag: bey tines may exceed the brow tine in length, and the top occasionally terminates in a tree-forked crown. **Yarkand deer**: as above, averaging 90–105 cm (35½–41½ in). Brow and bay tines may be very long although some may only carry a brow tine, and whether or not a 3-point crown is ever produced is uncertain.
Antler cycle	Kashmir stags shed between the end of February and the end of March, with regrowth complete by the following September. The cycle for the other subspecies runs slightly later.
Lifespan	Around 14 years
Threats	Depending on their presence across the range of the Tarim red deer, its predators may include the Himalayan wolf, brown bear, dhole, leopard and snow leopard. Eurasian lynx and wild boar also represent a threat to calves. Illegal hunting remains the greatest threat in all cases, while across much of Central Asia habitat loss caused by illegal logging and grazing by livestock, as well as forest fires, are also problematic. Agricultural expansion and oil exploration are a cause for concern in China. Additionally, given the low numbers remaining of the Kashmir stag, the potential for inbreeding cannot be discounted.

A GUIDE TO THE DEER OF THE WORLD

Cervus nippon

Sika

ORDER	Artiodactyla
SUBORDER	Ruminantia
INFRAORDER	Pecora
FAMILY	Cervidae
SUBFAMILY	Cervinae

▲ A mature Japanese sika stag with three prickets, illustrating typical rump markings and metatarsal gland markings on the hocks of the hind legs.

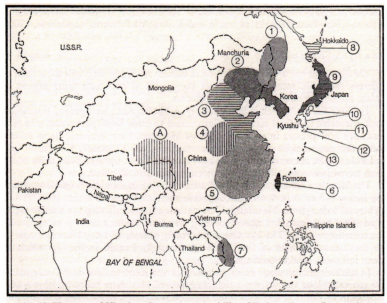

Map 12. The range of Sika deer *Cervus nippon*, and Thorold's deer, *Cervus albirostris* in ASIA

SIKA DEER. *Cervus nippon*

1. *Cervus nippon hortulorum* — Ussuri district, Manchuria
2. *C.n.mantchuricus* — Manchuria, Korea
3. *C.n. mandarinus* — Northern China
4. *C.n.grassianus* — Shansi district, China
5. *C.n.kopschi* — South-east China
6. *C.n.taiouanus* — Formosa
7. *C.n.pseudaxis* — Vietnam
8. *C.n. yesoënsis* — Hokkaido Island, Japan
9. *C.n.centralis* — Hondo (Honshu) Island, Japan
10. *C.n.nippon* — Kyushu Island, Japan
11. *C.n.mageshimae* — Mageshima Island, Japan
12. *C.n.yakushimae* — Yakushima Island, Japan
13. *C.n.keramae* — Ryukyu Islands, Japan

THOROLD'S DEER. *Cervus albirostris*

A. *C.albirostris* — Eastern Tibet, western China

▶ The 1972 distribution of sika, along with the subspecies recognised at that time, taken from G. Kenneth Whitehead's *Deer of the World* (Constable 1972).

ONCE COMMON AND widespread across eastern Asia, the sika has all but disappeared on much of the mainland and is now only truly numerous on the main Japanese islands. It is a medium-sized deer which varies considerably in size between subspecies; generally it bears a spotted summer coat, darker winter coat and a rump patch of erectile hair that can be fluffed out when alarmed. Typical mature stags carry antlers with a total of eight points, although more are occasionally seen on some subspecies. By rights, the species should be referred to simply as sika, as its name is taken from the Japanese word *shika* which itself means 'deer'.

The taxonomy of the sika has been subject to a great deal of change. Genetic mixing is widely believed to have taken place, especially in China, and as a result there remains some discussion regarding the exact status of the subspecies. There are potentially twelve of these, although some may already be extinct; the status of a thirteenth, Dybowski's sika, is uncertain. In general terms, deer size tends to decrease as natural ranges move southwards:

▼ Dybowski's sika hind, Moscow Zoo.
Photograph: Klaus Rudloff

Species		Distribution	Remarks
Japanese sika	C. n. nippon	Southern Honshu, Shikoku and Kyushu, Japan.	Average shoulder height for a stag is around 81 cm (32 in), a good specimen weighing up to 55 kg (121 lb).
North Honshu sika	C. n. aplodontus	Northern Honshu, Japan.	Somewhat larger than the Japanese sika of the southern end of Honshu Island, a typical stag stands around 86 cm (34 in) at the shoulder and weighs 70 kg (154 lb).
Manchurian sika	C. n. mantchuricus	Primorsky Krai, eastern Russia. Population stable and estimated at 8,500–9,000 animals. Once also found in north-eastern China and Korea, but now extinct in these places.	A large sika: average shoulder height for a stag 86–96 cm (34–38 in) and weight 72–109 kg (160–240 lb) with animals up to 160 kg (350 lb) recorded.
North China sika	C. n. mandarinus	Last recorded in Jilin Province, north-eastern China in 1992. Now considered extinct.	A small sika similar to more southern forms.
Shansi sika	C. n. grassianus	Last recorded in Shanxi Province, eastern China in the 1980s. Now considered extinct.	
Sichuan sika	C. n. sichuanicus	Sichuan Province, south-western China. A newer subspecies, first recognised in 1978. The overall population is probably no more than 400–500 animals.	An average stag will weigh around 150 kg (334 lb).
Hokkaido sika	C. n. yesoensis	Hokkaido, Japan. Common and widespread, with numbers increasing.	A more yellowish-red colour and heavily spotted in the summer coat. Average shoulder height for a stag is 88–90 cm (34½–35½ in) and weight 70–80 kg (172–176 lb).

Species		Distribution	Remarks
Formosan or Taiwan sika	C. n. taiouanus	Taiwan. Once free ranging across the island but eradicated in the wild by 1969; reintroduced to the Kenting National Park in 1986 using stock from Taipei Zoo.	Average shoulder height for a stag is 86–96 cm (34–38 in) and weight 72–83 kg (160–180 lb).
Vietnamese or Tonkin sika	C. n. pseudaxis	Northern Vietnam. The last few wild-living animals were reported in 1990. The subspecies is probably now extinct in the wild, though some animals are maintained in captivity and there is a breeding and conservation plan.	
South China or Kopschi sika	C. n. kopschi	South-eastern China; numbers extremely low and only found in 5 very isolated populations.	Average shoulder height of stag 85 cm (33 in).
Ryukyu or Kerama sika	C. n. keramae	Kerama Islands, Japan. Introduced during the seventeenth century and considered to have developed as a distinct insular form. Numbers are very low and it is considered to be endangered.	One of the smaller subspecies, which may be entirely melanistic: unspotted, small dark metatarsal glands, dark bellies and light napes. The average shoulder height for a stag is 65–71 cm (25½–28 in).
Tsushima sika	C. n. pulchellus	Tsushima Islands, Japan.	A smaller island race, similar to the Ryukyu sika in size.
Dybowski's sika	C. n. hortulorum	Far-eastern Russia. *Status as a distinct subspecies is uncertain and it may in fact be of mixed origin.*	Very large; average shoulder height for a stag is 106–112 cm (42–44 in) and weight 117–132 kg (257–288 lb).

> Japanese sika stag in summer coat at Nara Park, Japan.
Photograph: Alistair McLellan

The categorisation of the sika as Least Concern should not be taken at face value. Although abundant and increasing in much of Japan and stable in Russia, elsewhere populations are very seriously threatened. On the mainland some subspecies may indeed have disappeared completely, while others are in a perilous state, as a comparison of the current distribution map and that from 1972 shows all too clearly. Sika once ranged widely across eastern China, but over the past 50 years their distribution has shrunk radically and now only small, isolated populations exist in a few places.

It is only on the main Japanese islands that sika are truly thriving – in 2015 the Japanese Ministry of the Environment estimated the overall population to be

◀ A Japanese sika hind at the Tōdai-ji Temple in Nara Park, Japan.
Photograph: Pen Ash

▼ Hokkaido sika stag in winter.
Photograph: Saron Ang

over 3 million – and while heavily industrialised areas may offer only fragmented habitats, elsewhere the sika is considered to be over-abundant. Nowhere is this more true than in Hokkaido in the north: whereas for so many other deer species over-hunting is a major threat, the exact opposite is true on Japan's northern main island. A largely unchecked sika population in Hokkaido is held responsible for growing levels of agricultural, plantation and forest damage. Hunting is now actively encouraged there in an attempt to reduce numbers, though this has been restricted in the past by strict firearms ownership laws and only a limited market for venison. One form of forestry damage particularly associated with sika is bole scoring, where the trunk of a tree is extensively gouged with a stag's brow tines.

One of the main reasons for the sika's success in Japan has been the extinction of what were once its main predators, the Honshū wolf *Canis lupus hodophilax* and Hokkaido wolf *Canis lupus hattai*. The sika also benefits from a strong religious significance, the most famous illustration of this being at Nara Park to the south of Kyoto. Here the sika once enjoyed a divine and sacred status as a messenger of the Gods. Today they are still listed as National Treasures and over a thousand wander freely among visiting tourists, who feed them specially prepared *shika-senbei* or deer crackers after exchanging formal bows with the deer, which have learned to bow in return. Care needs to be taken, though, as some animals have been known to interpret a bow as a prelude to a head butt and reciprocate. Because of the tameness of these deer and the danger of injury to human residents and visitors, a ceremony has taken place at Nara every year since 1671 in which stags are captured and a Shinto priest supervises the cutting off of their antlers which, as they consist of hard, dead material by this time, causes the animal no pain.

In some parts of the world, introductions have been hugely successful. This is a highly adaptable and robust species, which quickly established well away from its natural range. In some countries the deer are now held to be a threat to woodland, while in the United Kingdom there are continuing concerns over hybridisation with the indigenous red deer *C. e. elaphus*. Sika in the UK are generally treated as the Japanese subspecies but have come from a number of sources and tend to be somewhat larger; they may also contain the genes of others, including Manchurian

A GUIDE TO THE DEER OF THE WORLD

▲ (*left*) A group of captive Manchurian sika in summer coat, the stag showing the distinctive rusty-red colour of the subspecies' antler velvet.
Photograph: Alexander F Meyer

▲ (*right*) A Manchurian sika stag pictured during the rut in Woburn Park, England.

▼ (*left*) Vietnamese sika stag, pictured in San Diego Zoo.
Photographs: Alexander F Meyer

▼ (*right*) Formosan sika stag and hind, pictured in San Diego Zoo.

and Formosan. Sika can subsist on poorer forage than some other deer species, having a digestive system which copes more efficiently with coarser fibres. This has helped them to become a dominant species in places, and they have been known to displace white-tailed deer *Odocoileus virginianus* in some parts of the USA where they have been introduced.

Much of the decline of the mainland sika can be attributed to hunting pressure, coupled with habitat loss. The meat has a ready market, and the velvet that covers growing antlers, along with other body parts, has always been highly sought-after for traditional medicine in China. Japan is probably the only country in eastern Asia where deer are not farmed specifically for velvet, and the escape of red deer *Cervus elaphus* from some mainland farms has been suggested as a source of unwelcome hybridisation.

Captive breeding may become the only way forward for the survival of some of the more threatened sika subspecies that remain; this practice has already enabled the reintroduction of the Formosan sika to Taiwan after it disappeared in the wild, and the same may yet apply to the Vietnamese sika.

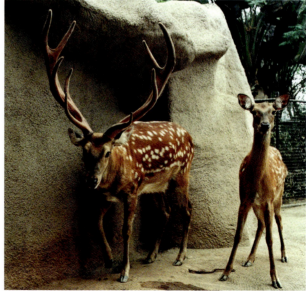

FACT BOX – *Sika*

World distribution	Native to China, Japan and Russia Reintroduced to Taiwan Possibly extinct in DPR Korea and Vietnam Extinct in the Republic of Korea Introduced to Armenia, Austria, Azerbaijan, Czechia, Denmark, Finland, France, Germany, Ireland, Lithuania, Madagascar, New Zealand, the Philippines, Poland, Ukraine, United Kingdom and the United States.
IUCN Red List Status 2022	**Least Concern**, population increasing (*though see main text*) (last formal assessment 2014).
Sexes	*Male:* Stag *Female:* Hind *Young:* Calf
Also known as	Spotted deer, Japanese deer Bulgarian *Elen sika*; Chinese *Mei-hua-lu*; Croatian *Jelen sika*; Danish *Sika*; French *Cerf sika*; German *Sikahirsch*; Hungarian *Szika szarvas*; Irish *Fia leapànach*; Japanese *Ezo-shika, Hanashika, Honshu-jika, Karoku kerama-jika, Khu-a-lu, Kyusyu-jika, Mage-shika, Nihon-jika, Ryukyu-inoshishi* or *Yaku-shika*; Korean *Sika sareum*; Lithuanian *Dèmètasis elnias*; Montenegrin *Elen sika*; Norwegian *Sikahjort*; Polish *Sika*; Russian *Pjatnisstij olen*; Serb *Jelen sika*; Slovakian *Sika zvěř*; Slovenian *Jelen sika*; Spanish *Sika*; Swedish *Sika* or *Sikahjort*; Taiwan *Kwaroku*; Yugoslavian *Sika jelen*.
Recognition features	A medium-sized, compact and slim-legged deer. The summer coat is typically a rich chestnut red with white spots, changing to a deep brown or sooty brown in winter with spots often barely visible (if at all), with a white caudal disc edged with black. The belly, chin and throat are usually grey or off-white, while the tail is typically white with a black central stripe. The muzzle is narrow and brow markings can give a 'frowning' appearance. Pale metatarsal markings on the hocks of the hind legs are usually apparent. Stags have thicker necks and produce rudimentary canine tusks; some subspecies develop a shaggy mane as the rut approaches. The rump patch is composed of erectile hair which can be flared when alarmed, and sika often depart with a 'pronking' gait, involving all four feet leaving the ground at the same time.
Height (at shoulder)	Widely variable between around 65 cm (25 ½ in) for some of the island races to over 100 cm (39 in) for more northerly subspecies. Sexual dimorphism is pronounced, with males considerably larger than females (*see subspecies*).
Weight	Variable (*see subspecies*)
Food	Takes a wide variety of foodstuffs including buds, leaves, seeds and new plant growth. Dwarf bamboos are an important food source in Japan.
Habitat	A secretive deer that prefers dense forested areas, but will also use thick scrub, freshwater marshes or grassland. Usually found at lower elevations up to 1,500 metres above sea level.
Voice	A highly vocal deer, especially the stags. Sounds made include bleating, cackling, whickering and snorting. Stags make a shrill, rising-and-falling whistle during the rut, and both sexes make a loud, carrying squeak when alarmed.

FACT BOX – *Sika*

Annual behaviour	A crepuscular deer, which may become almost entirely nocturnal when put under heavy hunting pressure or faced with other sustained disturbance. The sexes tend to live in separate herds throughout the year, coming together only for the rut.
	The sika is more prone to hide rather than flee where circumstances permit; it has poor endurance when chased and is vulnerable to attacks by wolf or domestic dog packs. An excellent swimmer, it readily takes to water to escape pursuit.
Rut	Both sexes reach sexual maturity at between 16–18 months, although stags are unlikely to breed until they achieve the dominance which comes with full maturity and antler development. The rut takes place between August and November depending on the geographical location. Stags will usually gather and defend harems but have been known to employ lekking strategies in the manner of fallow deer *Dama dama*, especially where densities are high. Territories are marked by digging with forefeet, urinating, and thrashing ground vegetation with antlers. Fighting between competing stags is fierce and occasionally results in fatalities.
Gestation and birthing	Most birthing takes place between May and July after a gestation period of between 210–230 days. The calf is spotted and weighs between 4.5–7 kg (10–15½ lb); twins are occasionally born. The hind will leave the main herd to give birth to her calf, initially hiding it in thick undergrowth while she goes off to feed.
Antlers (typical)	The antlers are robust and a mature stag typically produces a total of 8 points although 10 or even 12 have been known (especially among the northern subspecies). The smaller southerly species may normally only produce 6 points and the antlers are lighter. The brow tine tends to leave the main beam at an acute angle, with long front and back points.
	The largest antlers tend to be produced by the Hokkaido sika, where a good set might measure 74 cm (29 in). Manchurian sika average 66 cm (66 in), while the Japanese sika is closer to 50 cm (19½ in).
	The colour of the velvet which covers the growing antlers varies between subspecies: that of Manchurian animals is a bright rusty red, while the Formosan is browner and that of many of the Japanese subspecies is almost black.
Antler cycle	Casting takes place between March and May with older animals usually dropping their antlers first. Regrowth is normally complete and clean of velvet by early September.
Lifespan	Reportedly up to 25 years, though around 15 years is probably more usual.
Threats	Preyed on by tigers, leopards, wolves and brown bears where they occur across its range. There are no significant natural predators in Japan.
	Hunting and habitat loss are the main human threats.

Dama dama
Fallow deer

ORDER	Artiodactyla
SUBORDER	Ruminantia
INFRAORDER	Pecora
FAMILY	Cervidae
SUBFAMILY	Cervinae

THE FALLOW IS probably the most familiar of the deer to many of us. It has been transplanted around the world by humans since Roman times or even earlier and has adapted readily to many new habitats and climates. It became an important feature of many medieval deer parks and enclosures where it was kept, firstly as a food resource and then as a status symbol prized for its looks. Many wild fallow populations today have their origins in escapes from these early deer parks. Elsewhere, and most particularly across Europe, it was also once an important beast of the chase, the right to hunt it being jealously guarded by the nobility of the time and surrounded by a chivalric language of its own. The terms *buck* and *doe*, which are applied to so many other species of deer, have their origins as specific titles for the fallow.

In more recent times it has been introduced to places as far apart as New Zealand and South Africa by colonial settlers anxious to take reminders of their homelands to their adopted countries. Such introductions have not necessarily turned out to be benign: New Zealand in particular, a country which hitherto had no native mammals other than bats, has since suffered serious ecological problems because of a proliferation of various deer and other non-native species. In South Africa, they occur widely across the Western and Northern Cape regions where they are considered to be an invasive species, and their movement is now heavily regulated.

While common and successful worldwide, the species has suffered major declines within its historic native range. In Turkey there is believed to be one very small original native

▲ (*left*) A menil master buck during the rut.

Distributrion map: The European range of the fallow deer; other introduced populations exist elsewhere (*see World distribution*).

▼ Richmond Park, London. Fallow have always been an important park deer species.

population remaining, and although there are signs of population recovery on the Greek island of Rhodes, concerns persist for the genetically distinct animals there.

Among all the deer, the fallow has the widest variety of coat colours: these have their origins in selective breeding throughout a long history of semi-domestication. Although the natural form and probably the most well-known, the common variety with its attractive summer coat of russet brown patterned with pale spots may not actually be the most numerous in some places and herds can consist of animals in several different colours. Very often they will not breed true to type, and the fawn may be of an entirely different colour from either of its parents.

(*clockwise from top*)
Mature buck, common colour variety.
Photograph: Klaus Rudloff

A mixed herd of colour varieties in winter coat: common (*far left*), white (*second from left*), black (*front*) and menil (*second, third and fourth from right*). The variations in rump patterns are a good guide to colour variety.

A young black buck and a menil doe in summer coat.

Fallow do not always breed true to their colour variety. A menil doe with her common variety fawn.

◀ Long-haired fallow bucks, a mature animal of the black colour variety and a common pricket, pictured in the Mortimer Forest near Ludlow, England. The longer hairs on the crown of the head, ear tufts and the extended tail hair are typical of this unusual and very localised variation.
Photographs: Andrew Fusek Peters

A unique, long-haired variety of fallow can be found in the vicinity of Ludlow, England, the only place in the world where it is known to exist. The coat of the long-haired fallow can be as much as three times longer than that of a normal specimen. Typically, the length of the hair is most striking on the crown of the head, with long tufts also growing out of the ears, while the tail can also look especially lengthy. The bodies of young animals in their first winter can appear particularly shaggy and, being longer and finer than those found on regular animals, the hairs tend to be easily saturated, making the animal more prone to chilling. Otherwise there seem to be no other adverse effects and long-haired fallow will breed with the normal varieties. Just as with the regular colour variants, the offspring of a mating between two long-haired fallow may not necessarily produce a long-haired fawn. The fallow is the only deer species where polymorphism of this kind is known to occur.

Some localities do not seem regularly to produce classic, widely palmated fallow antlers, for any number of reasons. The annual growth of such structures demands considerable resources, and if the animal is not finding quality forage, along with essential trace elements, it follows that antler growth may not be as impressive as elsewhere. Genetics and stress, be it because of over-population or human pressures, can also affect antler growth.

▼ (*left*) The menil buck in front has just cast his antlers; his companion has yet to do so. Older animals generally cast first.

▼ (*right*) Pronking is a gait used by fallow and some other species, in which all four hooves leave the ground at the same time and the animal departs in a bouncing motion
Photograph: Coke Smith

A GUIDE TO THE DEER OF THE WORLD

FACT BOX – *Fallow deer*

World distribution	Original range uncertain, but probably included parts of southern Europe and Turkey (where it has now almost disappeared).
	Introduced widely across Europe, also Argentina, Australia, Canada, Chile, Fiji, New Zealand, Peru, South Africa, the United States, Uruguay and elsewhere.
IUCN Red List Status 2022	**Least Concern**, population trend unknown (last formal assessment 2008).
Sexes	*Male:* Buck *Female:* Doe *Young:* Fawn
Also known as	Forest deer, Mediterranean deer, spotted deer.
	Albanian *Dreri lobatar*; Argentina *Ciervo dama*; Bulgarian *Elen lopatar*; Croatian *Jelen lanjac*; Czech *Danrk skvrnity*; Danish *Danyr*; Dutch *Damhert*; Estonian *Hirvpodr*; Finnish *Kuusipeura*; French *Daim*; German *Damwild* or *damhirsch*; Greek *Platini*; Hebrew *Jackmur*; Hungarian *Damszarvas*; Iranian *Jackmur*; Irish *Fia bui*; Italian *Daino*; Latvian *Dambriedis*; Lithuanian *Danielius*; Montenegran *Elen lopatar*; Norwegian *Dadyr*; Polish *Danile*; Romanian *Cerb lopator*; Serbian *Jelen lopator*; Slovak *Danieli Zver*; Spanish *Gamo*; Swedish *Dovvilt*; Turkish *Alageyik*, *Jigin* or *Yagmurca*.
Recognition features	Coat colouration can vary considerably. There are 4 main varieties:
	✦ **Common** – red/brown with white or cream spots in summer, spots often merging to form a line along the flank, turning to an unspotted two-tone of dark brown upper body with a lighter grey below in winter. Dark dorsal line from the nape of the neck to the tail. The rump patch is pale, with an inverted black horseshoe marking surrounding it and a thick black line down the centre of the long tail.
	✦ **Menil** – similar to common, though somewhat paler; spotting remains visible on the paler but coarser winter coat. Rump and tail markings are light brown/caramel-coloured.
	✦ **Black (melanistic)** – summer coat is a glossy black with dark grey underparts, changing to more of a matt black in winter. The rump and tail are black with no markings clearly visible. Sometimes referred to as *Norwegian* or *Forest* fallow.
	✦ **White** – remain white/cream throughout the year. No tail or rump markings are clearly visible. They have normal dark eyes and hooves and are not albino.
	Other colourations may include a sooty dun (liver-coloured), blue-grey, silver-grey, sandy, and more.
	The tail is active and frequently twitched from side to side. Disturbed animals have a characteristic pronking or stotting gait, in which the deer departs with a bouncing motion as all 4 feet leave the ground at the same time.
Height (at shoulder)	Bucks 85–95 cm (33–37 in), does 75–85 cm (30–33 in). Fallow deer native to the Greek island of Rhodes are smaller on average than those elsewhere.
Weight	Bucks average 60–100 kg (130–220 lb), though a large specimen might attain 150 kg (330 lb). Does are significantly smaller at 30–50 kg (66–110 lb).
Food	Primarily a grazing deer but will also browse trees and shrubs
Habitat	Highly adaptable: found in forestry, woodland, shrubland and plantations. Broadleaf woodland with associated cultivated land is favoured.

FACT BOX – *Fallow deer*

Voice	Not highly vocal outside the rut, when the buck emits a rhythmic grunt, variously described as groaning or belching. Does and fawns communicate with soft bleats, and all sexes may utter a gruff bark if alarmed.
Annual behaviour	Fallow live in single sex herds for most of the year, coming together only at the time of the rut, and otherwise remaining loyal to their discrete home ranges. Very large herds numbering over 100 animals, often comprised mainly of does and fawns, are not uncommon. Buck fawns may stay with their mother for up to 2 years. Where subject to persecution or excessive pressure, most feeding and movement may take place under cover of darkness.
Rut	In Europe the rut takes place in October and November (April and May in Australasia). Bucks develop thickened neck muscles and their larynx (Adam's apple) becomes more prominent. They usually establish rutting stands (often on traditional sites) where they pace up and down groaning rhythmically to attract does to them. The pitch and frequency of groans is considered to have a direct effect on breeding success. In areas of high deer densities (such as in parks) rutting stands may be in close proximity to each other, and fighting can be frequent. Bucks will walk parallel to each other before either breaking off or, if well matched, turning to lock antlers for a pushing contest. Bucks eat less during the rut and rapidly lose condition as a result of their exertions; afterwards they often spend long periods of immobility while recovering.
Gestation and birthing	Gestation lasts between 225 and 230 days, after which a single fawn weighing about 4.5 kg (10 lb) is born. Twins are occasionally produced. Does are more tolerant of being suckled by the fawn of another, often giving the false impression of a multiple birth.
Antlers (typical)	The antlers of a mature buck are typically broad and palmate (spade-shaped) with rear protrusions (spellers) with prominent brow and secondary tines. Yearling animals seldom bear more than simple spike antlers, which develop over subsequent casting and regrowth until they reach full adult dimensions by around their sixth or seventh year. In some places palmation is not universal, and antlers may have no more than flattened tips, even on mature animals. Traditional names for the various age classes are: 1st head – pricket 2nd head – sorrel 3rd head – sore 4th head – bare buck 5th head – buck 6th head and thereafter – master *or* great buck.
Antler cycle	In the Northern Hemisphere fallow typically cast during April and May and antlers are fully regrown and clean of velvet by August or September. Elsewhere, the cycle may vary – in New Zealand, for instance, casting takes place in October and November.
Lifespan	Typically 12–16 years
Threats	In some places where they have been introduced, large predators may take adult fallow, though elsewhere only the younger fawns are vulnerable to foxes, boar and other opportunists. The small native population in Turkey is threatened by in-breeding and hunting, while that on Rhodes is subject to pressure from poaching and regular forest fires with additional concerns over cross-breeding with non-native stock that have escaped from enclosures. Elsewhere the species is generally not considered to be threatened.

Dama mesopotamica
Persian fallow deer

ORDER	Artiodactyla
SUBORDER	Ruminantia
INFRAORDER	Pecora
FAMILY	Cervidae
SUBFAMILY	Cervinae

▲ Mature Persian fallow buck.
Photograph: Alexander F Meyer

IT WAS ONCE considered that fallow deer were divided into two subspecies, *Dama dama dama* and *D. d. mesopotamica*, but following studies into the evolution of the Old World deer they now tend to be treated as distinct species. Although superficially similar in appearance, and having broadly similar habits, there are certainly notable differences between the two. Not only is the Persian fallow a rather larger animal, but its antlers are also far less prone to palmation and take a different overall form; furthermore, having not been subjected to such high levels of selective captive breeding as *Dama dama*, it does not occur in the wider colour variations that the latter does.

▶ A mature doe, showing the rump markings, less distinct than those of *Dama dama*, and the shorter tail.
Photograph: Ron Rabinovich

Ancient depictions on objects including Bronze Age pottery found in Cyprus (where humans may have introduced the animals 10,000 years ago), from wine cups and gaming boards there to temple walls and mosaics elsewhere, suggest that the Persian fallow deer once enjoyed a very wide distribution to the east of the Mediterranean. It may even have extended its range onto the African continent, as seems to be indicated by inscriptions on ancient monuments in Egypt and Ethiopia. Deer would have represented an important natural resource to the ancient inhabitants of these regions and also had an important cultural significance. The Persian fallow was probably the original 'roebuck' of the Bible, with the name misattributed during translations into English.

In more recent times, the species certainly occurred across the countries of the Levant and possibly beyond, but by the early twentieth century it was entering a catastrophic decline as a result of over-hunting and other predominantly human pressures. It was only first described scientifically in 1875 but by then was already restricted to west and south-west Iran. By the early 1970s it was believed that the world population consisted of no more than 50 animals, including those in captivity, and that the 1973 wild population was just 25, which existed in two adjoining Iranian reserves. The present status of these truly wild animals is unsure, and it is very possible that they may have died out and long since disappeared completely.

Fortunately, captive breeding ensured that the species survived. Early concerns that genetic integrity had been compromised by hybridisation with *Dama dama* have been dispelled, and it is felt that all of the animals involved in Iran and Israel reintroductions, as well as in European breeding projects, are genetically pure.

◄ Portrait of a well-grown fawn (the remains of an identification tag can be seen in its right ear).
Photograph: Ron Rabinovich

◄ A doe at an advanced stage of pregnancy.
Photograph: Brent Huffman

In Iran, reintroductions have taken place in a number of reserves – the Dasht-e-Naz Wildlife Refuge and Semeskandeh Wildlife Refuge in northern Iran, Ashk and Kaboudan Islands in Lake Uromiyeh, and the Miankotal enclosure in Arjan and Parishan Protected Area. All are either maintained in enclosures or on islands; in the case of the latter, care has been taken to trap and remove any natural predators that may potentially threaten the deer. Other introductions were attempted on islands in the Persian Gulf, but these do not appear to have been successful.

In Israel, a reintroduction programme started in 1996 in two main sites, one in the Carmel Hai-Bar Nature Reserve in the north of the country and another in the Judean Hills to the south of Jerusalem. These both proved successful, although concerns remain over human interactions, the danger of road traffic accidents, and the potential for predation by native wolves, which have also recovered from a much-reduced population and started to recolonise. Deer numbers are growing, however, and the Persian fallow is slowly expanding its range.

The world population has now increased to well over 1,000, many of which are in captive breeding programmes, and hopes continue to rise for the future of the species – although strict protective measures will still be needed to ensure success.

▶ Typical mature buck, in Israel's Carmel Hai-Bar Nature Reserve.
Photographs: Ron Rabinovich

▼ A buck in summer coat and full velvet, pictured in the Jerusalem Mountains.

FACT BOX – *Persian Fallow deer*

World distribution	Iran, but only on islands and in other semi-captive conditions Reintroduced to Israel Extinct in Iraq, Jordan, Lebanon, Palestine, Syria and Turkey.
IUCN Red List Status 2022	**Endangered**, population increasing (last formal assessment 2015).
Sexes	*Male:* Buck *Female:* Doe *Young:* Fawn
Also known as	Mesopotamian fallow deer, Bubale deer/Bubalos (Biblical), Arabian *Jackmur*; French *Daim de Perse/Daim de Mesopotamie*; German *Mesopotamischer damhirsch*; Hebrew *Jackmur* or *yachmur*; Iranian *Gavza-E-zard*.
Recognition features	Coat a dark reddish-brown with white spots, with a dark dorsal line from the nape of the neck to the tail. Very similar to the fallow deer *Dama dama* but tail shorter with less distinct black markings (often entirely white) and rump markings are usually less pronounced. Darker in winter. Unlike *D. dama*, no distinct colour varieties.
Height (at shoulder)	Slightly larger than *Dama dama*: bucks 95–110 cm (37½ –43 in), does 80–90 cm (31–35 in).
Weight	Bucks 70–100 kg (154–220 lb): does are significantly smaller.
Food	A grazing herbivore, which will also browse trees and shrubs, though grasses tend to form over 60 per cent of the diet.
Habitat	Prefers light woodland of oak, pistachio or tamarisk.
Voice, Annual behaviour and Rut	Similar to that of *D. dama* though the rut takes place earlier, in August and September.
Gestation and birthing	Gestation lasts around 229 days. A single fawn is usual, occasionally twins, with birthing taking place between late March and May.
Antlers (typical)	Noticeably different to those of *D. dama*, less palmated and a tendency towards forked tops, and with a shorter brow tine but a longer trez tine above it.
Antler cycle	Casting takes place between early February and mid-March
Lifespan	Around 11 years
Threats	Intensive hunting, habitat degradation, competition with livestock and poaching have all contributed to the extinction of this species across most of its natural range. Predation by wolves and other canids is still a threat in those places where deer are not maintained in enclosures. In-breeding and a lack of genetic diversity may yet be an issue, given the very small number of individuals from which present-day populations are derived.

Elaphodus cephalophus
Tufted deer

ORDER	Artiodactyla
SUBORDER	Ruminantia
INFRAORDER	Pecora
FAMILY	Cervidae
SUBFAMILY	Cervinae

▲ Mature buck, main race.
Photograph: Alexander F Meyer

WITH ITS DARK colouration and unusual crest of hair on the forehead, the tufted deer is a distinctive cervid which stands in a genus of its own, although it is superficially similar to the closely related muntjacs of the same subfamily, the *Cervinae*. At first glance the tufted deer certainly appears muntjac-like, with its very short antlers and long canine tusks, but it is a little larger than most muntjacs and the canines are more robust with a larger circumference at the base. It is most likely to be confused with the black muntjac *Muntiacus crinifrons*, with which the eastern part of its range coincides; both have distinctive tufts of hair on the forehead, though the tufted deer's is black while that of the black muntjac is ginger. Only male muntjacs have prominent facial ridges leading up to their longer pedicles.

▶ Mature doe, main race.
Photographs: Brent Huffman

Wherever there is geographic overlap between tufted deer and various muntjac species, the tufted deer tends to occupy the more elevated locations. Some of the musk deer also have a similar appearance and prominent canine tusks, particularly the black musk deer *Moschus fuscus*, though all are considerably smaller and have no hair tuft.

The generic name of *Elaphodus* is taken from the Greek *elaphus* meaning deer, and *odous* meaning tooth. Likewise, *cephalophus* comes from *kephale* or head, and *lophos* which refers to the crest or tuft of hair.

◄ An adult buck of the main race *E. c. cephalophus* with antlers and canine tusk visible.
Photograph: Brent Huffman

◄ An image of a doe captured on a trail camera in northern Myanmar, 2011. The continued presence in Myanmar is unconfirmed.
Photograph: Fauna & Flora International

Unlike the muntjacs, the taxonomy of the tufted deer has remained largely stable for well over 100 years. There are three recognised subspecies and a fourth whose status is uncertain. All are broadly similar in appearance and behaviour. The main race, *E. c. cephalophus*, is the larger of the three by a slight margin and occurs across south-western China as far as the border with north-eastern Myanmar, where its presence is currently uncertain despite repeated attempts to verify it. It is replaced by the Ichang tufted deer *E. c. ichangensis* in central and southern China, which itself gives way to Michie's tufted deer *E. c. michianus* in south-eastern China as far as the coastal provinces. Michie's tufted deer is rather lighter in colour than the others with less white on the tail. The fourth subspecies was described as *E. c. fociensus* in 1904,

▲ (*left*) Portrait of a Michie's tufted deer buck.
Photographs: Klaus Rudloff

▲ (*right*) Michie's tufted deer doe.

but its distribution is uncertain and the taxonomic status is considered to be doubtful. It appears that the original description was based on just a single specimen, and it is increasingly thought to be probably part of the same subspecies as Michie's tufted deer.

A preference for living in more inaccessible mountainous forests and valleys at very high altitudes makes the tufted deer challenging to study, and as a result our knowledge of this species is incomplete. It is well adapted to such higher, colder habitats, with a coat consisting of longer guard hairs that encourage water shedding and heat retention, in contrast to the lighter coats of the muntjacs which are more suited to temperate or tropical conditions.

The main threat to the tufted deer is most likely to be over-hunting. Its meat is widely sought, and skins are said to attract a special premium as high-end products. Some estimates put the Chinese population at somewhere between 300,000 and 500,000, but a very large number are killed every year. Although there is no way of quantifying actual numbers, something like 100,000 were estimated as killed each year during the 1970s and 1980s, the vast majority taken in the Hunan, Guizhou and Sichuan Provinces of southern central China. There is no reason to suppose that this pressure has lessened. The species is already declining, and such continued, unsustainable pressure will probably result in the tufted deer's move from Near Threatened into the Vulnerable category in the near future.

FACT BOX – *Tufted deer*

World distribution	Native to China Presence uncertain in Myanmar
IUCN Red List Status 2022	**Near Threatened**, population decreasing (last formal assessment 2014).
Sexes	*Male:* Buck *Female:* Doe *Young:* Fawn
Also known as	Burmese *Chick naw*; Chinese *Hei-chi-Tze* or *Maoguan-lu*; French *Élaphode* or *Cerf touffé*; German *Chinesischer schopfhirsch* or *Kluifhert kuifmuntjak*; Spanish *Eláfodo*.

FACT BOX – Tufted deer

Recognition features	A small deer, with a dark grey or chocolate-brown pelage of coarse hair.
	The characteristic tuft of black hair on the forehead can grow to as much as 17cm (6½ in) long in some cases. The ears are rounded with extensive white internal markings, are rimmed with white and have external white tips. There may also (though not always) be white surrounds to the eyes and white patches on either side of the muzzle. These markings can contrast sharply with the overall dark colour of the body.
	The long tail measures around 10–16 cm (4–6 in) long, is white on the underside and fringed with white. It is raised in flight and wagged or flopped.
	The hairs on the head, main body and tail can be flared during interactions with others.
	The canine tusks are robust and dagger-like. Those of mature males are very prominent; female tusks are smaller and less likely to be visible on a living animal.
Height (at shoulder)	55–70 cm (21½–27½ in): both sexes are similar in size.
Weight	17–30 kg (37½–66 lb)
Food	A generalist feeder, which eats evergreen shrubs, flowers, bamboos, seeds, herbs, grasses and fruits.
Habitat	Mountainous terrain with dense, wet forests or in rain forests in high valleys. Sometimes found at altitudes up to 4,750 metres above sea level (although it has been recorded as low as 300 metres in the more easterly parts of its range). A source of water is important.
Voice	Both sexes bark during the rut and when alarmed. Captive animals have been known to make a high-pitched whine when faced with a more dominant one, or clicking sounds during social interactions.
Annual behaviour	A solitary, territorial and crepuscular deer which is usually seen alone or in pairs. The small territories are defended aggressively, regularly patrolled along well-used trails, and marked with scent and dung piles. Dominant males chase and head butt others. Its flight is said to be with cat-like bounds.
Rut	The rut takes place between September and December. The very small antlers suggest that sparring is unlikely to occur and that the canine tusks are the main weapons used during fighting between rival bucks.
Gestation and birthing	Gestation has been variously reported as between 180–240 days; it is generally accepted that it lasts around 210 days. One fawn, sometimes 2, are born between April and July. They are similar to their parents in colour, but have a line of spots along each side of the upper body and appear to be born with the distinctive crest of hair on the head already present. Growth is fast and they are sexually mature at about 9 months old.
Antlers (typical)	Very short spikes, seldom exceeding 2–3 cm (¾–1 in), grown on low pedicles and often completely concealed by the tuft of forehead hair.
Antler cycle	Captive animals have been recorded casting regularly in April and May, with regrowth complete and clean of velvet by late July or early August. Some observers assert that casting may be irregular or not take place at all in some cases.
Lifespan	10–12 years in the wild; exceptionally, over 20 years recorded in captivity.
Threats	Major natural predators include leopards and dhole.
	As its preferred habitat can often be largely inaccessible, deforestation is not the same level of threat as it can be for other deer species but still occurs at lower altitudes. Hunting is, however, extensive and its habit of using regular trails makes it especially susceptible to snaring.

Elaphurus davidianus
Père David's deer

ORDER	Artiodactyla
SUBORDER	Ruminantia
INFRAORDER	Pecora
FAMILY	Cervidae
SUBFAMILY	Cervinae

▲ Stag and hind.
Photograph: Brent Huffman

Distribution map: Locations of main Chinese nature reserves containing reintroduced populations.

CLASSIFIED AS EXTINCT in the Wild by the IUCN, the Père David's deer has been cited as a classic example of modern conservation and has only been saved from complete extinction by captive breeding programmes. It probably once lived wild in north-eastern and central-eastern China; it may also have occurred on Hainan Island off the south coast, but whether this population consisted of wild or imported animals is uncertain. Commentators are divided but the general consensus is that it may have been largely extinct in the wild by around 200 AD, the main cause being over-hunting. Since then the species was only maintained in captivity, most notably at the 200-square-kilometre Nanyuang Royal Hunting Garden, to the south of Beijing. It was there that French Jesuit missionary Père Armand David found the deer in 1864 and realised that they were a species unrecognised by science. He arranged for specimens to be sent to France, and the species was named for him in 1866.

▶ Much time is spent in or close to water; a herd of hinds crosses a lake.
Photograph: Brent Huffman

Some 30 years later, the walls of Nanyuang were destroyed by flooding, allowing most of the deer to escape. Denied their sanctuary, they were subsequently hunted to a point where no more than 30 remained. Shortly afterwards, during the 1900 Boxer Rebellion, troops occupied the Royal Garden and any animals still there were shot and eaten. Fortunately, in the preceding years live specimens had been sent to collections in Belgium, France, Germany and the United Kingdom, and the last 18 animals remaining were eventually collected into a single breeding herd by the 11th Duke of Bedford at Woburn Park in England. There the animals settled, and bred to the extent that eventually there were enough to be shared with other collections.

▲ Stags in Woburn Park, England in April, with antlers almost fully grown and shedding winter coats.

Formal reintroductions to China commenced during the 1980s, though animals were initially maintained in paddocks. The first releases from enclosures into a more natural environment were at the Dafeng Milu Nature Park on the Yellow Sea coast of eastern China in 1998, and more have followed since. Meanwhile the Beijing Milu Reserve has maintained a breeding nucleus of animals which are distributed to a wide number of paddocks elsewhere. The first wild living populations appear to be in the Hubei and Hunan provinces, where animals escaped from the Shishou Nature Reserve as a result of flooding; in 2015 the reserve was estimated to hold 600 individuals and a 2021 report put numbers at around 2,000. Overall, an estimate in November 2021 suggested that there might be as many as 9,000 animals living in nature reserves across China.

It is hoped that the Père David's deer will continue to thrive to the point that they are no longer categorised as Extinct in the Wild. They are not prolific breeders which, to encourage success, need to be maintained in larger herds with sizeable open spaces, although birthing complications have been known to cause high mortality among calves. It is an odd-looking cervid, for which one of the Chinese names is *sibuxiang* meaning 'four unlikes', an allusion to the deer having the antlers of a stag, feet of a cow, neck of a camel and tail of a donkey.

▼ (*left*) A stag in summer coat digs in mud during the rut. **Photographs: Brent Huffman**

▼ (*right*) A hind and her newly born calf; the afterbirth is still visible.

FACT BOX – Père David's deer

World distribution	Native to China
IUCN Red List Status 2022	**Extinct in the Wild**, population trend unspecified (last formal assessment 2016).
Sexes	*Male:* Stag *Female:* Hind *Young:* Calf
Also known as	Milu, Elaphure Chinese *Mi-lu, Sen-pou-siang, Ssu-pa-hsiang* or *Sibuxiang*; French *Cerf de Père David*; German *Davidshirsch*.
Recognition features	A large deer with reddish pelage and pale underparts in summer, turning a dark grey in winter. A dark stripe runs down the spine. The tail is unusually long for a deer, measuring up to 66 cm (26 in) and ending in a dark tassel. The face is long, with large preorbital glands and proportionally short, pointed ears. The jaw contains rudimentary canine teeth which are not large enough to be visible outside the lips. Hooves are large and spreading, and the metacarpal bones make a clicking sound during movement, a trait which they share with the reindeer *Rangifer tarandus* and white-lipped deer *Cervus albirostris*.
Height (at shoulder)	Stags 114–122 cm (45–48 in), hinds 106–115 cm (42–45 in).
Weight	Stags up to 200kg (440 lb), hinds smaller at around 159 kg (350 lb).
Food	Predominantly grasses, reeds, foliage and aquatic growth.
Habitat	The natural habitat is grassland, river valleys, swampy areas and reed beds, often in places which experience seasonal flooding.
Voice	Mostly quiet; stags roar with a distinctively abrupt sound, and challenge with a series of grunts. Both sexes will bark if suspicious. Nursing hinds communicate with their calves by bleating.
Annual behaviour	The sexes live in separated herds outside the rut. This species prefers to live a semi-aquatic existence, spending long periods in water where it is available and grazing on aquatic plants. Scent-marking is conducted mainly by stags, using their preorbital glands and by spraying urine.
Rut	Males will endeavour to defend groups of females against challengers. Fighting between stags is preceded by parallel walking; it can be highly aggressive and fatalities have been recorded. Stags stop feeding almost entirely during the rut and lose weight rapidly, eventually giving way to stronger rivals.
Gestation and birthing	Gestation is around 283 days and a single calf weighing around 12 kg (26½ lb) is born in April or May. Twins are rare. Calves are a light, yellowish-red with pale spots. They are not weaned until around 10 or 11 months old.
Antlers (typical)	The antlers are unusual in having no forward-pointing tines and an extremely long back tine, which may itself bear further tines or subsidiary small points along its underside. Average length is between 55–80 cm (21½–31½ in).
Antler cycle	Shed from October onwards and are fully grown by May. Unusually, deer under well-fed park conditions may grow 2 sets of antlers during the year, producing a rudimentary set that are shed around January, followed by full antlers which are then clean in time for the rut.
Lifespan	Around 18 years
Threats	Low genetic diversity is considered to be a long-term threat. There is also some doubt over how much appropriate available habitat remains in China to support a free-ranging wild population.

DEER SPECIES | CERVIDAE – CERVINAE

Muntiacus atherodes

Bornean yellow muntjac

ORDER	Artiodactyla
SUBORDER	Ruminantia
INFRAORDER	Pecora
FAMILY	Cervidae
SUBFAMILY	Cervinae

THE BORNEAN YELLOW muntjac is one of several species within the genus *Muntiacus* that has not been subjected to any great depth of study. It is found only in the humid forests of Borneo, which it shares with the larger southern red muntjac *Muntiacus muntjak* and, like so many of its relatives, its taxonomy has been confused in the past. Once considered to be a subspecies of the southern red muntjac and described as *M. muntjak pleiharicus*, it was only finally recognised as a separate species in 1982 despite having clearly differing features. It is assumed to be present in Brunei although there has been no formal confirmation of this.

Bornean yellow muntjac are hunted intensively in some parts of Borneo, an activity which often increases considerably in association with logging camps. Logging itself is a major source of serious disturbance and habitat loss, though much needs to be discovered about this species' resilience to the changes it causes. It has been noted in at least one study that southern red muntjac populations frequently increased significantly after logging permitted the rapid establishment of more dense secondary growth, which provided both food and cover. Conversely, in the case of local Bornean yellow muntjac, two separate studies have suggested that intensive logging causes significant reductions in their populations, which can persist for some years after logging operations have finished.

Even where protected areas and legislation exists (all muntjacs are protected by Indonesian forestry law) poaching is a persistent problem. Though traditional hunting involved the use of

▲ A selection of camera trap images: this is a mature buck.
Photograph: John Mathai

▼ A buck in typical Sarawak jungle habitat.
Photograph: Oliver Wearn/SAFE Project

traps, dogs, blowpipes and spears, the use of guns now predominates. Shotguns, some of them home-made, are widely owned across much of Borneo and used in conjunction with dogs, or with spotlights along logging roads at night, and probably account for most of the animals killed. Hunting tends, however, to be largely indiscriminate and other species such as pigs and porcupines form the greater part of the animals that fall victim to snares and guns. Although some ethnic groups have traditional constraints against eating muntjac meat, much of it goes to markets rather than for personal consumption, and demand remains high for 'bush meat' of all kinds.

As is the case for so many animal species that live in less accessible areas, much of what we know about the Bornean yellow muntjac comes from camera trapping. These remote cameras, triggered by movement, can be left *in situ* over long periods and their photographic memories checked periodically. Camera traps have indeed been the source of a great deal of evidence regarding many species' presence and movements and are a mainstay of most field research activity. Camera trapping in a number of reserves already suggests that Bornean yellow muntjac numbers are at their highest in the gentler terrain of lowland sites, with animals using both primary and secondary forest, whilst much reduced sightings are recorded at higher elevations or in forest that has recently been subjected to logging. There is concern, as noted above, that the Bornean yellow muntjac may be severely affected when its habitat is converted through clearance, and evidence is still needed regarding the species' general resistance to habitat degradation and fragmentation.

➤ A well-grown fawn, probably around two months old, captured on a camera trap. The bottle fixed to the tree by researchers contains a scent lure to attract small carnivores.
Photograph: John Mathai

➤ Mature doe.
Photograph: Oliver Wearn/SAFE Project

This is yet another deer species that needs a great deal of further examination if we are to build up sufficient knowledge to understand it properly. While it does appear to be quite common in some places, it is nevertheless categorised as Near Threatened overall and the general trend appears to be a declining population. There are serious concerns about the actual rate of decline, and it is very possible that the species may yet be moved into the Vulnerable category; much more detailed research is required if the species is to be properly protected in the future.

DEER SPECIES | CERVIDAE – CERVINAE

FACT BOX – *Bornean yellow muntjac*

World distribution	Native to Indonesia (Kalimantan) and Malaysia (Sabah and Sarawak): presence unconfirmed but likely in Brunei Darussalam.
IUCN Red List Status 2022	**Near Threatened**, population decreasing (last formal assessment 2015).
Sexes	*Male:* Buck *Female:* Doe *Young:* Fawn
Also known as	French *Muntjac jaune de Bornéo*; German *Muntjak*; Malay *Kidang*
Recognition features	The coat is a yellowish-orange with a faint darker line running along the line of the spine, particularly noticeable on the back of the neck. The underparts are a paler yellow with white inner haunches, but the legs do not contrast as darkly against the main body colour as those of the southern red muntjac. The tail has a white underside and measures 14–20 cm (5½–8 in). The faces of both sexes are dark with prominent preorbital glands below the eyes. Males have long pedicles up to 8.7 cm (3½ in) in length from which their antlers grow and visible canine tusks; females have a darker patch on the forehead.
Height (at shoulder)	Up to 50 cm (19½ in), females marginally smaller.
Weight	Between 13–17 kg (28½–37½ lb).
Food	Diet includes herbs, seeds, new leaf growth, grasses and fruits.
Habitat	Lowland rain forest; not believed to venture readily into more mountainous areas.
Voice	A sharp bark. Females with young may make a high-pitched mewing sound.
Annual behaviour, Rut, Gestation and birthing.	Mostly active throughout the day but may also move at night. Solitary by nature, it lives in small territories and is only seen alone or in male/female or female/fawn pairs. Little is known about the seasonality of breeding but it is likely that rutting and birthing can occur at any time of year. Bucks appear to fight for breeding rights, taking part in pushing contests in an attempt to unbalance a rival before slashing with canine tusks. Gestation lasts around 7 months and the single fawn is born with lines of white spots on the upper body, which fade at around 2 months old.
Antlers (typical)	Simple spikes set on long pedicles, usually no more than 5 cm (2 in) in length.
Antler cycle	The antler cycle is not understood; some observers suggest that antlers may be cast only rarely.
Lifespan	Not known; probably around 12 years.
Threats	The principal natural predator is the clouded leopard; others include the Bengal tiger and sun bear, while smaller carnivores may take fawns.
	The main human threats are habitat encroachment, mainly through logging, and widespread hunting for meat, hides and traditional remedies.

Muntiacus crinifrons

Black muntjac

ORDER	Artiodactyla
SUBORDER	Ruminantia
INFRAORDER	Pecora
FAMILY	Cervidae
SUBFAMILY	Cervinae

▲ Mature black muntjac buck in summer coat, Beijing Zoo.
Photograph: Alexander F Meyer

LARGER THAN MOST other muntjacs and standing longer-legged, the black muntjac has a more deer-like and less porcine appearance. It is notable for its dark body colour and the ginger tufts of longer hair that adorn its forehead, giving rise to its alternative name of hairy-fronted muntjac. It also has a longer tail than is usual for its genus. A notable feature is that it is one of the very few species that reverse the normal trend of sexual dimorphism among deer, in that the males tend to be smaller than their female counterparts. This characteristic is shared with Fea's muntjac *M. feae* and it is of note that both species are considered to be 'younger' and more recently evolved than the other *Muntiacus* species. Again like Fea's muntjac, the black muntjac has less well-developed antlers and it appears that sparring is less important in contests between males: they prefer instead to rely more on increased agility and the use of sharp canine tusks rather than taking part in pushing matches where weight provides an advantage.

▶ Mature black muntjac doe.
Photograph: Alexander F Meyer

The black muntjac's range covers a limited mountainous region of eastern China. It probably once extended as far as Guangdong Province just above Hong Kong in the south, and eastwards to the coast at Ningpo where the Yangtze River discharges into the East China Sea. Today, though, distribution has contracted to approximately half of its former size, leaving just a small, isolated pocket behind at Ningpo. Reports of its presence over 1,000 miles away from its accepted range in northern Myanmar and the border area of south-western China have persisted until quite recently, but may be due to confusion with the newly described Gongshan muntjac *Muntiacus gongshanensis*, now considered to be a distinct species.

The reduction of the black muntjac's distribution is largely attributable to deforestation and the expansion of agricultural activities. While hunting cannot be discounted as a threat, it is probably not as great an issue within the black muntjac's range as it is in other parts of southern China and South East Asia where hunting pressure is more intensive. In its part of eastern China, there is less of a hunting culture, the ownership of firearms appears to be more strictly controlled, and an improving economy have combined to encourage less dependence on subsistence hunting. In addition, much of the black muntjac's present distribution now lies within protected areas where the enforcement of conservation measures is more effective.

The black muntjac appears to prefer mountainous, densely forested areas with high levels of ground cover, and where this is cleared for human use the muntjac may still adapt to secondary growth as long as they are not heavily disturbed or persecuted. It does not appear to interact with the Reeves' muntjac *M. reevesi* that occurs in the same region, and which is more adaptable and tolerant of human presence. Nor does it appear to coexist with the tufted deer *Elaphodus cephalophus* (a superficially similar species of around the same size, also dark in colour but with a tuft of hair, albeit black rather than ginger, on its forehead) in those places where both are found. In some of the more remote areas it has been noted that an abandonment of human activities is allowing the habitat to slowly recover and reforestation to occur. It is hoped that many of the present populations are secure, although there is no room for complacency.

▼ (*left*) Portrait of a mature buck.
Photograph: Alexander F Meyer

▼ (*right*) Black muntjac doe in its distinctively dark winter coat, Beijing Zoo.
Photograph: Roland Wirth

	FACT BOX – *Black muntjac*
World distribution	Native to China
IUCN Red List Status 2022	**Vulnerable**, population decreasing (last formal assessment 2015).
Sexes	*Male:* Buck *Female:* Doe *Young:* Fawn
Also known as	Hairy-fronted muntjac Chinese *Chi-tze* or *Hei-ji*; French *Muntjac noire*; German *Schwartzer muntjac*; Spanish *Muntjac negro*.
Recognition features	A large muntjac, with longer legs and a more cervine appearance than other species. Coat is a blackish-brown, darker and thicker in winter while lighter in colour during the summer. Both sexes have an extensive tuft of long, ginger or cinnamon-coloured hair on the forehead above the eyes and between the ears, which can sometimes obscure the pedicles of males. The ears are rounded and hairless inside. The tail measures some 21 cm (8 in), almost twice the length of more typical muntjacs, is edged with an extensive white fringe, and has a white underside. Both sexes have prominent preorbital glands, and males have visible canine tusks.
Height (at shoulder)	58–62 cm (22½–24¼ in), **males tending on average to be 5–10 cm (2–4 in) smaller than females.**
Weight	18–19 kg (39½–42 lb), males on average around 1kg less than females.
Food	A generalist browser of leaves, shoots, herbs, grasses and fruits.
Habitat	Largely habitat-specific, the black muntjac prefers dense, evergreen forest with high canopy cover, in higher mountainous areas up to around 1,000 metres above sea level. It is also known to inhabit dense scrub and mixed forest, with increased use of conifer forests recorded during winter.
Voice	A sharp bark
Annual behaviour, Rut, Gestation and birthing.	Little has been studied about behaviour and breeding in the black muntjac, but it is probably similar to that of other *Muntiacus* species, featuring solitary habits and the aggressive defence of small territories. An alarmed animal will raise its frontal hair tuft and display the white underside of the tail. Rutting does not appear to be seasonal and the female is believed to come into season and mate again shortly after giving birth. Gestation is around 210 days; the single fawn is darker than those of other muntjacs, though similarly marked with pale spots.
Antlers (typical)	Short spikes, often with a stubby brow tine at the base of the antler, rarely measuring more than 6 cm (2½ in) and grown on thin, converging pedicles.
Antler cycle	There is no confirmed information concerning a cycle for casting and regrowth, although this is presumed to be seasonal. Some authorities even suggest that antlers may be shed only rarely.
Lifespan	Probably 10–12 years
Threats	Natural predators include leopard and yellow-throated marten. Fawns may be taken by foxes and other smaller carnivores. The main human threats come from habitat loss through deforestation and agricultural expansion. It is also hunted for its meat and skin, though possibly not as intensively as other muntjacs are elsewhere.

DEER SPECIES | CERVIDAE – CERVINAE

Muntiacus feae

Fea's muntjac

ORDER	Artiodactyla
SUBORDER	Ruminantia
INFRAORDER	Pecora
FAMILY	Cervidae
SUBFAMILY	Cervinae

LIKE MANY OF the other muntjacs, Fea's muntjac has not been extensively studied and information on its ecology is scarce. It is a secretive animal which is reluctant to leave dense cover and so is seldom seen. Its presence is regularly recorded on camera traps, though, suggesting that it is relatively common across much of its known range, although it remains categorised as Data Deficient by the IUCN. Though it coexists with both the northern and southern red muntjacs *Muntiacus vaginalis* and *M. muntjak* across its distribution, there seems to be little competition between the species, the latter two preferring more openly wooded areas while Fea's muntjac is very much a creature of the denser, tropical evergreen forest.

It is named for the Italian naturalist and explorer Leonardo Fea (1852–1903), who also has a number of species ranging from reptiles, amphibians and mammals to a genus of woodlice bearing his name. Working for the Museum of Natural History in Genoa, Fea made several overseas trips to collect specimens, spending four years in Burma (now Myanmar) in the process. His extensive collections are still held in the Genoa museum.

Fea's muntjac reverses the rule regarding sexual dimorphism among deer. In the vast majority of the other species the male is larger than the female to varying degrees, an adaptation primarily intended to enable dominance over rivals when it comes to breeding rights. Fea's muntjac are different and the male is noticeably smaller than the female. It is thought that this allows greater agility

▲ Fea's muntjac buck, Dusit Zoo, Bangkok.
Photograph: Roland Wirth

▼ Fea's muntjac doe, Dusit Zoo, Bangkok.
Photograph: Alexander F Meyer

Fea's muntjac buck. Note the characteristic tuft of hair between the pedicles.
Photograph: Roland Wirth

Buck in velvet.
Photograph: Alexander F Meyer

during fighting, where the sharp canine tusks are used as the main weapon and trials of strength are not so important. It shares this characteristic with the black muntjac *Muntiacus crinifrons*, another 'young' species which has only evolved more recently. Other features shared with the black muntjac are the tufts of longer hair on the forehead and along the front of the pedicles, and shorter, less well-developed antlers on thinner pedicles – another physical sign that the antlers are of less significance to these two species.

The distribution of Fea's muntjac appears to be centred on the Tenasserim Hills, a 1,700 kilometre mountain chain with an average width of around 130 kilometres, running from north to south with their northern and central ranges forming a natural border between southern Myanmar and western Thailand. In these hills Fea's muntjac appears to prefer to live in the evergreen forests at elevations below 1,500 metres. It has been claimed that they may also exist elsewhere, possibly as far afield as China and Tibet, though any evidence to support this contention is scarce and disputed. The situation is also complicated by some recent recognition of other newer muntjac species which may have been misidentified as Fea's in the past, though it may indeed prove to be the case that the species has a wider range in Myanmar than is currently thought. A few live specimens are maintained in captivity, mostly in Thai zoos.

FACT BOX – *Fea's muntjac*

World distribution	Native to Myanmar and Thailand
IUCN Red List Status 2022	**Data Deficient**, population trend unknown (last formal assessment 2015).
Sexes	*Male:* Buck *Female:* Doe *Young:* Fawn
Also known as	Tenasserim muntjac Burmese *Gutra* (male) or *gutri* (female); French *Muntjac de Fea*; Thai *E-Keng* or *Fan*.
Recognition features	A medium-sized muntjac, similar in size to the Reeves' muntjac though darker, and appears longer-legged than the other muntjac species. Uniform brown in colour, with lighter shading along the back of the legs. Longer dark hair forms tufts on the forehead, and up the pedicles of males, with yellow hairs around the centre of the crown and pedicles and the base of the ears. The tail is relatively long for a muntjac with a dark, almost black, upper surface, is white underneath, and has a distinct white fringe. Males have the canine tusks common to all the muntjac species, measuring around 24 mm (1 in) in length.
Height (at shoulder)	Around 57 cm (22 in): **males are on average some 6 cm (2 in) smaller than females.**
Weight	19–22 kg (42–48 lb)
Food	A selective browser, taking new growth, fruits, and leaves.
Habitat	Prefers thicker evergreen, mixed or shrub forest; avoids more open forest types.
Voice	A loud bark
Annual behaviour	Largely nocturnal and solitary, though often seen during daylight. Frequently uses regular, well-trodden trails.
Rut	Little is known about the breeding habits of Fea's muntjac but it is assumed that they are similar to those of other muntjac species. Males will fight for breeding rights but with more emphasis on using their canine tusks rather than on trials of physical strength. It is likely that males will seek to establish territories which overlap with the home ranges of a number of females. Rutting can take place at any time of the year but activity may be more intense during the winter months.
Gestation and birthing	Gestation is believed to be around 240 days. The single fawn is usually born in dense undergrowth where it remains until able to travel with its mother.
Antlers (typical)	Usually simple, short, incurved spikes not exceeding 8 cm (3 in) on long pedicles.
Antler cycle	Most adult males probably cast their antlers around May, with new growth complete by late August.
Lifespan	Around 12 years
Threats	Preyed on by tigers, leopards, dholes, wild dogs and pythons. Localised hunting for skins and meat undoubtedly occurs. May be threatened by clearance and logging in some of its Thailand range, though much if its known habitat is now under protection. Oil palm plantations in southern Myanmar, along with heavier levels of hunting, usually with snares, is also a significant potential threat.

Muntiacus muntjak
Southern red muntjac

ORDER	Artiodactyla
SUBORDER	Ruminantia
INFRAORDER	Pecora
FAMILY	Cervidae
SUBFAMILY	Cervinae

▲ Southern red muntjac buck, Taman Safari Indonesia.
Photograph: Roland Wirth

▶ Markings may vary between localities; this doe is a Javan animal.
Photograph: Roland Wirth

ONCE CONSIDERED TO have a far wider distribution across the Indian subcontinent and Asia, recent reclassifications have split what used to be known as the Indian muntjac with around 15 subspecies into just two species, the Northern and Southern red muntjacs. Broadly speaking, the Northern red muntjac *Muntiacus vaginalis* exists only on the mainland and Sri Lanka, while that which occurs across the islands to the south is the Southern red muntjac *Muntiacus muntjak*. The Southern red muntjac is broadly similar to its northern relation in appearance and behaviour.

The Southern red muntjac is found only in the very southern end of Thailand below the Kra Isthmus, and then across Malaysia. It is also present on the main islands of the Greater Sundas – Bali, Borneo, Java and Sumatra – and many of the lesser ones, though it is now extinct in Singapore. Suggestions that it may also exist in Myanmar are unproven. The general name of muntjac applied across the whole genus comes from this region, having its origins in *mēncēk*, meaning 'small deer' in the Sundanese language of Java. It has also been translated as 'something graceful and bounding'.

Even some of the more recent deer literature can be confusing, as can much of what is currently available through Internet resources. For the sake of clarity, the classifications adopted by the IUCN in 2008 have been used as a template to work against when describing these species, but scientific opinion still remains divided in places. The status of subspecies is a further matter for potential controversy and much work remains to be done regarding this species before we can begin to understand its taxonomy better. There certainly appear to be local variations in size, markings, antler form, behaviour and habitat preferences, most of which are probably related to living an island existence and adapting to differing environments and available resources.

This species is remarkable for having the lowest recorded chromosome numbers for any mammal: males have 7, and females only 6. This compares with the Reeves' muntjac which has 46 chromosomes (most mammals have between 36 and 60). Despite this, the two species have been known to hybridise in captivity, although none of the resulting offspring have ever proven to be fertile.

The Southern red muntjac remains common across much of its range and has demonstrated a strong resilience to hunting and clearances resulting from logging and other human activities, adapting readily to living in more open habitats. In some cases, clearance work can allow a thicker forest understorey to spring up, with a resulting increase in suitable habitat, associated with a corresponding rise in the muntjac population. Being prepared to live on higher ground also allows it to seek appropriate environments when displaced.

It does remain vulnerable to increasing hunting pressure, however, and is widely persecuted across its range. It is the most sought-after wild meat on the Malay Peninsula, and among the most preferred across Indonesia. Though much hunting is conducted at a local subsistence level using archaic methods, there is also a lucrative trade in bush meat, skins and body parts for traditional medicine, this demand being met by the widespread use of snares and firearms. The potential for wider declines cannot be dismissed.

▲ Southern red muntjac doe, Taman Safari Indonesia.
Photograph: Alexander F Meyer

FACT BOX – Southern red muntjac

World distribution	Native to Indonesia, Malaysia, Thailand and Brunei. Extinct in Singapore, presence uncertain in Myanmar.
IUCN Red List Status 2022	**Least Concern**, population decreasing (last formal assessment 2015).
Sexes	*Male:* Buck *Female:* Doe *Young:* Fawn
Also known as	Barking deer, Bornean red muntjac, Common muntjac, Indian muntjac, Red muntjac, Sundaland red muntjac. French *Muntjac des Indes*; German *Muntjak* or *Indischer muntjak*; Malay *Kldang*; Sundanese *Mencek*; Thai *E-Keng* or *Fan*. (**Note**: a mischievous entry on a Wikipedia Internet page dating from 2011 provided 'Mastreani deer' as an alternative name for the muntjac genus. Although this is incorrect it has been widely perpetuated.)
Recognition features	The main body colour is a deep golden red, with darker shading on the front of legs, and with pale underparts. The winter coat is slightly darker. Tail 18–23 cm (7–9 in), dark brown above and white underneath. Ears are rounded and have very little hair on the inside. Bucks have notably long pedicles for a muntjac species, and canine tusks around 2.5 cm (1 in) long.
Height (at shoulder)	50–65 cm (19½–26 in), females around 7.5 cm (3 in) smaller.
Weight	14–18 kg (31–39 ½lb), males larger than females.
Food	Includes fruits, buds, tender leaves, flowers, herbs and young grass. Also said to feed on birds' eggs and small mammals.
Habitat	Mostly associated with forest, but frequently found in more open habitats, often adjacent to plantations and cultivated land. Most likely to be encountered at lower altitudes although human pressure can push animals onto higher ground.
Voice	A short, loud and sharp bark which can be repeated over long periods extending up to an hour. Barking is often stimulated by the known presence of a predator and can be welcomed by humans in the vicinity who recognise the warning.
Annual behaviour	Generally a cathemeral feeder, taking food at irregular intervals throughout both day and night. Usually solitary within set home ranges; not known to be fiercely territorial and bucks may tolerate others when not breeding. May form loose groups in places where food is abundant.
Rut	Polygamous and with no fixed breeding season
Gestation and birthing	A single fawn is born after a gestation of about 180 days. The doe returns to oestrus shortly after giving birth and mates again, hence most females spend their adult lives in some state of pregnancy. Fawns stay with their mothers until around 6 months of age.
Antlers (typical)	Short and usually incurved, typically with a very short brow tine, and carried on long pedicles. Average length 10 cm (4 in). The antlers of animals on Sumatra are reputed to be smaller than average, often poorly developed with simple spikes.
Antler cycle	Antlers are typically cast around April and regrown by late August or September.
Lifespan	Up to 16 years
Threats	Natural predators include tigers, leopards, dhole and pythons. Smaller carnivores and wild boar take fawns. Hunting, logging and other habitat clearance are among the most significant human threats.

Muntiacus putaoensis
Leaf muntjac

ORDER	Artiodactyla
SUBORDER	Ruminantia
INFRAORDER	Pecora
FAMILY	Cervidae
SUBFAMILY	Cervinae

AT AROUND THE same time that other new species of muntjac were also being recognised elsewhere, the diminutive leaf muntjac was first documented by the late Alan Rabinowitz, a field biologist working in the remote Naungmung Township of northern Myanmar in 1998. The first specimen examined was initially thought to be a juvenile of another muntjac species but DNA analysis revealed it to be an adult female belonging to an entirely new one. It was given its name for the local hunter's habit of wrapping one in a single large leaf of the shrub *Phrynium capitatum*, also known as the Packing Leaf, a plant which has long been of great local importance for the wrapping and transport of edible items. The *putaoensis* of the scientific name is taken from Putao, a town in northern Myanmar close to where it was first discovered.

The leaf muntjac seems to have a very limited distribution which is not yet fully understood, most sightings coming from camera trap recordings, and many of them are inconclusive. It is one of the smallest, and possibly the most primitive, of the living muntjacs. DNA analysis has also identified its presence just across Myanmar's border with India and its range may extend eastwards into China. It seems to prefer to live in dense forests between 700–1,220 metres above sea level; reports elsewhere may have confused it with other muntjac

These photographs, taken by Wildlife Conservation Society biologists Alan and Salisa Rabinowitz, were obtained during a 1997 field study in the remote Naungmung Township in northern Myanmar. They show an immature leaf muntjac which had been caught in a trap and was subsequently released, and are believed to be the only images of a living animal in existence. Samples taken during this expedition permitted DNA analysis which proved this to be a new species.
Photographs: Alan and Salisa Rabinowitz

species. Although numbers have not been accurately assessed, anecdotal evidence from the villagers who hunt the leaf muntjac suggest that, while it remains relatively common, numbers have reduced over time.

Unlike some of the other more adaptable muntjacs which share its range, the leaf muntjac appears to be more tied to forest habitats and rather less able to adjust to others. It may also be less capable of recovering numbers quickly when put under hunting pressure. Although the places where it is thought to occur in India are subject to habitat loss and human expansion, the forests of Myanmar are not so badly affected in this respect although this may yet change in the future. Leaf muntjac may not be hunted specifically, but they are often taken in the course of such activity directed at more abundant species, and if their regular ranges become further fragmented by forest clearance this could have a serious effect on their future status. Where they are known to occur in the Arunachal Pradesh area of India, hunting has been prohibited since 1973 but it still continues; in Myanmar, they frequently occupy regions which are not afforded any meaningful levels of protection.

As this is a newly discovered species, much remains to be learned about its biology, ecology, distribution and resistance to threats. Increasing our understanding in these areas will lead to a far better idea of what needs to be done to ensure its conservation. In particular it will tell us how far the leaf muntjac needs to be protected from present levels of largely uncontrolled hunting, and so only underlines the urgent need for further biological surveys and research.

▶ Skull sections from male animals which had been retained by local hunters. The one on the left is probably the older of the two; the pedicles of most muntjac species typically shorten and thicken over the years with subsequent antler castings. The tendency of the pedicles of this species to curve inwards can clearly be seen.
Photographs: Alan and Salisa Rabinowitz

DEER SPECIES | CERVIDAE – CERVINAE

FACT BOX – *Leaf muntjac*

World distribution	Native to India and Myanmar Presence in China uncertain
IUCN Red List Status 2022	**Data Deficient**, population decreasing (last formal assessment 2015).
Sexes	*Male:* Buck *Female:* Doe *Young:* Fawn
Also known as	Leaf deer, Putao muntjac Burmese *Phet-gyi*; NE India – Lissu *Lugi-che*; Mossang *Ling-pun*; Tikhak *Lang wu* or *Ko koi*.
Recognition features	A small muntjac with reddish-yellow pelage, small, rounded ears, a short tail about 10 cm (4 in) in length, and a darker anterior to the legs. The face is darker with a raised tuft of hair in the forehead region and well-developed suborbital glands. Coat colour can be variable, and females have been noted as darker in early spring than in summer. Unlike other muntjacs, both sexes appear to bear pronounced canine tusks, measuring some 2.4 cm (1 in), though only males bear antlers.
Height (at shoulder)	One of the smallest of the muntjacs, averaging no more than 50cm (19½ in). There appears to be no marked sexual dimorphism in either size or weight.
Weight	12 kg (26½ lb) on average
Food	Probably selective browsers; analysis of stomach contents suggests that fruit forms a major part of its diet. This could mean that they are important seed dispersal agents within their ecosystem.
Habitat	A variety of forest types, including tropical evergreen, sub-tropical and temperate. The availability of dense cover is important and open ground is avoided.
Voice	Probably similar to other muntjacs, making sharp, dog-like barks.
Annual behaviour	While little is known about the ecology of this species, it is reasonable to assume that it is similar to that of other muntjacs and features solitary behaviour although it has been suggested that the male remains with the female throughout her pregnancy. The high proportion of animals observed with ripped ears suggests that a large amount of fighting takes place between territorial individuals; some females also exhibit torn ears, so they too may indulge in this behaviour and be more fiercely territorial than the females of other muntjac species. Such a possibility is also suggested by their unusual possession of pronounced, rather than simply vestigial, canine tusks.
Rut and birthing	Little is understood about rutting and subsequent birthing times, but fawns can be born at any time of the year. A high proportion of pregnant and lactating females observed in early May suggests that a peak time for rutting may be around October. Unusually among muntjacs, newly born fawns bear no spots but are a rich chestnut colour which fades to the adult colouration with age.
Antlers	Unlike other muntjac species, the pedicles from which the antlers grow curve inwards. The antlers themselves are short, usually little more than 2.5 cm (1 in) and consist of simple spikes. Because of the pedicle shape the gap between antler tips tends to be small. The timing of the adult antler cycle is currently not understood.
Lifespan	Not known
Threats	Potential predators within the leaf muntjac's range include tiger, leopard, clouded leopard, Asian golden cat, dhole and python. Hunting for meat and skins is felt to be the most significant human threat, although the species is probably largely taken in the course of pursuing more abundant species. Habitat degradation may also be a cause of decline.

Muntiacus reevesi
Reeves' muntjac

ORDER	Artiodactyla
SUBORDER	Ruminantia
INFRAORDER	Pecora
FAMILY	Cervidae
SUBFAMILY	Cervinae

▲ Reeves' muntjac doe.
Photograph: Alexander F Meyer

The map shows the natural distribution of the Reeves' muntjac.

A SMALL AND rather primitive deer, the Reeves' muntjac is a native of south-east China and Taiwan. It is very much a forest creature that inhabits the subtropical forests of the region, where it appears to favour habitats in the vicinity of streams. Like all the muntjacs it is a primitive deer, and the bucks carry short, basic antlers and well-developed upper canine teeth. Although female muntjac also have canines, these are vestigial and not readily visible without close examination. Fossil evidence suggests that the muntjac species have changed little in appearance for at least the past 15 million years. The Reeves' muntjac is named for John Russell Reeves, a nineteenth century inspector of tea who worked for the British East India Company in Canton. A prominent amateur naturalist, his name is also associated with the Reeves' pheasant as well as four species of reptile.

➤ Adult buck, showing the upper canines.
Photograph: Brent Huffman

The tusk-like canines are important to the bucks, as they seek to establish exclusive territories that overlap with the home ranges of as many does as possible, to maximise their breeding opportunities. Fierce fighting can take place in defence of these territories with antlers used for pushing and parrying, but it is the canine tusks which are of greatest importance in disputes. Significant damage can be inflicted on an opponent with them: and a buck who breaks one or both canines, as frequently occurs, will almost immediately sacrifice his dominance, even if he is otherwise stronger and heavier than a rival. Although other bucks are generally not tolerated within a territory, a younger one who is not a potential competitor may be.

◂ Mating is usually preceded by protracted chasing. A mature muntjac doe seen with a buck in close attendance is likely to have only recently given birth and come into oestrus again.
Photographs: Klaus Rudloff

▾ Fawns are born spotted – these markings disappear at around two months old.

Being aseasonal breeders which can mate and give birth at any time of year, reproductive rates are potentially high. The fawn weighs around 1.2 kg (2lb 10 oz) at birth but grows rapidly, is weaned by the age of two months and fully independent by the time it is around six months old. Only one fawn is normally born at a time, but there have been occasional claims of twins.

As a group, the muntjacs are also known as barking deer with good reason. They are very vocal and their voices carry well in open areas, but studies have found that their frequency range prevents the barks from carrying so well in dense vegetation. Barking can be sustained for periods lasting up to an hour: seemingly it serves various functions, as a form of warning that a predator might be in the vicinity, as a form of general communication between individuals, or maybe just an expression of general anxiety. Alongside this, scent-marking is a very important alternative form of communication, mainly via the highly developed and very obvious preorbital glands in front of each eye, which can appear to be turned virtually inside-out as scent is deposited on twigs and

◂ The tail is wide, and is raised to display the white underside when alarmed.

▲ Reeves' muntjac buck in velvet, with preorbital gland and canine tusks clearly visible.

▼ A buck in open woodland habitat.

other vegetation. The chemicals laid down in this process can send important signals to other deer in the area about the bearer's identity, dominance, territory, and sexual condition.

There are four known subspecies of the Reeves' muntjac. Three, *Muntiacus reevesi reevesi*, *M. r. jiangkouensis* and *M. r. sinensis* are found in mainland China, while the fourth, *M. r. micrurus*, occurs in Taiwan. All are broadly similar. While the IUCN classifies the species as being of Least Concern, it has been suggested that it may yet need to be listed as Near Threatened or Vulnerable in some locations. Its status varies considerably between regions across the wide Chinese distribution, and although numbers appear stable in well-managed reserves and on Taiwan, habitat loss and severe hunting pressure may be taking their toll elsewhere.

Although the population in its native habitat shows some signs of decreasing, the same cannot be said of the situation in the United Kingdom, where escapes and deliberate releases over the past century have led to the Reeves' muntjac becoming abundant with a range that continues to expand. It is increasingly found living in towns and cities where waste ground, parks and overgrown gardens offer habitats acceptable to it. Actual numbers are difficult to assess, however, given the secretive nature of this adaptable and elusive deer which makes accurate counting virtually impossible. Its presence was originally considered to be benign; in 1949 the 12th Duke of Bedford, whose father had been responsible for the first English introductions at Woburn half-a-century earlier, wrote in his autobiography: 'It must be admitted that where they occur in numbers they are *not* very good neighbours either to young hardwood plantations or market gardens; but an animal no bigger than a terrier, producing but one young once a year, not very wary, and capable of being excluded by any wire fence that will really exclude a rabbit, is hardly likely, as has been suggested by one well-known writer on Natural History subjects, to join the grey squirrel in becoming a menace to the countryside!'

Even by the 1970s, the UK population was officially considered to be no more than 5,000 animals. Today some estimates put it closer to 250,000 and the animal is increasingly implicated as a significant cause of environmental and economic damage. The Reeves' muntjac has become an object lesson in ill-advised introductions to an ecosystem that is unable to restrict population growth. It is now officially classified within Europe as an Invasive Alien Species with specific legislation aimed at limiting further spread, but it is generally accepted that the Reeves' muntjac is in the UK to stay. Likewise, escapes in Japan, specifically on the Bōsō Peninsula of Honshu and the island of Izu Ōshima, have seen numbers subsequently rise to damaging proportions, and attempts to eradicate the muntjac as an undesirable species have so far failed. Historic attempts to introduce the species to France appear to have been unsuccessful, though there is evidence of small populations in some parts of Western Europe, and in the Republic of Ireland.

◀ All of the muntjacs are most comfortable either in or close to cover.

FACT BOX – *Reeves' muntjac*

World distribution	Native to south-east China and Taiwan
	Introduced elsewhere, most notably in the United Kingdom and Japan, as well as Belgium, the Netherlands and the Republic of Ireland.
IUCN Red List Status 2022	**Least Concern**, population decreasing (last formal assessment 2016).
Sexes	*Male:* Buck *Female:* Doe *Young:* Fawn
Also known as	Chinese muntjac, Barking deer, Rib-faced deer, Formosan muntjac
	Chinese *Huang-ji* or *Xiao-ji*.
	(**Note**: a mischievous 2011 Wikipedia entry led to the proliferation of an erroneous alternative name of 'Mastreani deer' for muntjacs in general.)

FACT BOX – *Reeves' muntjac*

Recognition features	A small, stocky, and short-legged deer with a pig-like appearance. The coat is reddish-brown, becoming slightly darker in winter. Dark markings on the insides of the pedicles create a V on the face of the buck, while the doe has a dark crown on the forehead and between the ears. The wide tail has a white underside and is held erect when the animal is alarmed or fleeing. Both sexes have prominent suborbital glands.
Height (at shoulder)	45–50 cm (17¾–19½ in); female slightly smaller.
Weight	12–17 kg (26¼–37 lbs)
Food	A browsing deer which feeds selectively on shoots, leaves, herbs, fungi, fruits and nuts. The eggs of ground-nesting birds have also been recorded as taken during opportunistic feeding, and it has even been suggested that they will eat the flesh of birds and small mammals on occasion.
Habitat	A deer of forest, woodland and shrubland, it prefers areas which offer dense ground cover. Where suitable local cover exists, such as that provided by waste land or overgrown gardens, it is prepared to live in close proximity to human habitation.
Voice	A rasping bark, repeated every few seconds, and often kept up over long periods of time. Both sexes bark primarily as a warning and to communicate their presence.
Annual behaviour	A solitary deer most often encountered alone, otherwise in rutting pairs or a doe with her fawn. Both sexes are territorial, scent-marking with their pronounced preorbital glands on foliage, although numbers can sometimes congregate in areas of preferred feeding with little animosity usually shown between individuals. Dominant bucks will fight furiously, indulging in pushing matches while endeavouring to push their opponent off-balance, before slashing at them with their sharp canine tusks. Ripped ears and scars to heads, necks, flanks and rumps are commonplace, especially in areas where densities are high.
Rut	There is no fixed season for rutting which can occur at any time of year. Both sexes achieve sexual maturity by around 7 months of age.
Gestation and birthing	Gestation lasts some 210 days. Following the birth of the single fawn the doe will come into oestrus and mate again within a couple of days.
Antlers (typical)	Antlers are simple incurved spikes, sometimes with a short brow tine, measuring around 10 cm (4 in) long.
Antler cycle	Casting takes place between May and July, then new antlers are regrown throughout the summer and usually clean of velvet by late August or early September. As a young buck can be born at any time of year, he may sometimes not be able to synchronise with the adult antler cycle until he is 2 years of age.
Lifespan	Normally around 10–12 years, though over 20 years recorded in captivity.
Threats	Significant natural predators include the leopard, dhole and yellow-throated marten. Other threats come from habitat loss and hunting; at one point, before it became illegal, some 650,000 muntjac were killed for their skins every year in China out of an estimated population of just over 2 million and they are still heavily hunted.

Muntiacus vaginalis
Northern red muntjac

ORDER	Artiodactyla
SUBORDER	Ruminantia
INFRAORDER	Pecora
FAMILY	Cervidae
SUBFAMILY	Cervinae

THE NORTHERN RED muntjac has by far the widest distribution of any of the muntjacs. It is found across most of India, ranging from as far west as the Thar desert and bounded by the Himalayas in the north. Its territory extends eastwards as far as southern China, and south to all of the countries surrounding the Gulf of Thailand. It is also present in Sri Lanka and may overlap slightly with the range of the Southern red muntjac in Malaysia and Thailand, before the latter becomes the predominant muntjac species throughout Indonesia. The Northern red can exist in a wide variety of habitats.

Until fairly recently, this particular species was described as just one of 15 subspecies of what is now recognised as the Southern red muntjac *Muntiacus muntjak*, but the two have now been broadly separated into two distinct species. The IUCN Red List decided to embrace the reclassification in 2008, though the taxonomy of muntjac remains somewhat confused and open to dispute, as noted. Further changes cannot be discounted: one possibility is that Northern red muntjac found in Sri Lanka may yet prove to be a distinct species in their own right, and there are certainly some subtle regional variations in pelage.

There have been few attempts to introduce the Northern red muntjac outside its natural range. It appears that it has been successfully introduced to the Andaman Islands in the Bay of Bengal, along with chital *Axis axis* and sambur *Rusa unicolor*, although the latter species

▲ Mature buck.
Photograph: Klaus Rudloff

▼ A Northern red muntjac doe, photographed by a camera trap.
Photograph: Leibniz-IZW Southern Institute of Ecology Bidoup Nui Ba NP

did not survive. Released into the woods both within and outside Woburn Park, England, around 1900, a number of muntjac, described as Indian muntjac but with their exact provenance uncertain, initially thrived but were found to be aggressive. The 12th Duke of Bedford, whose father was responsible for the releases, recorded in his memoirs that a decision was made to replace them with Reeves' muntjac: this was partly because the Reeves' were perceived to be rarer, and partly because of the danger the so-called Indian species posed to small dogs, the Park ratcatcher's terrier having been killed by a buck in an unprovoked attack. While the Reeves' muntjac has gone on to colonise much of England, none of the Indian animals are known to have survived beyond the 1930s.

As the Northern red muntjac is the most widespread of the genus *Muntiacus*, it is appropriate to offer some generalised comments here which also apply across the various species. Muntjac are generally speaking small, primitive deer which have evolved very little over many millions of years. To put this into context, the European roe *Capreolus capreolus* has probably only existed in its current form for some one million years, and the fallow *Dama dama* for only some 100,000 years. The muntjacs first appeared during the Miocene epoch, and once occurred naturally in Europe; fossil deposits have been discovered in France, Germany and Poland. Since then, however, their distribution gradually shrank to Asia which remains their natural range today. One of their ancient ancestors was probably a small deer called *Dicrocerus*, an important instance of deer evolution which existed up to some 21 million years ago. It shared the muntjac's typically long pedicles, simple antler structure and canine tusks. *Dicrocerus* is also important as being one of the earliest examples of deer which cast and regrow their antlers annually.

▼ A mature buck, showing the long pedicles and pronounced frontal and preorbital glands in between and forward of the eyes which are common to most muntjac.
Photograph: Brent Huffman

Males of all species are typically distinguished by their prominent canine tusks (females possess small, vestigial tusks which are not visible on the live animal) and simple antlers set on long pedicles. The latter are often no more than a single spike, perhaps with a short brow tine, ranging in typical length from 8 to 17 cm depending on the species involved. They all share other similar characteristics, being mostly small deer with a tail of moderate length, that is typically white or very pale on the underside; this is erected as a warning signal when the animal is alarmed or disturbed.

While all deer have preorbital glands situated just forward of the eyes, those of the muntjac are especially highly developed and sit in deep pits in the skull. These scent glands are important for chemical communication and are used frequently to anoint vegetation with secretions. Readily visible on most of the muntjac species, they are present though not so obvious among other members of the *Cervidae*.

None of the muntjacs appear to have a fixed season for rutting and birthing though there are often seasonal peaks, and although males do tend to have a regular antler-casting cycle this does not affect their year-round fertility. A single fawn is the norm at each birthing. Breeding is almost continuous with the doe coming into season almost immediately after giving birth. One captive Reeves' muntjac female reared a total of 19 fawns by the time she was 14 years old and there is no reason to suggest that this would be any different from what occurs in the wild.

Until the early 1990s, it was generally accepted that there were six known muntjac species occurring naturally across India and Asia, but the opening up of some countries to scientific exploration has brought yet more to light. This has been coupled with fresh understandings of muntjac taxonomy, and there are now considered to be a possible 13 distinct species. Given the secretive nature of the muntjac and the remote, densely forested nature of its natural habitats, we cannot discount the possibility that there may be yet more species waiting to be discovered. However, concern continues to exist about muntjac conservation because, as one observer noted, 'their taxonomy is in a mess, and therefore species of high conservation need may exist but remain unrecognised'.

The two predominant threats to all of the *Muntiacus* both stem from human activity: loss of habitat and hunting. Paradoxically, forests that are disturbed by logging or similar activities may not necessarily be to the complete detriment of such small

▲ An adult doe self-grooming, showing the long tongue.
Photograph: Brent Huffman

▲ Mature buck (*left*) and mature doe captured on remote cameras.
Photographs: Minh Nguyen

deer. Subsequent regeneration at ground level may actually produce more food and cover for the deer. Hunting is a much greater worry. Deer in south-east Asia have long been subjected to low levels of subsistence hunting but an increasing demand for wild meat has produced massive pressures on wild populations. Furthermore, this demand is no longer confined to a local level; modern means allow for supply to markets a long distance away from the deer's origin. The rapidly developing Chinese market is especially significant, not simply because of a long-standing traditional value attached

▶ The summer coat is a deep golden-red.
Photograph: Leibniz-IZW Southern Institute of Ecology Bidoup Nui Ba N

to the properties of 'bush meat' but also the demand for various body parts for use in traditional medicine.

Snaring in particular is sometimes carried out, on at what can only be described as industrial levels, and accounts for vast numbers of animal deaths; it goes without saying that this is an indiscriminate method, and even when targeted at more plentiful species is likely to account for others of a similar size. Muntjac, once considered to be of low market value because of their small size, have become subject to a phenomenon known as 'hunting down'; in effect, as larger species become too scarce to be economically viable to commercial hunters, attention has turned to smaller and (currently) more numerous species.

FACT BOX – *Northern red muntjac*

World distribution	Native to Bangladesh, Bhutan, Cambodia, China, Hong Kong, India, Laos, Myanmar, Nepal, Pakistan, Sri Lanka, Thailand, and Vietnam.
	Presence in Malaysia is uncertain.
	Introduced to the Andaman Islands.
IUCN Red List Status 2022	**Least Concern**, population decreasing (last formal assessment 2015).
Sexes	*Male:* Buck *Female:* Doe *Young:* Fawn
Also known as	Red muntjac, Barking deer, Indian muntjac, Indian red muntjac, Rib-faced deer, Jungle sheep (Sri Lanka)
	Annamese *Con meng*; Assamese *Hugeri*; Bengali *Maya*; Bhutan *Karrisar* or *Karsair*; Cambodia *Klug*; Chinese *Chi-tze*; French *Muntjac des Indes*; German *Muntjak* or *Indischer muntjac*; Gond *Bherki*, *Gutra* or *Korta*; Hindi *Bukra*, *Jangli-bakeri*, *Kakar* or *Kakur*; Kannada *Chali*, *Kankari*, *Kardkari*, *Kard koorie*, *Kaukari*, or *Kond kari*; Korku *Menda*; Lepcha *Sikku*; Madhya Pradesh *Kolri*; Malay *Kidang*; Marathi *Bekar*, *Bekra* or *Bhekad*; Nepalese *Kegan*, *Mriga*, *Ratuwa*, *Ratwa* or *Ruthwa*; Sinhalese *Hula-muha*, *Olu muwa*, *Ubi*, *Weli* or *Weli-mawa*; Southern India *Jungli bukri*; Tamil *Kalai*, *Katu-ardu* or *Simblimann*; Telugu *Kuka-gori*; Thai *E-Keng* or *Fan*.

FACT BOX – *Northern red muntjac*

Recognition features	One of the larger muntjacs, the main body colour is a deep golden-red, with dark fronts to the legs and with pale underparts. The winter coat is darker. Tail 18–23 cm (7–9 in), dark brown above and white underneath. Bucks have notably long pedicles for a muntjac species.
Height (at shoulder)	50–65 cm (19½–26 in), females around 7.5 cm (3 in) smaller.
Weight	14–18 kg (31–39 ½ lb), males larger than females.
Food	A selective browser, taking buds, seed pods, tender leaves and young grasses, also fallen fruits and seeds. Suggested it also feeds opportunistically on the eggs and fledglings of ground-nesting birds and small mammals. Considered to be an important seed dispersal agent for fruit-producing plants across much of its range.
Habitat	Inhabits a wide variety of habitats, including dense woodland, scrub, thorny shrubland, open forest, evergreen and deciduous areas, sometimes venturing onto more open ground or into agricultural crops and capable of existing in largely deforested areas. Appears to prefer lower altitudes below 1,500 m above sea level, but there have been sightings at over 3,000 m.
Voice	A short, loud and sharp bark which can be repeated over long periods.
Annual behaviour	Like all muntjacs, mostly solitary and retiring but also encountered in breeding pairs or as doe and fawn. Occasionally small groups may be encountered in places where food is unusually abundant. Although loyal to home ranges, this species does not appear to be as fiercely territorial as some others. Behaviour can be nocturnal in some places and diurnal in others, probably dependent on local disturbance, prevalent predators and other factors.
Rut	Largely an aseasonal breeder, but defined breeding seasons have been suggested among some populations, particularly those in the more northern parts of the species' range where seasonal changes in vegetation are more marked. Most rutting activity appears to peak during the winter months. At such times rival males will fight for breeding rights, first indulging in pushing matches to shove an opponent off balance before slashing at it with canine tusks. Like all muntjacs, females are polyoestrous, each cycle lasting 2–3 weeks.
Gestation and birthing	A single fawn weighing around 650 g (1½ lb) is born after a gestation period lasting around 180 days.
Antlers (typical)	Short and usually incurved, typically with a very short brow tine, and carried on long pedicles. Average length 10 cm (4 in). Animals in Myanmar are reputed to produce the longest antlers, measuring up to 17 cm (6½ in).
Antler cycle	Antlers are typically cast around April and regrown by late August or September.
Lifespan	Up to 16 years
Threats	An important prey item for a wide range of predators, including tiger, leopard and dhole. Widely hunted, intensively in places, both legally and illegally for its meat, skin and body parts for use in traditional medicine. Capable of recovering quickly where such persecution is controlled.

Muntiacus vuquangensis

Giant muntjac

ORDER	Artiodactyla
SUBORDER	Ruminantia
INFRAORDER	Pecora
FAMILY	Cervidae
SUBFAMILY	Cervinae

▲ A mature buck with typical antlers passing a remote camera.
Photograph: Minh Nguyen

▼ The skull of the giant muntjac (in this case a museum-quality resin copy) shown against that of a Reeves' muntjac (left) for comparison.

THE GIANT OR large-antlered muntjac is one of the 'new' muntjac species. It was only identified by researchers in 1994 when the Annamite mountain range of southeast Asia, which sweeps from central Laos, through Vietnam, and taking in a small part of eastern Cambodia, was opened up to field biologists after decades of political conflict. The area has a wide and surprising natural diversity with plant and animal species found nowhere else on earth, and amongst these yielded the Annamite muntjac. Another new species, the saola (a large bovine related to cattle) was also discovered there at about the same time, hinting at the potential presence of more large mammals which have yet to be recognised by science.

The first suggestion of the giant muntjac's existence came when unusual antlers were spotted hanging in a dwelling by ecologists carrying out surveys in Laos. Live animals were encountered soon afterwards, and a specimen was even located in a small local zoo. It is named for the Vu Quang district of Vietnam, where the first living specimens were confirmed. It was assigned its own genus *Megamuntiacus* at first, but subsequent studies have placed it with the other *Muntiacus* species.

It is clear that the species was known to local hunters long before it came to the attention of scientists. Illegal hunting with snares, dogs by day and night shooting with lamps, remains a serious cause for concern, as this and other species are sought not just by subsistence hunters but also those who supply the lucrative bush-meat market as far afield as China. The giant muntjac is of course an attractive target because of its larger body size; but its ability to recover from sustained hunting appears lower than that of the Northern red muntjac *Muntiacus vaginalis* with which it shares its range.

Snaring pressure is considered to be especially intense throughout the forests of central Vietnam, where over a period of six years from 2011 onwards more than 100,000 wire snares were removed by rangers and forest guards in two nature reserves alone. Elsewhere, in a single Cambodian national park, rangers found almost 28,000 snares in one year (2015) at a density of seven snares to every square kilometre.

Such snares are easily made from cheap materials such as bicycle brake cable, are simple to set, but kill indiscriminately.

The 'slash and burn' agriculture practised by many ethnic groups has long been considered a severe threat to the forest areas in which the giant muntjac exists, and shifting cultivation in Laos alone is estimated to claim 100,000 hectares of primary forest and 300,000 hectares of secondary forest every year. Furthermore, commercial developments, particularly hydroelectric projects and logging, are opening up previously inaccessible areas to yet more settlement and hunting pressure – all this against a backdrop of growing human populations. Vital habitat is disappearing at a frequently alarming pace.

By 2016 the decline of the giant muntjac was such that its classification was changed from Endangered to Critically Endangered on the IUCN Red List of Threatened Species, and it has become increasingly more likely to be found only in those places that are less accessible to humans and subsequently under less pressure from hunting. Meanwhile, though, the widespread development of new roads not just improves access to previously remote areas but also provides routes to take the products of poaching onward to their markets.

The survival of the giant muntjac currently depends heavily on maintaining viable populations in properly protected areas. A lack of more secure populations in other countries which have more effective levels of protection, or in captivity with breeding programmes, is an important concern. Without such a safety net, there is no means of preserving the species in the event of further declines in the wild. There are no known captive giant muntjac at the time of writing (2022). A combination of extensive study to understand the species properly, coupled with meaningful and effective conservation measures, offer the only hope before extinction becomes an all-too-real possibility.

▲ A mature buck pictured passing a camera trap.
Photographs: Leibniz-IZW Southern Institute of Ecology Bidoup Nui Ba NP

◄ Camera trap image of a doe.

▼ (*left*) Doe with a well-grown fawn.
Photographs: Minh Nguyen

▼ (*right*) Young buck.

A GUIDE TO THE DEER OF THE WORLD

FACT BOX – Giant muntjac

World distribution	Native to Cambodia, Laos and Vietnam.
IUCN Red List Status 2022	**Critically Endangered**, population decreasing (last formal assessment 2015).
Sexes	*Male:* Buck *Female:* Doe *Young:* Fawn
Also known as	Large-antlered muntjac Danish *Kaempemuntjak*; Dutch *Indochinese muntjac*; French *Muntjac géant*; German *Riesenmuntjak*; Spanish *Muntjac gigante*; Swedish *Jattemuntjak*.
Recognition features	A very large and distinctive muntjac, which has similar proportions to other members of *Muntiacus* though on a much greater scale. Size similar to that of a female fallow deer *Dama dama*, though with shorter legs. Coat is a dark brown with pale underparts and a medium-length tail, dark above with a white underside. Bucks bear their antlers on noticeably long pedicles and have canine tusks of around 4 cm (1½ in) in length. The dark muzzle colouration extends up the inner front of the buck's pedicle hair, giving the impression of a V-shape. Females have a dark forehead patch, and the inside of the ears carry very little hair.
Height (at shoulder)	Up to 75 cm (29½ in), females smaller.
Weight	30–50 kg (66–110 lb), females smaller.
General ecology	Shy and extremely wary of humans, very little is known about the giant muntjac. Its ecology is probably similar to most other muntjac species, featuring solitary habits, aseasonal breeding and single fawns. Likewise little is understood about its territorial habits. Feeding is believed to be based on selective browsing on new shrub growth, fruits, and other plant material.
Habitat	Most commonly encountered in evergreen and semi-evergreen forest with an understorey of bamboo, saplings and other growth, although it may also use other habitats. Considered to be rarer where habitats are degraded or disturbed. Camera trap records suggest that they rarely venture further than 1,000 m above sea level.
Rut	Believed to be polygynous in line with other muntjac species, with rutting activity possible at any time of year.
Gestation and birthing	The gestation period is unknown and females have only been observed with single fawns. The young of most other muntjac are born weighing in the region of 1 kg (2 lb 3 oz) but given the size of the giant muntjac it can probably be safely assumed that their fawns are larger.
Antlers (typical)	Typically long but simple and lyre-shaped, consisting of a main beam measuring 17–28 cm (7–11 in) with brow tines of up to 10 cm (4 in).
Antler cycle	Not fully understood, but mature animals are likely to cast their antlers around April and have them fully regrown by September.
Lifespan	Unknown
Threats	The main natural predator within the giant muntjac's range is probably the leopard. Large scale illegal hunting for meat, mostly with snares, is considered to be the most dominant and severe threat. There also appears to be a strong demand for body parts for traditional medicine as well as a trade in antlers as trophies or curiosities. 'Slash and burn' clearance for local agriculture is responsible for habitat loss.

Muntiacus gongshanensis, M. rooseveltorum, M. truongsonensis, M. puhoatensis and M. montanus

Gongshan, Roosevelts', Annamite, Puhoat and Sumatran muntjacs

TO DATE, MANY of the muntjacs have not been extensively studied and we have much to learn about them. As they are broadly similar in both habits and appearance, five of the less well understood species are covered here. There is great uncertainty regarding their actual distribution, and all are categorised as Data Deficient by the IUCN – although their population status is considered to be unknown at best, or decreasing where sufficient information exists. Illegal hunting stands high amongst the human threats that they face, along with habitat loss or degradation.

The sexes are known as buck and doe, and the young is a fawn. All are generally shy, solitary and elusive animals, preferring to live in dense cover; they are usually seen alone, or in pairs consisting of a breeding buck and doe, or a doe and her fawn. There appears to be no set time for the rut, although there are certainly seasonal peaks, so breeding and subsequent birthing can take place at any time of the year, with a single fawn typically being produced. The degree of spotting on a fawn's coat can vary between species. Gestation is presumed to generally last around seven months and twins are extremely rare.

All of the muntjacs considered here are small deer with a porcine appearance, that tend to carry the head low with the rump higher than the shoulders. The coat is generally a chestnut to dark brown, with paler underparts, and the tail is erected in flight to display the white underside. Sexual dimorphism is not marked, though males are generally slightly larger, and most of the species described here stand between 45–50 cm (17¾–19½ in) at the shoulder and weigh between 10–15 kg (22–33 lb). Both sexes have prominent preorbital glands which are used for scent-marking, and although both have canine tusks only those of the males are prominent in many of this group. The antlers of bucks are small and grow on long pedicles whose ridges extend along the front of the skull. Their call is a sharp bark, often repeated over long periods. The lifespan of all these species is unlikely to exceed 15 years.

Among the *Muntiacus* species in general, antlers are seldom longer than 8 cm (3 in) and typically consist of simple, incurved spikes, sometimes with a short brow tine. The muntjacs of the *Muntiacus rooseveltorum* group which also includes *M. truongsonensis*, *M. putaoensis*, and possibly also *M. puhoatensis*, are something of an exception and considered to form their own clade, being genetically and morphologically close. Females tend to have well-developed canines; the pedicles of bucks are also relatively shorter than those of other muntjacs, and their antlers tend to be straight, seldom exceeding 2.5 cm (1 inch) in length.

The following five species are covered under this generalised category, though it is stressed that there is still a great deal of taxonomic uncertainty regarding the actual status of some, with potentially major upheavals in classifications expected in the future: The first four species occur to the north of mainland south-east Asia, in the region that was once more commonly known as Indochina. Some are closely related to the extent that there is still some considerable taxonomic uncertainty and may yet require reclassification in the future.

Muntiacus gongshanensis
Gongshan muntjac

ORDER	Artiodactyla
SUBORDER	Ruminantia
INFRAORDER	Pecora
FAMILY	Cervidae
SUBFAMILY	Cervinae

▲ This camera trap image from north-east Kachin, Myanmar, shows what is likely to be a genuine female **Gongshan muntjac**. It appears to be a little larger than animals belonging to the *M. rooseveltorum* clade but still has a stout appearance and relatively short legs. The mid-dorsal dark band on the crown of the head and slight hair tufting indicate an affinity with the Gongshan muntjac but sadly the tail, which would be very dark and white-edged in the latter, is not visible to confirm the identification
Photograph: Flora & Fauna International

The currently accepted distribution of the Gongshan muntjac *M. gongshanensis* compared to those of the black muntjac *M. crinifrons* (yellow circle) and Fea's muntjac *M. feae* (blue oval) and showing the considerable geographical separation of the three species. In truth, however, much of the intervening areas remain poorly studied for muntjacs and the last few decades have already produced many surprises.

In 1988 an unusual muntjac buck was captured in the mountainous area of Gongshan County in the south-western province of Yunnan, China, leading to the recognition of a new species in 1990. The **Gongshan muntjac** *M. gongshanensis* is believed to be related to the black muntjac *M. crinifrons* although the former is much smaller in size and lacks the long central crown tuft of the latter, as well as the reversal of the dorsal neck hair that distinguishes the black muntjac and Fea's muntjac *M. feae*. Several features of the skull also differ and it may stand as high as 60 cm (23½ in) at the shoulder. Genuine Gongshan muntjac are a little larger than *M. rooseveltorum* clade animals and the Reeves' muntjac *M. reevesi*, but noticeably smaller than most northern red muntjac *M. vaginalis* populations.

The taxonomy of the Gongshan muntjac remains very confused; it has been claimed by some (although the IUCN Red List has never considered it conspecific) to be of the same species as the black muntjac, despite being morphologically very different and occurring well away from the accepted range of the latter, which lies over 1,000 miles distant in eastern China. Certainly there are distinct differences between the two and the new classification is now generally accepted. Like the black muntjac, though, it appears to favour higher ground and lives in the elevated subtropical forests and thick mountain forests that occur across its range, possibly even as far up as the Himalayan alpine shrubland. Just how sensitive it is to hunting pressure needs to be evaluated, but its skins are actively sought and traded by professional hunters in addition to more localised subsistence hunting for its meat. Although it is thought to occur in protected areas in both China and Myanmar, it has no special status as a protected species in the former and conservation measures in the latter are still evolving.

DEER SPECIES | CERVIDAE – CERVINAE

This series of photographs, of what appears to be a young male muntjac, present something of a mystery and are a good illustration of the confusion surrounding much muntjac classification. They were taken in Bomi County, Tibet, within the assumed range of the Gongshan muntjac, an identification that was originally suggested. Its stature, however, is more similar to that of Fea's muntjac *M. feae* and the black muntjac *M. crinifrons* but it lacks the characteristic forehead hair tuft of those species. It is possible that it belongs to an as yet unidentified member of the Fea's and black muntjac clade although it was encountered well away from their known ranges (*see Gongshan muntjac distribution map*). It is notable, though, that some authors have previously listed Fea's muntjac as present in eastern Tibet and south-western China, largely as a result of sightings of animals very similar to this one.
Photographs: Yi Lin

◀ This female animal, pictured at a roadside in Yunnan Province, China, is considered to represent a typical Gongshan muntjac. The blackish dorsal surface to the tail, a relatively dark head (especially the frontal area) with a very dark forecrown and small lateral tufts, and the animal's relatively small stature, are all features that closely correspond with the *M. gongshanensis* type.
Photograph: Brian Jones

Distribution	China and Myanmar Presence uncertain in India and, though suggested, there is no evidence that it occurs in Bhutan
IUCN Red List Status 2022	**Data deficient**, population decreasing (last formal assessment 2015)

Muntiacus rooseveltorum

Roosevelts' muntjac

ORDER	Artiodactyla
SUBORDER	Ruminantia
INFRAORDER	Pecora
FAMILY	Cervidae
SUBFAMILY	Cervinae

▲ The taxonomy of the Roosevelts', Annamite and Puhoat group of muntjacs remains confused and unresolved – the following images of animals which have the characteristics of the clade were captured on remote camera traps in the Saola Natural Reserve in Quang Nam Province, Vietnam. This is a **Roosevelts'/Annamite/Puhoat clade** buck.
Photograph: Quang Nam Saola NRWWF – Viet Nam GWC

Roosevelts' muntjac *M. rooseveltorum* has a rather longer pedigree as a recognised species. It is named after Theodore and Kermit Roosevelt who presented a specimen to the Field Museum of Natural History, Chicago in 1929 following one of their many famous hunting expeditions and the plural form of its name deliberately recognises both of them. Since then there has been some controversy regarding its status as a species in its own right, and although this now seems to be largely resolved by genetic analysis there is still uncertainty that needs to be addressed. At one point it was even suggested that this species be extinct, though this is now known not to be the case. Certainly it is morphologically distinct from the other well-established muntjac species. Nevertheless, its distribution does remain uncertain. The situation is not helped by its confusing similarity to other closely related muntjac species,

▶ **Roosevelts'/Annamite/ Puhoat clade** muntjac doe with her well-grown fawn.
Photograph: Quang Nam Saola NRWWF – Viet Nam GWC

rendering camera-trap records difficult to assess, whilst its genetic relationship with more recently named species (the Annamite, Puhoat and leaf muntjacs) complicates matters still further.

With a shoulder height of around 45–50 cm (17¾–19½ in) and weighing 10–15 kg (26¼–33 lb), Roosevelts' muntjac is very similar in size to the Reeves' muntjac *M. reevesi*.

◂ **Roosevelts'/Annamite/Puhoat clade** doe.
Photographs: Quang Nam Saola NRWWF – Viet Nam GWC

◂ **Roosevelts'/Annamite/Puhoat clade** muntjac doe with a fawn of probably less than two months old.

▾ This camera trap image of a buck, though of low definition, is a useful illustration of typical pelage, rump markings and tail length within the **Roosevelts'/Annamite/Puhoat muntjac clade**. It was taken in Pù Mát National Park, Vietnam.
Photograph: Leibniz Institute for Zoo and Wildlife Research & Save Vietnam's Wildlife & Pù Mát National Park

Distribution	Laos
	Presence uncertain in China, Myanmar and Vietnam
IUCN Red List Status 2022	**Data deficient**, population decreasing (last formal assessment 2015)
Also known as	Roosevelts' barking deer
	Chinese *Luoshi-ji*

Muntiacus truongsonensis

Annamite muntjac

ORDER	Artiodactyla
SUBORDER	Ruminantia
INFRAORDER	Pecora
FAMILY	Cervidae
SUBFAMILY	Cervinae

The uncertain taxonomy of the **Annamite muntjac** *M. truongsonensis* reflects the confusion over Roosevelts' muntjac. It is another recently named species, first identified in the Annamite mountains of Vietnam in 1997, and appears to differ from Roosevelts' muntjac in that it has a dark coat rather than the brown or reddish one of the latter, as well as a blacker top surface to the tail and a subtly different skull structure. For now its distribution remains extremely uncertain; although only known in very limited parts of Laos and Vietnam, it may actually extend much further across both countries and possibly as far as China.

Distribution	Laos and Vietnam
	Presence uncertain in China
IUCN Red List Status 2022	**Data deficient**, population decreasing (last formal assessment 2014)
Also known as	Annam Black muntjac, Annamite dark muntjac, Pygmy muntjac, Truong Son muntjac or Truongson muntjac
	French *Muntjac de Truong Son*; Vietnamese *Mang Truong Son*

Muntiacus puhoatensis

Puhoat muntjac

ORDER	Artiodactyla
SUBORDER	Ruminantia
INFRAORDER	Pecora
FAMILY	Cervidae
SUBFAMILY	Cervinae

The **Puhoat muntjac** *M. puhoatensis* is one of the many potentially 'new' animal and plant species that came to scientific attention after political borders were relaxed towards the end of the last century, although there is considerable doubt over its validity. It is only included here for completeness as it is included in the IUCN Red List. Its description was based on some very limited material collected in the mountainous Pu Hoat region of northern Vietnam, which lies on the border with Laos; the new name was applied in 1997 only after accidental publication in a magazine article. What little evidence there is suggests that, if it is indeed a separate species, like the Annamite muntjac it is closely linked to Roosevelts' muntjac, with which it may yet prove to be conspecific. They share many features, appearing to be very similar in both size and appearance.

The status of the Puhoat muntjac remains under investigation, though for now it remains listed as a separate species. There are no definitive photographs available. The distribution map showing its presumed range within Vietnam must be treated as indicative only and it is very likely that this species may yet be discounted.

Distribution	Vietnam
	Presence uncertain in Laos (*see main text*)
IUCN Red List Status 2022	**Data deficient**, population trend unknown (last formal assessment 2014)

Muntiacus montanus

Sumatran muntjac

ORDER	Artiodactyla
SUBORDER	Ruminantia
INFRAORDER	Pecora
FAMILY	Cervidae
SUBFAMILY	Cervinae

The fifth and final species of muntjac covered here is more distinct taxonomically and set well apart from the previous three, being more closely related to the black and Gongshan muntjacs. The status of the **Sumatran muntjac** *M. montanus* has been unclear until relatively recently, when an image was captured on a trail camera on the slopes of Gunung Tujuh volcano, Sumatra, in 1998; two years later a live animal was discovered and freed from a poacher's snare not far away in the Kerinci Seblat National Park in 2000. Since then there have been further sightings, but little remains known about the ecology of the species.

There is still uncertainty about this species' current status within Sumatra. The animals appear to be confined to higher ground on the west of the island and records suggest that they might inhabit broadleaf forest habitat in the montane forests of higher elevations, and the range may extend far further than is presently understood. Some 30,000 square kilometres of land lie more than 1,000 metres above sea level in Sumatra, but just how much of this is occupied by this muntjac (or indeed whether these deer habitually live above this altitude) is unknown. Being similar in size and appearance to the Southern red muntjac also found on the island, the species was probably overlooked on many occasions before its presence was once again confirmed.

It is potentially preyed upon by the naturally occurring predators of Sumatra, which include the Sumatran tiger, clouded leopard, golden cat, dhole and yellow-throated marten. Deforestation and human settlements outside the national parks may have an effect on habitat, and although Sumatran law affords unambiguous protection to all muntjacs, the deer may still be susceptible to poaching pressure (which largely comes from the setting of snares). However, if it proves to prefer living at higher elevations, less accessible to easy human access, this will mitigate that risk.

To date, just how numerous or threatened the Sumatran muntjac remains is still a subject for conjecture. If it does prove to be more widespread and preferring to live at higher (and thus safer) altitudes, it may actually be of Least Concern. A more restricted range at lower altitudes could, however, lead to it being placed in a higher threat category: and without further study it may have to remain classified as Data Deficient.

▲ This picture, captured by a trail camera at Gunung Tujuh, Sumatra, in 1998, was the first indication of the Sumatran muntjac's continuing existence as a distinct species.
Photograph: Jeremy Holden/Fauna & Flora International

Distribution

Western Sumatra

IUCN Red List Status 2022

Data Deficient, population trend unknown (last formal assessment 2015)

Also known as

Sumatran mountain muntjac

Indonesian *Kijang sumatra* or *kijang gunung*

Rucervus duvaucelii
Barasingha

ORDER	Artiodactyla
SUBORDER	Ruminantia
INFRAORDER	Pecora
FAMILY	Cervidae
SUBFAMILY	Cervinae

▲ A western barasingha stag, his antlers in velvet and still in the process of growing.
Photograph: Klaus Rudloff

In the distribution map the three smaller current populations are circled to assist visibility. The green line indicates the extent of the barasingha's nineteenth century distribution.

▼ (*left*) Western barasingha hinds.

▼ (*right*) Western barasingha hind and calf.
Photographs: Klaus Rudloff

AT THE TURN of the nineteenth century, the barasingha ranged widely across much of central and northern India as far as the southern foothills of the Himalayas, extending west into Pakistan and well into Bangladesh in the east wherever there was habitat that suited it. The conversion of grasslands to agriculture and other forms of habitat loss, coupled with extensive hunting, saw massive reductions in numbers throughout the middle of the twentieth century. This once-abundant deer has now been reduced to just a few fragmented populations: it is extinct in Bangladesh and Pakistan and its presence in Bhutan is doubtful.

There are three recognised subspecies. The **western barasingha** R. d. duvaucelii is the most numerous (though this is only relative), and it now occupies just a handful of localities in Uttar Pradesh in northern India. It is also present just across India's border in Nepal, though overall numbers are probably in the low thousands. The impression of a contiguous main range given by the distribution map is misleading, because in reality the remaining populations are extremely fragmented. This subspecies is the most specialised for a marshland habitat, possessing slightly longer legs and hooves that splay for walking on the soft ground of the swamps it prefers, although it can also be found in some forest areas.

Until recently, the **southern** or **hard-ground barasingha** *R. d. branderi* was found only in the 940 square kilometres (360 square miles) of the Kanha Tiger Reserve in Madhya Pradesh, where it is accorded the position of a key species and 'Bhoorsingh the barasingha' is the reserve's mascot. It is also the state animal of Madhya Pradesh itself (as is the western barasingha in Uttar Pradesh). Unlike the other two subspecies, its hooves are more specifically adapted for hard ground. By 1938 only around 3,000 remained in the Kanha area and numbers continued to drop to a low of 66 in 1970, but since then they have steadily risen and the population is now estimated to stand at around 1,000 animals. Translocations of deer from Kanha to the Satpura Tiger Reserve just over 100 miles away commenced in 2015 and by 2021 some 58 animals had been established there. These remain, for now, the only places where southern barasingha are known to survive in the wild.

▲ Southern barasingha hinds 'boxing'. Many female deer, particularly those of the herding species, will do this to assert dominance, as can stags with sensitive growing antlers.
Photographs: Brent Huffman

◄ Southern or hard-ground barasingha stag, in hard horn.

▼ A female herd of southern barasingha in typical habitat.

▲ Eastern barasingha in Kaziranga National Park, Assam.
Photograph: Coke Smith

▶ Eastern barasingha hind.
Photograph: Roland Wirth

The **eastern barasingha** *R. d. ranjitsinhi* once extended its range as far as Bangladesh. Today it can only be found in Assam, where its population had declined to just a few hundred animals by 1994; its continued presence in Bhutan is doubtful. Present numbers for this subspecies are not known, but a 2016 census put them at an estimated 1,148 in the main remaining stronghold, the Kaziranga National Park, where it inhabits grassy flood plains. There it shares its range with the Indian one-horned rhinoceros; Kaziranga hosts some two-thirds of the world population of this equally Vulnerable species. Otherwise the eastern barasingha's presence is patchy at best and more usually uncertain elsewhere.

Originally placed within the genus *Cervus*, the barasingha is now classified alongside Eld's deer *R. eldii* and the extinct Schomburgk's deer *R. schomburgki* in a group more generally referred to as the swamp deer. The common name of barasingha comes from the Hindi *bārah* meaning 12 and *singgā* meaning horns, a reference to the typical antler formation, although a stag may carry more tines than this. Its scientific name is given in honour of French naturalist Alfred Duvaucel by his stepfather Georges Cuvier, who himself was a highly regarded zoologist and naturalist; indeed he is often referred to as the founding father of palaeontology, and first described the species in 1823.

Once protected by the malarial conditions that prevailed in the wet, swampy areas that the barasingha largely prefers and which discouraged human settlement and development, modern technology and medicines began to remove this natural defence from the 1930s onwards. From that point, as suitable habitat became increasingly converted for human use, the range of the barasingha shrank. The deer now live largely in the isolated pockets of wetland that remain.

Compared to the meat of the chital *Axis axis* and the hog deer *A. porcinus*, that of the barasingha is considered to be less palatable, although this does not prevent poaching for antlers, meat and hides. Hunting is believed to have been the main cause of its extinction in Bangladesh and elsewhere, and remains a significant threat, especially outside those preserves which offer more heightened levels of protection.

For the moment barasingha numbers appear to be relatively stable, but two of the subspecies are probably already down to just one or two remaining herds and highly vulnerable to natural events such as unusual levels of flooding or disease. If the barasingha is not to succumb to these, or to pressures created by a rapidly growing human population in so many of the places where it is already precarious, it will need both effective protection as well as sufficient suitable habitat if it is to flourish. It is of some encouragement that forward-thinking conservationists are all too aware that other iconic species such as the tiger depend on it, and the habitat that they share, if they too are to survive in the wild.

FACT BOX – *Barasingha*

World distribution	Native to India and Nepal Extinct in Bangladesh and Pakistan Presence uncertain in Bhutan
IUCN Red List Status 2022	**Vulnerable**, population decreasing (last formal assessment 2015).
Sexes	*Male:* Stag *Female:* Hind *Young:* Calf
Also known as	Swamp deer, spotted rusa Assamese *Bhelingi-puhu*, *Bheelwah* or *Dolhorina*; French *Barasinga* or *Cerf de Duvaucel*; German *Indischer sumpfhirsch*; Hindi *Bárasingha*, *Máhá* or *Gond*; Madhya Pradesh *Bahrainge*, *Bára-newari*, *Goin-jak* (male), *Gaoni* (female) or *Salsamar*; Monghyr *Potiya haran*; Nepalese *Baraya*, *Barriya*, *Gonda*, *Ghos*, *Gonn*, *Gonr* or *Gour*; Sindhi *Goin*; Spanish *Barasinga* or *Ciervo de Duvaucel*; Tamil *Catuppunila man*; Uttar Pradesh *Nerwari* or *Sál-sámar*.
Recognition features	A large and long-legged deer, its pelage is a rich, reddish- or golden-brown in summer, becoming a duller yellow-brown in winter and quite woolly in texture. Faint white spots may become visible on the body as the hot season advances and are most pronounced along either side of the dorsal ridge; this is most notable among the southern barasingha. The underparts are paler and the underside of the short tail is white or a light yellow. The neck of the stag is maned. The barasingha is reputed to have a distinctive, strong smell at close quarters.
Height (at shoulder)	120–124 cm (47–49 in), hinds smaller.
Weight	Stags 170–280 kg (370–620 lb), hinds 130–145 kg (287–320 lb).
Food	A grazing deer that feeds mainly on grasses and aquatic plants, according to habitat.
Habitat	Primarily marshes, reed beds and other wetlands; occasionally found in open forest. In Madhya Pradesh there are no swamps, and the hoof adaptation for hard ground among the southern barasingha that live there reflects its reliance on grassy plains.

	FACT BOX – *Barasingha*
Voice	The stag makes a donkey-like roar during the rut: alarmed animals make a shrill, braying scream or bark.
Annual behaviour	A social deer; herds usually comprise 10–20 animals but may number over 50 depending on local abundance. Summer herds usually consist of hinds and their current young, with stags living separately in bachelor groups. Feeding takes place throughout the day with animals resting during the hottest periods. The barasingha is a vigilant, nervous deer which is easily alarmed but can become regular in its daily habits if undisturbed. A deer spotting a predator will characteristically stamp its foot, bark in alarm and stott before fleeing.
Rut	Rutting dates vary between subspecies. The western barasingha ruts around August and September, the southern barasingha in December and the eastern barasingha in April. The same rutting sites tend to be revisited every year, even sometimes where they have already been given over to cultivation. As the rut begins, herds start to break up and stags will consort with receptive females which are defended against rivals. There is much displaying, calling and fighting among the stags, which use their antlers in trials of strength as they assert dominance and claim ownership of hinds. At this time the stags will wallow frequently and, unlike some other species, are more likely to feed throughout the rut. Once the rut is over the stags may become solitary, or band up with other stags; hinds return to their separate herds.
Gestation and birthing	Gestation is 240–250 days, and a single calf is normally born although twins are very occasionally recorded. The calves are brown and strongly spotted at birth, but these markings fade fast as the calf grows, and they are weaned at about 6 months old. Sexual maturity is reached by around 2 years old, although a stag is unlikely to succeed in competition with others until he is at least 4 or 5 years old.
Antlers (typical)	There can be considerable variation in the form of antlers. The main beam tends to curve backward from the skull before reaching slightly forward again towards the tip, though viewed from the front there is little incurving. Between 10 and 15 points are normal, though up to 20 have been recorded. An average antler will measure some 76–89cm (30–35 in), although exceptional examples may reach around 100 cm (39 in).
Antler cycle	As with rutting activity, the antler cycle varies between subspecies. The western barasingha starts casting around mid-January, the southern barasingha in late April or May and the eastern barasingha in October. The growing antlers are covered in velvet, ranging from a pale, reddish tinge to a rich red. Tall grasses and small shrubs are used for cleaning velvet rather than larger trees.
Lifespan	15–20 years; up to 23 years recorded in captivity.
Threats	The tiger is a major natural predator, and barasingha may also be taken by leopards and dhole. Calves are vulnerable to golden jackal predation. Seasonal flooding can also be a cause of mortality. Habitat loss to agricultural development is the most significant current human threat. Poaching also occurs outside the better-protected preserve areas.

DEER SPECIES | CERVIDAE – CERVINAE

Rucervus eldii

Eld's deer

ORDER	Artiodactyla
SUBORDER	Ruminantia
INFRAORDER	Pecora
FAMILY	Cervidae
SUBFAMILY	Cervinae

ELD'S DEER IS a medium-sized, graceful and seriously endangered deer of Southeast Asia. It takes its English name from Lieutenant Percy Eld, a British officer attached to the residency in Manipur who was instrumental in its scientific description. The alternative name of brow-antlered deer highlights an antler configuration which is unique among deer (*see panel for description*). For a long time it was placed within the genus *Cervus* before being moved to *Panolia*, but today it is accepted as being grouped in *Rucervus* along with the barasingha *R. duvaucelii* and the extinct Schomburgk's deer *R. schomburgki*. It was once considered to be a tropical wetland specialist species, but such a description only really applies to one of the subspecies.

There are considered to be three subspecies, which were once far more widely distributed than the seriously fragmented populations of today. The **Manipuri brow-antlered deer *R. e. eldii*** once ranged widely across the Manipur region of north-east India but is now restricted to a small population at the southern end of Loktak Lake

▲ Thamin stag.
Photograph: Wich'yanan Limparungpatthanakij

Distribution map – Note smaller populations are circled to assist visibility.
Green: reintroduced,
Purple: possibly extinct.

◄ Captive Manipuri *R. e. eldii* stags.
Photograph: Bishnu Sarangi

A GUIDE TO THE DEER OF THE WORLD

1. Captive Thamin stags *R. e. thamin*, their antlers almost completely grown but still in velvet, pictured at the Huai Kha Khaeng Nature Reserve, Thailand.
   Photograph: Coke Smith

2. A captive-bred Thamin calf in the process of losing its spots.
   Photograph: Marcel Langthim

3. Thamin hind.
   Photograph: Brent Huffman

4. A mature Thamin stag almost clean of velvet. He is fitted with a radio collar to enable researchers to follow his movements.
   Photograph: Coke Smith

5. A group of Thamin with a young stag on the right.
   Photograph: Coke Smith

just to the south of Imphal. There it is known locally as *sangai*, literally 'the deer that looks at you'. Heavily dependent on wetland habitats with *phumdis* – massive floating islands of matted vegetation, soil and other organic matter that reeds and grasses grow on, which the deer use as refuges – the animal was actually considered to be extinct by the 1950s but has since been rediscovered in the area. Its large, spreading hooves show far greater adaptation to living in marshland than the other subspecies. Although numbers are probably in the low hundreds, it is actively protected against poaching and an increase in local support for its conservation seems encouraging. It is now hoped that numbers are stable and may even be increasing.

The **Thamin** or **Burmese brow-antlered deer *R. e. thamin*** remains the most widely distributed of the subspecies. It was still considered to be abundant in some places as recently as the 1980s, but its range has shrunk considerably. At one time its continuous range covered much of southern Myanmar across to Thailand, though this has since decreased to the vicinity of the central plains of the Irrawaddy. Its continued presence in Thailand is considered to be increasingly unlikely. It does not seem to be as dependent on a wetland habitat as the Manipuri subspecies, being more inclined to use deciduous forest.

The third subspecies is the **Thai brow-antlered deer *R. e. siamensis*** which occupies a similar habitat to the Thamin and is found mostly in central Cambodia, although the last remaining animals in the south-west of the country are now believed to be extinct. It is said to have been used as a major food source for the Khmer Rouge army during Cambodia's civil war which raged between 1967 and 1975; if this were so, it would account for much of the rapid depletion of numbers. A small fragmented and localised population exists further north in Laos, but it is feared that the species no longer survives in Vietnam. A very small number also exists on China's Hainan Island, where the deer are confined to limited areas of scrub and dry grassland. A suggestion that they represent an entirely separate subspecies currently has no evidence to support it.

▼ Thai brow-antlered deer pictured on Hainan.
Photograph: Qin Huang

▶ A captive group of Thai brow-antlered deer *R. e. siamensis*, illustrating the marked dimorphism between the sexes and the characteristic lyre-shaped sweep of the stag's antlers.
Photograph: Alex Kantorovich

Eld's deer remains in a perilous state across Southeast Asia. Some populations only contain a handful of animals, with the largest numbering no more than a few hundred. All three subspecies are kept in captivity, the majority being of the Thamin subspecies, and a number of breeding programmes continue. These may yet provide an essential element of conservation efforts although, in the places where the Eld's deer has disappeared completely, unless the appetite for effective protection increases it is unlikely that they will be successfully reintroduced. It is, regrettably, a very short step from the current situation to Critically Endangered status. Urgent steps need to be taken if the Eld's deer is not to go the same way as Schomburgk's deer already has, in much the same part of the world and for very similar reasons.

FACT BOX – Eld's deer

World distribution	Native to Cambodia, China (Hainan Island), India, Laos and Myanmar. Possibly extinct in Thailand and Vietnam.
IUCN Red List Status 2022	**Endangered**, population decreasing (last formal assessment 2014).
Sexes	*Male:* Stag *Female:* Hind *Young:* Calf
Also known as	Brow-antlered deer, Hillside or Flying deer (Hainan Island), Thamin (Myanmar). Burmese *Tamin*, *thameng* or *thaming*; Cambodia *Panolia*, *polu* or *romeang*; Chinese *Po-lu*; French *Cerf d'Eld*; German *Leierhirsch*; Manipur *Sangai*, *sangnai*, *sungai*, *sungnai* or *sungrai*; Spanish *Ciervo de Eld* or *Tamin*; Tamil *Man*; Thai Hthamin, *lamang* or *la-ong*.
Recognition features	A medium-sized deer. Mature stags carry very distinctive antlers (*details overleaf*). The coat is generally a reddish-brown or grey-brown, with pale brown or cream underparts, animals of the Thai subspecies having a more rufous appearance. Hinds tend to be slightly paler in all cases. The coat darkens in winter. The tail is short at between 20–30 cm (8–12 in) and there is no pronounced rump patch. The feet of the Manipuri subspecies are adapted for a more aquatic habitat with splaying hooves and cornified skin on the back of digits, the other subspecies less so.

DEER SPECIES | CERVIDAE – CERVINAE

FACT BOX – *Eld's deer*

Height (at shoulder)	110–125 cm (43–49 in). Sexually dimorphic with males notably larger than the more lightly-built females.
Weight	110–130 kg (242–286 lb), exceptionally up to 170 kg (375 lb).
Food	A grazer and opportunistic browser, taking grasses, shoots and other new growth as well as fruits as available. Aquatic plants are widely eaten according to habitat. Cultivated crops including maize, rice, peas and others are often raided.
Habitat	Swampland (Manipuri ssp); other subspecies inhabit firmer ground including deciduous forest and (in the case of Hainan Island populations of the Thai subspecies) scrub and grassland.
Voice	There is no specific call associated with rutting stags. Both sexes make a barking grunt as an alarm call; the bark of stags is louder and more drawn out.
Annual behaviour	The larger stags are largely solitary apart from during the rut, while hinds and juveniles will form herds which can be large but are inevitably influenced by population densities.
	Daily and seasonal movement can vary between populations; some do not move widely and tend to remain constant to relatively small home ranges, while others are more heavily influenced by food and water availability, and by seasonal flooding. Stags in particular seem to enjoy wallowing.
	Animals kept in captivity have a reputation for nervous and excitable behaviour.
Rut	The rut takes place between mid-March and mid-May, stags attempting to gather and then defend their own group of hinds. At this time fighting between rival stags is frequent.
Gestation and birthing	After a gestation period of around 242 days, a single, spotted calf is born away from the herd. Twins are occasionally born but in such cases early mortality can be high. They are weaned at between 4 and 5 months old, and become sexually mature at around 18 months.
Antlers (typical)	The antlers of Eld's deer have a unique structure, with a long upward-curving brow tine, and a main beam which curves backwards and then forward again in a graceful, lyre-shaped sweep. From the side profile, the appearance is bow-like. The main beam often forks towards its tip; older stags can produce a number of small projections from the upper surface of the lower fork.
	A good pair of antlers may measure as long as 100 cm (39 in). The brow tine can measure as much as 38 cm (15 in). The Manipuri subspecies has the smallest antlers.
Antler cycle	Casting may take place as early as late June in Manipur, though further south it may be as much as 2 months later. Normally, mature stags will have fully regrown their antlers and cleaned them of velvet by the end of the year.
Lifespan	Probably around 12 years in the wild. In captivity, a male of the Thai subspecies lived for almost 15 years and females for more than 19 years.
Threats	Natural predators include tigers, leopards and dholes.
	The predominant human threat is hunting for their meat, hides and distinctive antlers, some products bound for commercial 'bush meat' markets and traditional medicine. Illegal hunting is a major issue across much of the Eld's deer range, and the antlers have a particular trophy value.
	Habitat loss in some places, associated with displacement by seasonal flooding, may also be a localised issue. A hydro-electric project in Loktak Lake, the last refuge of the Manipuri subspecies, has affected the ecology of the floating marshes on which the deer rely.
	Because Eld's deer readily graze on agricultural crops such as rice, there is a potential for conflict with farmers and then retaliatory killing. A reducing gene pool, especially in low density populations such as that on Hainan, may also prove a longer-term threat.

Rucervus schomburgki

Schomburgk's deer

ORDER	Artiodactyla
SUBORDER	Ruminantia
INFRAORDER	Pecora
FAMILY	Cervidae
SUBFAMILY	Cervinae

▶ Schomburgk's deer photographed in Berlin Zoo c. 1905. The photograph is attributed to a Mr Chance of London.

The distribution map shows the probable former range of Schomburgk's deer.

▼ A collection of antlers showing typical forms, probably dating from the late nineteenth century. Photographic plate from *The Journal of Siam Society Natural History Supplement Vol XI No 1* dated 1937.

SADLY, SCHOMBURGK'S DEER exists within these pages only as a cautionary tale. Already considered to be on the verge of extinction by 1918, the last of the species had probably disappeared completely by 1938 – although it was not widely accepted that this was the case until some 40 years later.

Once abundant across the vast swampy plains of central Thailand, this deer was named for Sir Robert Schomburgk, the British consul in Bangkok between 1857 and 1864. Along with the barasingha *R. duvaucelii* and Eld's deer *R. eldii* it was part of a group commonly referred to as the swamp deer. Although still thought to be relatively common at the turn of the twentieth century, it was already suffering habitat loss by then: this was because of an increase in commercial rice farming in the late nineteenth century, which had seriously reduced and fragmented the swamps and grasslands on which the deer depended. The species then started to decline rapidly, and intensive hunting, both for its meat and to supply the Chinese medicine trade, sounded the death knell. Hunting was too easy: during the rainy season, flooding would cause the deer to become concentrated on islands of raised ground, from which they would be driven by large hunting parties in boats or mounted on water buffaloes, and then killed with clubs or spears while swimming away.

By 1924 the supply of antlers to the Bangkok trading centres, destined for the traditional medicine trade, had slowed dramatically. The last known wild specimen was a stag shot in 1932. Another fully grown stag – kept as a pet in a temple not far from Bangkok and which wore a piece of yellow robe and a bell around its neck – was allowed to wander freely around the temple and a local market, but it was killed with a club by a drunken local man who thought that it was wild. No living Schomburgk's deer has been seen since.

The antlers of Schomburgk's deer were described by Whitehead (1972) as 'probably the most beautiful of all species of deer, being moderately large and extremely complex in formation'.

Some thought to have come from a Schomburgk's deer were found in a Laos medicine shop in 1991, though their provenance was never satisfactorily explained and they, like so many other examples that had surfaced previously, are believed to be no more than relic stock from the trade in wildlife parts.

A few animals, probably numbering no more than eight in total, were maintained in zoos in Berlin, Cologne, London, Hamburg, Paris and Shanghai between 1862 and 1911, but there was only very limited captive breeding. This was probably the last point by which any concerted effort, such as that which ensured the survival of the Père David's deer *Elaphurus davidianus*, might have preserved the species.

Some still hope that a living Schomburgk's deer may yet emerge from the wilder parts of central Thailand, but in reality the chances of this are extremely remote. Rumours of a remnant population have been carefully investigated several times with no result, and the only real option left to anyone who wants to see one is to visit the *Muséum national d'histoire naturelle* in Paris. There, visitors can gaze on the only fully mounted specimen known to be in existence, an animal which lived in the museum's menagerie at the *Jardin des Plantes* until its death in 1868.

Barring the near-miracle that a small remnant population remains to be discovered, it must be accepted that Schomburgk's deer is now long gone. If there is one lesson that comes from its demise, it is just how quickly circumstances can conspire to reduce a once numerous species to a mere thing of the past. Schomburgk's deer represents an important wake-up call to look to the preservation of those species which remain.

FACT BOX – *Schomburgk's deer*

World distribution	Once native to Thailand
IUCN Red List Status 2022	**Extinct**
Sexes	*Male:* Stag *Female:* Hind *Young:* Calf
Also known as	French *Cerf de Schomburgk*; German *Schomburgkhirsch*; Thai *La-on*
Recognition features	Similar in appearance to the barasingha *R. duvaucelii*: a large deer with a uniform brown pelage, with off-white underparts and lower jaw. Hooves were large and could be spread widely to assist in swampy habitat.
Height (at shoulder)	102–104 cm (40–41 in) for a mature stag, hinds smaller.
Weight	Probably between 110–120 kg (220–264 lb)
Habitat	The swampy plains of central Thailand; it is believed to have avoided forest.
Voice	The voice of one animal kept in the Berlin Zoo was described as a short, high-pitched bleat.
Food, Annual behaviour, Rut, Gestation and birthing	Probably similar to the closely related barasingha *R. duvaucelii*.
Antlers	The antlers of Schomburgk's deer were complex and distinguished by the forking of all the main tines. Tines numbered more than 20 in a large specimen, with up to 33 recorded. A mature antler probably measured around 69 cm (27 in) with up to 83 cm (33 in) recorded. The antler cycle is unknown.

Rusa alfredi

Visayan spotted deer

ORDER	Artiodactyla
SUBORDER	Ruminantia
INFRAORDER	Pecora
FAMILY	Cervidae
SUBFAMILY	Cervinae

▲ Stag in hard horn.
Photograph: Klaus Rudloff

FOUND ONLY IN the western Visayan Islands of the Philippines, this species is now limited to just four fragmented populations on the islands of Panay, where it is confined to the western mountains, and a few remaining forest areas on Negros. Previously it had also existed on the islands of Guimaras, Cebu and Masbate, as well as possibly on Ticao; the last animals on Cebu were eradicated by the middle of the twentieth century, and those on Masbate probably disappeared during the 1990s. It was also thought to have become absent on Negros until 2009 when an expedition investigating the biodiversity of the North Negros National Park discovered evidence of two separate groups of deer, the first seen in over ten years. Previous to this the last major survey of the Visayan spotted deer, conducted in 1991, had determined that it had become extinct over 95 per cent of its former range as a result of over-hunting and widespread deforestation.

▶ Hind showing the extent of spots on the flanks and rump.

◀ Stag in velvet and about to clean.
Photographs: Klaus Rudloff

The Visayan spotted deer is now Endangered, and the wild population of mature animals is estimated to have reduced to probably no more than 700 from an estimated overall population of 2,500 in 1996. Once thought of as no more than a poorly understood variant of the much more widespread sambar *R. unicolor* – despite it being the only spotted species of deer found in the region – it was not given its own status as a distinct species until 1983. It is named for Prince Alfred, the second son of Queen Victoria, who is credited with sending the first known specimen to English zoologist Philip Sclater in 1870.

▼ A recently cast captive stag (right) with a fully grown hind, showing typical sexual dimorphism and the dark dorsal line of the coat.

The species once ranged from sea level up to 2,000 metres above sea level but is now confined to more remote, forested and mountainous slopes that are less accessible to humans. Hunting for meat and antlers, along with the regular taking of live specimens, are among the greatest threats to these deer. While fully protected in the Philippines, it is especially concerning that a high demand for living animals as pets is reflected even among local politicians, suggesting that any appetite for preservation, despite a growing awareness of the need to do so, still remains low. The very remoteness and inaccessibility of the few places where the Visayan spotted deer remains makes effective patrolling against illegal activity a difficult and often impossible task.

This is one of the most endangered and least widely distributed deer in the world. Given the scarcity of verified information regarding population numbers, it is possible that it is already in the Critically Endangered category. Some of the wild populations are already so badly reduced in numbers that they are probably no longer viable in any case.

➤ Hind with a well-grown calf. Calves are born spotted.
Photograph: Klaus Rudloff

A small hope remains that the species may yet be revived. A formal conservation programme was established in 1990 between the Philippines government and Mulhouse Zoo in France to initiate a captive breeding programme, which includes wildlife rescue and breeding centres on Panay and Negros. Furthermore there are growing numbers of breeding animals in various zoos across Europe. Captive breeding is only a buffer against potential extinction, though. Without a significant change in current practices and attitudes, the rigorous protection of existing wild populations and the habitats available to them to live in, along with an effective plan for reintroductions elsewhere, the future of the Visayan spotted deer is by no means secure.

DEER SPECIES | CERVIDAE – CERVINAE

FACT BOX – *Visayan spotted deer*

World distribution	Native to the Philippines (Western Visayan Islands)
IUCN Red List Status 2022	**Endangered**, population decreasing (last formal assessment 2016).
Sexes	Male: Stag Female: Hind Young: Calf
Also known as	Philippine spotted deer, Prince Alfred's deer. French *Sambar de Prince Alfred*; German *Prinz-Alfred-hirsch*; Philippines *Lasao* or *Usa*.
Recognition features	A small, heavily built deer with relatively short legs. The pelage is a dark brown coat, spotted on the back and flanks from behind the shoulders, consisting of soft, dense hair. It is the only true deer native to the Philippines in which the mature adult bears a spotted coat. The fur of the belly and inside the haunches is white or cream-coloured, and there are white markings on the chin and lower lip. The ears and tail are short.
Height (at shoulder)	Around 70–80 cm (28–31 in), females smaller.
Weight	50–80 kg (110–176 lb), females smaller.
Food	Primarily a browser which also grazes, the main food items include leaves, buds and grasses. New growth emerging after fires, earthquakes and other natural events that have allowed the forest canopy to open up is particularly attractive to them. They are also said to lick the ashes of recently burned areas, most probably for their mineral content.
Habitat	Although it once ranged as far as the shoreline, human pressure has now encouraged it onto higher ground where it inhabits dense grassland and forest on largely inaccessible slopes and steep escarpments. While it will visit more open areas to feed, the close proximity of thick cover is important.
Voice	Stags roar during the rutting season
Annual behaviour	Very little is known about the ecology and behaviour of the Visayan spotted deer. It is largely nocturnal, emerging from cover as night falls to feed. Although considered to be a social deer, it is usually seen in groups of not more than 8 animals or smaller family parties. Mature stags are often seen alone. This may be a result of dwindling numbers and human disturbance, as larger captive groups have been maintained without any signs of stress or undue aggression.
Rut	The rut takes place in November and December, with stags sparring for access to individual hinds.
Gestation and birthing	Gestation is around 240 days, with young born in May and June. The single calf is spotted and is weaned at about 6 months old. Breeding has been recorded at all times of the year in captive animals.
Antlers	Typical antlers are short and heavy, rarely exceeding 25 cm (10 in) with a pronounced brow tine and a shorter back tine. Casting is probably during the spring with regrowth during the summer months.
Lifespan	Probably 12–15 years
Threats	There are no significant natural predators. Despite being fully protected under Philippine law, the Visayan spotted deer is still intensively hunted for subsistence by locals and by recreational hunters from cities. Their meat is widely traded in markets and sought by speciality restaurants. There is a strong demand for animals that are kept as pets, with some locals specialising in live capture, and often the orphaned young of adults killed by hunters are taken. High levels of snaring are evidenced by a proportion of captive animals missing lower limbs. Enforcement of protective legislation is generally ineffective. Habitat destruction from logging and land clearance for agriculture are also significant threats.

Rusa marianna
Philippine sambar

ORDER	Artiodactyla
SUBORDER	Ruminantia
INFRAORDER	Pecora
FAMILY	Cervidae
SUBFAMILY	Cervinae

▲ A stag, which has recently cast its antlers, with a hind in Avilon Zoo, Philippines.
Photograph: Alexander F Meyer

Distribution in the Philippines (introduced locations in Guam, Micronesia and the Northern Mariana Islands not shown). Circled areas: red – extinct, purple – possibly extinct.

AS ITS NAME suggests, this species is a native of the Philippine islands: it is fairly widespread there, although with heavily fragmented populations and no longer present at all on some of them. At no point does its range overlap with the closely related Visayan spotted deer *R. alfredi*. This latter species is also endemic only to the Philippines, albeit just in the western islands where it is Endangered and declining, for much the same reasons that affect the Philippine sambar.

There have been introductions of Philippine sambar to a number of western Pacific islands, usually as a game animal for recreational hunting, and most notably on Guam where it has been successful to the point of becoming invasive. Some earlier literature mentions a potential subspecies that occurred on Bonin or Ogasawara Island, but it is now known that these animals were introduced from the Philippines around the late eighteenth or early nineteenth century. The deer established initially but did not flourish and were extinct there by 1925.

Once considered to be a subspecies of the sambar *R. unicolor*, the Philippine sambar has a complex taxonomic history and was not confirmed as a distinct species until 1993. Even then, the animals first described as *Cervus mariannus* in 1822 were actually those transplanted to the Mariana Islands rather than natives of the Philippines, hence the scientific name which remained after the species was placed in the *Rusa* genus. There are currently four described subspecies: two, *R. m. marianna* from Luzon and *R. m. barandana* from Mindoro, appear to be distinct, but there is some uncertainty about the others. *R. m. nigella* tends to inhabit upland sites on Mindanao while *R. m. nigricans* is more a deer of lowland Mindanao and the neighbouring island of Basilan. Within Mindanao there are highly variable body sizes, pelage colours and other attributes among the deer present; further animals exist on other isolated islands which may yet prove to be distinct and the relationship between the latter two subspecies is not fully understood. Additionally, there is a lightly coloured form on the island of Leyte, which has yet to be fully assessed.

The Philippine sambar suffers across most of its range from intensive hunting for its meat, hide and antlers, despite local legislation which is all too rarely enforced: and human encroachment means that much of its habitat is being lost. Although some hunting is conducted at subsistence levels by indigenous people, there is considerable commercial exploitation of the species. Some of the populations are felt to be under particular threat. On Mindoro alone, the available forest cover has been reduced to just ten per cent of its original levels and the already low numbers of deer there are felt to be especially endangered. There are also concerns that the live capture of animals to establish deer farms and for other commercial purposes are threats; this is because of the potential for the spread of diseases as well as hybridisation with other deer species kept in the same place.

◀ Mature hind.
Photograph: Alexander F Meyer

The Philippine sambar is declining alarmingly across most of its range but our understanding of this deer remains incomplete. An urgent evaluation is now considered essential to establish the species' true status, and then to ensure that full protective measures can be put in place to arrest further reductions.

FACT BOX – *Philippine sambar*

World distribution	Native to the Philippines Introduced to Guam, Micronesia and the Northern Mariana Islands.
IUCN Red List Status 2022	**Vulnerable**, population decreasing (last formal assessment 2014).
Sexes	*Male:* Stag *Female:* Hind *Young:* Calf
Also known as	Luzon sambar, Guam sambar, Marianne sambar, Philippine deer, Philippine brown deer. French *Cerf sambar*; German *Sambarhirsch*; Philippines *Lagsao*, *Saladong* or *Usa*.

FACT BOX – Philippine sambar

Recognition features	A medium-sized deer, similar in appearance to the sambar *R. unicolor* but much smaller, with small ears and a shorter tail, and the stags growing smaller antlers. The pelage can be variable even within localised populations but is generally a medium to dark brown (sometimes appearing almost black) with coarse hair. The underparts and insides of the legs may appear paler than the main body but there is no distinct rump patch. The insides of the relatively small ears and underside of the tail are white or pale brown. The head features pronounced preorbital glands in front of the eyes.
Height (at shoulder)	55–90 cm (21½–35½ in); stags some 12 per cent larger than hinds.
Weight	40–90 kg (88–198 lb); stags may be as much as 50 per cent heavier than hinds.
Food	Feeds widely on a variety of material including grasses, herbaceous plants, foliage, fruits and seeds. May also take agricultural crops where available and will visit burned ground to feed on new growth as it emerges.
Habitat	Very adaptable, but prefers primary and secondary forest with adjacent grassland for foraging. Often driven to inhabit higher ground up to 2,900 metres above sea level when subjected to regular disturbance or heavy poaching activity.
Voice	A loud bark, made most frequently during the night or at dawn and dusk.
Annual behaviour	Largely nocturnal, emerging in darkness to feed after spending the day laid up in dense forest cover. Hinds live in small herds of usually no more than 8 animals; stags are more solitary and tend to be less tolerant of each other.
Rut	Rutting activity is believed to peak between September and January, although breeding may take place all year round. When a hind is in oestrus, stags become particularly aggressive and compete among themselves, fighting frequently with their antlers.
Gestation and birthing	Gestation is around 6 months. The single fawn is born lightly spotted; there are no known records of twins.
Antlers (typical)	Typically slender with 3 tines on either side, with a single brow tine and a tine to the rear at the top fork. The length is usually 20–40 cm (8–16 in) but occasionally up to 55 cm (21½ in). Larger non-typical antlers are sometimes produced, especially on Rota and occasionally on Pohnpei, and may bear more than 5 points on either side and even become slightly palmate towards the top fork.
Antler cycle	The antler cycle has not been subjected to any depth of study, but it appears that they can be cast at any time of year.
Lifespan	Normally 8–10 years; up to 15 years recorded in captivity.
Threats	There are no significant natural predators, although feral dogs may predate them and have been noted as a particular threat among the introduced populations of Micronesia. The most significant human threats come from illegal hunting and a continuing severe habitat loss resulting from agricultural development, illegal logging and mining.

DEER SPECIES | CERVIDAE – CERVINAE

Rusa timorensis
Javan deer

ORDER	Artiodactyla
SUBORDER	Ruminantia
INFRAORDER	Pecora
FAMILY	Cervidae
SUBFAMILY	Cervinae

SMALLER THAN ITS close relation the sambar *R. unicolor*, the Javan deer was once thought to belong to the same species. There is some confusion over its true native range but it is now generally accepted that this is confined to Java and Bali, though it is now also widespread on many other Indonesian islands. These include Alor, Ambon, Banda, Batjan, Buru, Butung, Flores, Halmahera, Komodo, Lembeh, Lombok, Mangole, Muna, Papua, Sanana, Saparua, Seram, Sulawesi, Sumba, Sumbawa, Taliabu, Ternate, Timor and Wetar. Human agency is certainly responsible for its presence on many of these islands, the movements often rooted in antiquity, but the Javan deer is also a very capable swimmer which may have enabled some emigration between the islands east of Bali.

The animals currently found on New Caledonia were taken there in the 1870s, while the first to arrive on Réunion Island were released as far back as 1639 by European sailors who wanted to establish a source of fresh meat for longer voyages. There have been further transplantations since: the New Guinea population, for example, was introduced in the early 1900s. Further afield, the species has adapted successfully to conditions as far afield as Australia, Brazil, Malaysia, New Zealand and Thailand, with less successful introductions attempted elsewhere.

There has been continuing controversy over the taxonomy of the Javan deer; as many as seven subspecies have been described, though opponents suggest that apparent differences between animals occurring in various

▲ A mature Javan deer stag on the island of Sulawesi.
Photograph: Klaus Rudloff

The native distribution of the Javan deer on Java and Bali; locations of introduced populations elsewhere are not shown.

◀ Portrait of a mature hind.
Photograph: Alexander F Meyer

places can be more simply attributed to their adaptation to local conditions and the genetic limitations of relatively small, isolated populations. Of all these subspecies, the case for only two of them seems strongest and is based on the original source animals from Java (described as *R. t. russa*) becoming genetically distanced and developing different breeding seasons from those found on some of the Maluku Islands (*R. t. moluccensis*).

Unlike the other *Rusa* species, which tend to live in much smaller groups, the Javan deer is highly gregarious and once formed herds that may have numbered over 1,000 until as recently as a century ago. Since then its numbers have declined, though, and it is now more usual for them to be seen in herds of around 20 to 30 and they are rarely encountered alone. Compared to the more solitary sambar *R. unicolor* the Javan deer has a more pronounced mane in winter, a longer and thicker tail, and tends to grow relatively more impressive antlers, all of which are included among the 'social organs' which have greater importance to those deer species that habitually form structured social groups.

▲ (*left*) Mature stag in velvet at the Taman Safari Indonesia.
Photographs: Alexander F Meyer

▲ (*right*) Mature hind at the Taman Safari Indonesia.

▶ Java race hind and calf at the Tierpark, Berlin.
Photograph: Klaus Rudloff

The readiness of the Javan deer to live in large herds lends itself to commercial farming, which takes place in Australia, New Caledonia, Mauritius, Réunion, and Thailand, mainly to produce meat and velvet. It is also a prized trophy animal for sport hunters in New Caledonia, New Guinea, New Zealand and Australia; in some of these places numbers are high, and the deer are often regarded as invasive with hunting encouraged.

Despite being fully protected by Indonesian law and until the 1990s still considered to be numerous, the Javan deer has suffered badly from a relatively recent change in public attitudes within its native range where previously there had been strict gun control and effective policing. Social changes in the late 1990s, with a corresponding lessening of respect for the authorities, have led to increases in both uncontrolled habitat destruction and poaching. Accordingly, as a large deer which represents a high meat yield and an attractive cash value on the commercial market, the Javan deer has diminished significantly over the last two decades or so. Its Vulnerable status reflects the fact that, within its native range at least, the population is estimated to stand at less than 10,000 animals with a visible and steady decline. Without appropriate protective measures and, in particular, full and effective enforcement of the law, it is likely that this will continue.

◀ Mixed herd at a wildlife rescue centre on Sulawesi.
Photograph: Klaus Rudloff

FACT BOX – *Javan deer*

World distribution	Native to Indonesia (Bali and Java)
	Introduced to Australia, Brazil, Indonesia (Kalimantan, Sulawesi, Lesser Sunda & Maluku Islands), Malaysia, Mauritius, New Caledonia, New Zealand, Papua New Guinea, Réunion Island, Thailand and Timor-Leste.
IUCN Red List Status 2022	**Vulnerable**, population decreasing (last formal assessment 2014).
Sexes	*Male:* Stag *Female:* Hind *Young:* Calf
Also known as	Javan deer, Javan rusa, rusa, rusa deer, Sunda sambar, Sunda deer, Timor deer.
	Bahasa Java *Menjangan*; Bahasa Sunda *Umcal*; Balinese *Rusa*; French *Cerf de Timor*; German *Mähnenhirsch*; Javanese *Kijang*; Malay *Rusa*; Spanish *Sambar de Java*; Sundanese *Rusa*.
Recognition features	A medium-sized deer, the Javan deer is similar in appearance though smaller than the sambar *R. unicolor*. The reddish- or greyish-brown coat frequently has a coarse appearance and darkens in winter; the throat and underparts are a lighter grey. The tail is long and bushy with a white underside but is not held erect when fleeing. The ears are wide and slightly rounded, and the legs are relatively short. Stags grow a conspicuous mane in winter.

FACT BOX – *Javan deer*

Height (at shoulder)	Size and weight may vary considerably according to location and the available habitat. Stags average around 100 cm (39½ in), hinds are smaller at 88 cm (34½ in). Animals on Java are larger and a stag there can measure up to 120 cm (47 in).
Weight	Sexual dimorphism is marked. The average weight of a stag is around 120 kg (265 lb) with a hind weighing some 74 kg (163 lb). A Javan stag may weigh up to 160 kg (352 lb).
Food	Primarily grazes on grasses, but also browses on leaves and takes other material such as fallen fruit or seaweed.
Habitat	Where available, grass plains and parkland close to the forest edge appear to be preferred. Otherwise the species is flexible and will also inhabit deciduous forest, marshland, mountains and shrubland.
Voice	Stags emit a shrill roar during the rutting season. Hinds make a piercing cry when alarmed, stags make a loud honk.
Annual behaviour	Outside the rut the sexes live apart in separate herds. Behaviour can vary between locations; in some places they are largely nocturnal, in others they may feed heavily during the day especially where they are undisturbed. Javan deer are said to drink only infrequently, obtaining most of the moisture they need from their foodstuffs.
Rut	There is no fixed breeding season, although there are seasonal peaks to rutting which vary according to locality but are generally between June and October. Much rutting activity is nocturnal. Stags often decorate their antlers with grasses to enhance their appearance when competing for the attention of hinds in oestrus. At such times stags are extremely vocal and aggressive towards each other and fighting with antlers is common.
Gestation and birthing	Gestation is around 8 months and the calves are born unspotted. They are weaned at between 6 and 8 months and attain sexual maturity at 18 to 24 months.
Antlers (typical)	The antlers are lyre-shaped and usually consist of 3 simple points on each side, an upwardly curving brow tine and a forked top. Occasionally 4-point antlers, sometimes with slight palmation, have been known to occur. Length is usually 65–70 cm (25½–27½ in) although over 100 cm (39½ in) have been recorded.
Antler cycle	Casting can occur between October and February depending on location
Lifespan	Around 15 years, and only very rarely beyond 20 years
Threats	The main predators are the Javan leopard, dhole, crocodiles and pythons. They are also a main prey item of the Komodo dragon where the two species occur together on the islands of Flores and Komodo. The main human threats are land clearance, leading to some highly fragmented habitats, as well as both legal and illegal hunting. In many places, poaching activity for subsistence and at more commercial levels is the most significant cause of reductions in numbers despite legislation and protected areas.

DEER SPECIES | CERVIDAE – CERVINAE

Rusa unicolor

Sambar

ORDER	Artiodactyla
SUBORDER	Ruminantia
INFRAORDER	Pecora
FAMILY	Cervidae
SUBFAMILY	Cervinae

THE SAMBAR IS one of the world's largest deer, smaller only than the elk *Alces alces* and similar in size to the wapiti *Cervus canadensis*. It is an adaptable species with a natural range that extends across much of India and Asia, restricted only by the western deserts of India, the Himalayas and the northern arid uplands of China. It can also be found on the island of Taiwan in the east, and as far south as Sumatra, Borneo and some of the minor islands. Capable of living in a wide range of habitat types, it is the most widespread of all the deer of southern Asia although, despite the encouraging appearance of the distribution map, it is only locally common in some places while scarce and declining in others.

▲ An Indian sambar stag and hind pictured in Kanha National Park, Madhya Pradesh.
Photograph: Coke Smith

The distribution map shows the native range only; introduced populations not shown.

◂ (*left*) An Indian sambar stag with typical six-point antlers.
Photograph: Brent Huffman

◂ (*right*) Sambar are seldom found far from sources of water.
Photograph: Pixabay

A GUIDE TO THE DEER OF THE WORLD

> An Indian sambar stag in its short summer coat, pictured at the Tierpark, Berlin.
> Photograph: Klaus Rudloff

At one point there were widely thought to be around 15 subspecies, a number which included three which now have their own status as individual species – the Javan deer *R. timorensis*, Philippine sambar *R. marianna* and Visayan spotted deer *R. alfredi*. More recently some taxonomists have suggested that there might now be seven subspecies:

Species		Distribution
Bornean sambar	*R. u. brookei*	Borneo
Southeast Asian sambar	*R. u. cambojensis*	Mainland Southeast Asia
South China sambar	*R. u. dejeani*	South-west and southern China
Hainan sambar	*R. u. equina*	Sumatra
Formosan sambar	*R. u. swinhoii*	Taiwan
Indian or Sri Lankan sambar	*R. u. unicolor*	Bangladesh, India and Sri Lanka

The taxonomy of the sambar remains somewhat confused; a 2011 reclassification, for example, proposed dividing the sambar into just two separate species split between the majority of India, and then north-east India and the reminder of south-east Asia. It is likely that this list may yet be revised further, though for now the IUCN lists the species only as *R. unicolor* with different regional forms.

Another subspecies once described as *R. u. boninensis* occurred on the Bonin or Ogasawara Islands, which lie some 1,000 kilometres to the south of Tokyo. It is likely, though, that these animals were probably examples of the closely related Philippine sambar *R. marianna*, transplanted during the late eighteenth and nineteenth centuries and considered extinct by 1925.

The adaptability of the sambar has enabled its successful introduction to Australia, where it has spread steadily and is found in large numbers across the northern and eastern coastal areas. Here, it is considered a pest species in some states and year-round hunting is encouraged; the situation is the same on New Zealand's North

DEER SPECIES | CERVIDAE – CERVINAE

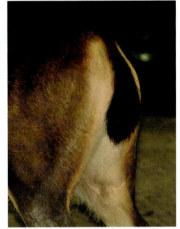

◄ A Southeast Asian sambar stag in swampy habitat.
Photograph: Brent Huffman

◄ (*left*) Malayan sambar hind.
Photograph: Roland Wirth

◄ (*right*) The tail is short, and its colour may vary between light and dark brown. This is a Malayan sambar.
Photograph: Klaus Rudloff

▼ Sambar hinds also develop manes, though to a lesser degree than stags. This one is in the company of a chital stag (*foreground*) showing the significant size difference between the two species.
Photograph: Nagesh Ramarao

Island. In South Africa's Western Cape they were also introduced to a private estate during the 1880s, from where they have extended their presence to across the area of Table Mountain. Numbers are not high and they are not felt to have any serious impact. In the USA, sambar were released onto the St Vincent Islands, Florida, in

1908 where they still live in small but viable numbers alongside the native white-tailed deer *Odocoileus virginianus*. They have also been released in parts of California and Texas, primarily for hunting on game ranches, where they are locally successful but never abundant.

Despite its wide distribution, the sambar is considered to be a Vulnerable species by the IUCN. Though locally abundant in some places, most especially within some of the better managed reserves and other protected areas and in Taiwan where hunting has been successfully restricted, it is heavily persecuted. Being a large-bodied deer with a high meat yield it is especially attractive to commercial hunters, and there is also a significant market for antlers as well as other body parts for use in traditional medicine. Although the situation is particularly concerning in some eastern and southern parts of its range, where numbers may have dropped by more than half during the past 30 years, nowhere can it be considered entirely safe from over-exploitation. Effective levels of protection are urgently needed.

FACT BOX – Sambar

World distribution	Native to Bangladesh, Bhutan, Brunei, Cambodia, China (Hainan, Hunan, Guanxi, Guizhou, Jiangxi, Sichuan and Yunnan provinces), India, Laos, Malaysia, Myanmar, Nepal, Sri Lanka, Sumatra, Taiwan, Thailand and Vietnam.
	Introduced to Australia, New Zealand, South Africa and the United States.
IUCN Red List Status 2022	**Vulnerable**, population decreasing (last formal assessment 2014).
Sexes	*Male:* Stag *Female:* Hind *Young:* Calf
Also known as	Indian sambar, Sambar deer, Mountain horse (plus a number of variations related to specific regions).
	Annamese *Con Hai* or *Kha-khowa-pohu*; Bengali *Bholongi Gaoj* or *Gous* (male); Borneo *Payoh*; Burmese *Connai*, *Sut* or *tshat*; Cambodia *Kadanh*; Chinese *Hai-lu*, *Twahé*, *Hei-lu*, or *Shui-lu*; French *Cerf sambar* or *Sambar de l'Indie*; German *Indischer sambarhirsch* or *Pferdehirsch*; Gond *Ma-ao* or *Mauk*; Himalayas *Jerao* or *Jerrow*; Hindi *Sabhar*, *Sámar* or *Sambar*; Holkar *Sáram*, *Sambhar* or *Sambhur*; Kanarese *Kadaba*, *Kadala*, *Kadave*, *Kaddama*, *Kadvi* or *Kudawe*; Karen *Hseukhan*, *Kheu* or *Takhau*; Kurukh *Dhalnar*; Madhya Pradesh *Sal-samar*; Malayalam *Kullay Marn*, *Rusa* or *Rusa etem*; Marathi *Meru* or *Samba*; Nepalese *Jarai* (female) *jarao* or *jaro* (male); Sinhalese *Gona Rusa* or *Phursa jarai*; Sri Lanka *Goma* or *Marrei*; Szechwan *Hei-lu* or *hei-lu-tze*; Tai (Formosa) *Cheeang* or *Tsui-roku*; Tamil *Kadumai*, *Kataman*, *Komboo* or *Kudoo marn*; Terai *Máhá*; Telugu *Kenadi* or *Kennadi*; Thai *Kwang* or *Kwang-paa*.
Recognition features	A very large deer. The coat tends to be shaggy in appearance, though sleeker in summer, and is uniform in colouration, ranging between yellowish-brown and dark grey with lighter underparts. The ears are large and rounded. The tail, which can be raised to signal alarm, is long for a deer and white on the underside with a darker upper surface. Stags grow a dense mane, hinds less so.
Height (at shoulder)	100–160 cm (39½–63 in), hinds smaller. In broad terms the western forms tend to be larger than those found in the east.
Weight	Between 100–350 kg (220–770 lb), more typically 185–260 kg (408–573 lb), though an exceptional stag may weigh considerably more. Hinds are around two-thirds the size of stags.
Food	A generalist feeder, its feeding habits depend on the habitat occupied and can include grasses, the shoots and leaves of a wide variety of bushes and trees, fruit, and aquatic plants.

FACT BOX – *Sambar*

Habitat	The sambar occupies a wide variety of habitats including dry, tropical and subtropical forest, marshland, scrub, grassland and alpine woodland up to altitudes of 3,900 metres above sea level, though it does not extend its range onto the barren plains typified by the Punjab or barer mountain slopes. It seldom moves far from a water source.
Voice	Generally quiet. Stags make a bellowing roar during the rut; both sexes emit a high-pitched scream or a ringing call when alarmed.
Annual behaviour	Largely crepuscular or entirely nocturnal, resting in heavy cover during the day. Females live in small herds based on family units for most of the year while stags tend to be more solitary and nomadic, though larger concentrations have been seen, especially in protected areas where densities are higher or located near large bodies of water at the peak of the summer. Sambar are excellent swimmers and will often seek water when pursued. They are more likely than most deer physically to attack predators such as dholes or feral dogs, and have also been known to form a defensive ring with rumps touching when threatened. Hinds can be unusually aggressive when defending their young.
Rut	There is no set breeding season but rutting activity peaks between September and January. In central India most rutting takes place in December, while in much of Indonesia the timing is several months earlier. The stags establish temporary territories, wallow frequently, scent-mark, and attempt to attract hinds to them though they do not collect harems. Rutting stags are particularly aggressive towards each other, fighting with locked antlers and also rearing up to crash downwards at opponents. They may cover nightly distances of up to 20 km during the rut. The hinds will also move widely between the territories of various stags in search of a suitable partner and several may remain in the vicinity of one while they are in oestrus.
Gestation and birthing	Gestation is between 8 and 9 months. The single calf is brown and usually unspotted, although some forms may have a light spotted pattern which quickly fades; it weighs between 6–10 kg (13–22 lb) at birth. It remains with its mother for up to 2 years.
Antlers (typical)	Antlers usually comprise a total of 6 or 8 tines including a forward-facing terminal fork and long brow tines. A good set will measure about 100 cm (40 in) in length. The largest antlers tend to be produced by Indian animals; the biggest recorded came from Madhya Pradesh and measured 127.6 cm (50¼ in).
Antler cycle	There is considerable variation in the timing of casting. Animals in central India tend to cast around late March or early April; those in Burma and Taiwan may be a month later. Further south there is more irregularity and mature stags might be encountered in hard horn at any time of year.
Lifespan	Seldom more than 12 years in the wild but up to 20 years; 26 years recorded in captivity.
Threats	The sambar is an important prey species of the tiger. Other predators, especially of young or infirm animals, include leopards, dholes and crocodiles. Habitat loss to human development and hunting are the most significant threats across most of the sambar's range and its meat is highly prized. For the latter reason poaching pressure can be intense where protective measures are inadequate. As a large deer, it represents a much higher quantity of meat than that obtained from a smaller species. Although sambar are not considered to raid crops to any significant degree, this may also be used as an excuse to kill animals. One exception to falling numbers is in Taiwan where, following the successful reduction of hunting, sambar populations have risen visibly. Hybridisation with the Javan deer *R. timorensis* may be a localised threat where the ranges of the two species overlap.

A GUIDE TO THE DEER OF THE WORLD

Moschidae

Musk deer

ORDER	Artiodactyla
SUBORDER	Ruminantia
INFRAORDER	Pecora
FAMILY	Moschidae

Also known as

Chinese *She* or *She-lú*; French *Cerf port-musc*, *Chevrotain port-musc* or *port-musc*; Dutch *Muskus hert*; German *Moschustier*; Hindi *Bena, Custura, Jako-sika, Kabanga, Kastura, Mushk, Mushknafa* or *Zako sika*; Ladakhi *Ribjo*; Pahari *Masak naba* or *Mussuck naba*; Spanish *Ciervo almizclero*; Tibetan *La, Láwa* or *Shawa*; Urdu *Kastura*

▲ A Siberian musk deer.
Photograph: Brent Huffman

WITH UPLAND RANGES that extend across the Himalayas and then through much of China and northwards into Siberia, the musk deer prefers to live in the colder forests and scrublands at higher altitudes of over 2,000 metres above sea level and beyond. The most favoured habitat appears to be that which provides suitable cover: this might include dwarf rhododendron, spruce, prickly oak or similar, at around 3,800 metres. It is not a true deer of the *Cervidae* family but is closely related to it, the *Moschidae* having evolved on a slightly different but broadly parallel path. One of the main differences between the two is that musk deer have gall bladders whereas the true deer do not; another is that female musk deer have only two teats compared to the four of a true deer.

Neither sex of the *Moschidae* ever produces antlers but they do bear upper canine teeth, which have developed into sharp tusks: those of the male can reach up to 10 cm (4 in) in length. These canines are mobile within their sockets but can break easily, and if this happens the male deer will suffer a loss in dominance among rivals for breeding rights. Females also have extended upper canines but these remain relatively short and are never long enough to protrude below the level of the lower lip.

There are seven recognised species of musk deer, all of which are broadly similar in appearance and behaviour. With an average shoulder height of 50–70 cm (20–28 in) and weighing up to 17 kg (37 lb) the body is compact and stocky, with the hindquarters held higher than the shoulders. Generally a dark brown, the pelage can vary between a lighter brown to almost black, speckled with a lighter grey and with paler underparts. There are often contrasting white chest markings that may extend from the chin and down the chest as far as the belly, and there may be light spotting on the back and sides. The face has a long, almost kangaroo-like appearance, and is carried low on a relatively long, thin neck; the ears are long and rounded. The feet have broad cleaves and well-developed dew claws that regularly show in the animal's tracks. Musk deer are largely silent but make a soft hiss if disturbed and can scream loudly when distressed.

The musk deer is well suited to living in high altitude mountainous regions. Its coat is coarse, dense and made up of hollow guard hairs which provide efficient insulation; the feet are adapted for negotiating rocky terrains and snow-covered landscapes; and the powerful hindquarters enable easy movement uphill and across difficult country. The tail is very short and can be hidden completely by the hair of the rump, a typical adaptation of deer that have evolved to live in cold conditions.

It is a solitary and largely nocturnal deer that is seldom seen in groups larger than three animals. Even then musk deer are shy, highly elusive and rarely encountered; one experienced researcher recorded just 65 sightings over the course of a dedicated three-year study, while others have enjoyed only marginally better success. Covering up to seven kilometres in the course of a night's feeding, a musk deer will generally return to its regular bedding spot each morning along regular paths, which can become well-trodden over time. Lichens can constitute virtually the entire diet during winter, though at other times grasses, leaves, shoots, bark and fungi are also eaten.

Their main predators include lynx, wolverines and yellow-throated martens but they may also be taken by larger carnivores. When pursued, a musk deer will usually head for an inaccessible crag, narrow gap or other rocky terrain; if this is not possible they may run in wide circles, though they are unable to sustain this for long and tire quickly after the first few hundred metres.

Most rutting appears to take place between November and January with a peak in December. One or two young are usual, occasionally up to three, and are born between May and July after a gestation period of around six-and-a-half months; the young are liberally spotted and wean at three to four months old, generally attaining sexual maturity by the time they are around 16 months old.

The main threat to the musk deer is illegal hunting, though not primarily for its meat even though this is considered a local delicacy. The mature male musk deer has a gland just forward of the penis about the size of a golf ball, also known as the 'musk pod', which produces a strongly smelling reddish-brown, waxy secretion: this is believed to be mixed with urine and used to stimulate females into entering oestrus. It is highly prized as a fixative by the perfume industry but is also used in oriental medicine and has been quoted as attracting a value of up to US$45,000 per kilogram; a single gland contains some 25–30 grams. When fresh, the musk has a pungent smell but is refined to produce a rich, sweet and aromatic scent. Although it can be extracted from the live animal, and musk farms have been established mainly in China and Russia for the purpose, captive animals can be expensive to maintain, prone to disease and are said to produce a poorer-quality musk. For these reasons it is far more common for wild deer to be killed and the entire sac removed. While the perfume industry has developed cheaper synthetic alternatives, genuine musk remains one of the most valuable animal-derived products known. Many female and immature deer are killed in addition to males in the course of hunting for musk, as snaring, the main form of poaching, is completely indiscriminate. Illegal and unsustainable hunting is considered to be the most significant threat to all of the *Moschidae* species and the main reason for their continuing declines.

As an animal that lives at higher altitudes, the musk deer is not so strongly threatened by habitat degradation as many of the other deer. Despite this, it can still be badly affected by logging and the disturbance caused by other activities such as mining, as well as forest loss to human settlement and agriculture. All or any of these factors can cause the displacement of this shy and furtive species, whilst fragmenting the existing habitat.

All the musk deer are difficult to identify by species using morphological characteristics alone and some of them are particularly easily confused. In some cases only genetic studies have confirmed specific species. The following table suggests some generalised distinguishing features (though it must be emphasised that the list is not definitive and individual animals can vary considerably):

	Anhui *M. anhuiensis*	Forest *M. berezovskii*	Alpine *M. chrysogaster*	Kashmir *M. cupreus*	Black *M. fuscus*	Himalayan *M. leucogaster*	Siberian *M. moschiferus*
Crown of head	Grey	Dark grey	Pale brown	Grey/coppery-red	Black	Grey/black	Grey/brown
Ear (outer)	Dark	Black	Pale brown	Dark brown	Black	Grey/brown	Dark brown
Ear (inner)	White	White	Grey	White and grey/black	White	Grey	White
Ear tip (outside)	Dark	Black	Yellow	Coppery-red	Black	Grey	Pale brown
Throat/neck	Strip	Three wide strips	White strip	White	No strip	Grey, no strip	Two white strips
Chin	Light grey	White	White	Grey	Black	Grey	White
Nape	Grey/brown	Grey/brown	Yellowish-brown	Coppery-red	Black	Grey/brown	Dark brown
Thigh	Grey/brown	Dark grey	Paler than black	Coppery-red	Black	Dark	Black/brown
Lower limbs	Light grey	Grey	Paler than body	White	Black	Dark	Grey
Upper limbs	Grey/brown	Grey/brown	Greyish-yellow	Coppery-red and grey	Black	Black/brown	Grey
Upper body	Grey/brown (pale spots)	Grey/brown	Yellowish-brown	Coppery-red (faint white spots)	Black	Grey/black	Black/brown (whitish spots)
Lower body/underside	Grey/brown	Grey/brown	Yellowish-brown and grey	Coppery-red	Black	Grey/black	Grey/brown
Rump	Grey/brown	Almost black	Paler than black	Dark grey	Ochre tones	Dark	Black/brown

Primary source of information: Singh, P.B., Khatiwada, J.R., Saud, P. *et al*. mtDNA analysis confirms the endangered Kashmir musk deer extends its range to Nepal. Sci Rep 9, 4895 (2019). https://doi.org/10.1038/s41598-019-41167-4

DEER SPECIES | MOSCHIDAE

Moschus anhuiensis

Anhui musk deer

ORDER	Artiodactyla
SUBORDER	Ruminantia
INFRAORDER	Pecora
FAMILY	Moschidae

The **Anhui musk deer** *M. anhuiensis* has a very limited distribution, being found only in a small western region of Anhui province of China, where it inhabits conifer, broadleaf and mixed forests at high elevations. It is not well understood but is reputed to mature more quickly than other species and may be capable of breeding at a year old. According to some researchers, it may also be more likely to produce twins than other musk deer. Once considered to be a subspecies of the Forest musk deer, with which it is easily confused because of a similar morphology and pelage colour, it is now recognised as a valid separate species and its known distribution lies well to the east of that of the latter. Like most of the musk deer it is classified as Endangered and, although there are no available population estimates, numbers may only lie between the mid-to-high-hundreds. Such is the species' scarcity that it has proven impossible to source a verified photograph.

▲ A watercolour representation of the Anhui musk deer.
Painting: Anni Sharp

Distribution	China
IUCN Red List Status 2022	**Endangered**, decreasing (last formal assessment 2015)

Moschus berezovskii

Forest musk deer

ORDER	Artiodactyla
SUBORDER	Ruminantia
INFRAORDER	Pecora
FAMILY	Moschidae

▲ A Forest musk deer passes a remote camera.
Photograph: VNUF IBF Leibniz IZW GWC HLNR

▶ Forest musk deer in the mountainous region to the west of Ya'an, Sichuan Province, China.
Photograph: Marc Faucher

▶ The skull of a Forest musk deer, showing the length of typical musk canines. This specimen is held in the United States National Museum and was collected in Wenchuan County, Sichuan China in 1934.
Photograph: David Huckaby/ Mammal Images Library of the American Society of Mammalogists

The **Forest musk deer** *M. berezovskii* is found in central and southern China and also north-eastern Vietnam; it may also be present in northern Laos but this is unconfirmed. It is a lighter coloured musk deer, being a grizzled yellowish-brown, and is one of the smaller species which seldom exceeds some 50 cm (28 in) in height. There are believed to be four subspecies, one of which *M. b. caobangis* might yet achieve the status of a separate species but has not been studied sufficiently to date.

Distribution	China and Vietnam Presence uncertain in Laos
IUCN Red List Status 2022	**Endangered**, decreasing (last formal assessment 2015)
Also known as	Chinese forest musk deer or Dwarf musk deer Chinese *Lin-she*

DEER SPECIES | MOSCHIDAE

Moschus chrysogaster

Alpine musk deer

ORDER	Artiodactyla
SUBORDER	Ruminantia
INFRAORDER	Pecora
FAMILY	Moschidae

The **Alpine musk deer** *M. chrysogaster* is generally a sandy-to-mid-brown colour. With a range that covers the central highlands of China and extends westwards along the Himalayas as far as Nepal, it is widely distributed but much of the population is disjointed. It is usually found on barren plateaus where it inhabits forests, shrublands and more open ground, typically on the steeper slopes.

▲ An Alpine musk deer in Sagarmatha National Park, Nepal, home to Mount Everest.
Photograph: Brian Long

◄ (*left*) Alpine musk deer in typical mountain habitat.
Photograph: Marc Faucher

◄ (*right*) Musk deer featured on a Nepalese banknote.

Distribution	Bhutan, China, India and Nepal
IUCN Red List Status 2022	**Endangered**, decreasing (last formal assessment 2014)
Also known as	Chinese *Ma-she*

Moschus cupreus

Kashmir musk deer

ORDER	Artiodactyla
SUBORDER	Ruminantia
INFRAORDER	Pecora
FAMILY	Moschidae

▲ Trail camera images of Kashmir musk deer, taken in the Mustang district of Nepal and identifying presence there.
Photographs: Paras Bikram Singh

Restricted to the Himalayas to the extreme north of Afghanistan, India and Pakistan, the **Kashmir musk deer** *M. cupreus* is another poorly understood species which is closely related taxonomically to the Alpine musk deer. Recent research has also indicated its presence in western Nepal. Within its known range it is likely that numbers are low and localised in many places, most particularly Afghanistan where any suitable remaining habitat is seriously fragmented.

Distribution	Afghanistan, India, Nepal and Pakistan
IUCN Red List Status 2022	**Endangered**, decreasing (last formal assessment 2014)
Also known as	Kashmiri *Rao, Raos, Rons, Rous* or *Rous*; Pashto *Hussai*

DEER SPECIES | MOSCHIDAE

Moschus fucus
Black musk deer

ORDER	Artiodactyla
SUBORDER	Ruminantia
INFRAORDER	Pecora
FAMILY	Moschidae

The **Black musk deer** *M. fuscus* lives on the tree-line at higher elevations, inhabiting rhododendron thickets and coniferous forests and preferring to live on the forest edge and on rocky ridges. Its range extends in a relatively narrow strip from north-west China and across the northern extremes of Myanmar, India and Bhutan as far as the eastern tip of Nepal. As its name implies, it is a very dark form of musk deer. Like many of the other species it has been poorly studied, and although no population estimates are available it is considered to be extremely rare.

▲ A rare photograph of a Black musk deer, of necessity taken at long range and then cropped. The image is from *The Mammals of North East India* by Anwaruddin Choudhury (Gibbon Books & The Rhino Foundation, 2013).
Photograph: Manoj Nair

◄ Typical musk deer habitat in Mustang, Nepal.
Photograph: Paras Bikram Singh

Distribution	Bhutan, China, India, Myanmar and Nepal
IUCN Red List Status 2022	**Endangered**, decreasing (last formal assessment 2015)
Also known as	Dusky musk deer

Moschus leucogaster

Himalayan musk deer

ORDER	Artiodactyla
SUBORDER	Ruminantia
INFRAORDER	Pecora
FAMILY	Moschidae

▲ (*above and right*) A female Himalayan musk deer, also pictured in Sagarmatha National Park. A lack of any neck markings distinguishes it from the Alpine musk deer.
Photographs: Martijn van Dijk

The **Himalayan musk deer** *M. leucogaster* occupies the Himalayas across China (where its presence is thought to be marginal), Bhutan, India and Nepal. Although there are no available population figures it can be reasonably assumed that numbers are very low wherever it occurs. The lowest altitude it has been recorded at is 2,500 metres above sea level, and it was once treated as a subspecies of the Alpine musk deer until it was reclassified because of the different skull proportions of the two.

Distribution	Bhutan, China, India and Nepal
IUCN Red List Status 2022	**Endangered**, decreasing (last formal assessment 2014)
Also known as	White-bellied musk deer Nepalese *Kasturi mriga*

DEER SPECIES | MOSCHIDAE

Moschus moschiferus
Siberian musk deer

ORDER	Artiodactyla
SUBORDER	Ruminantia
INFRAORDER	Pecora
FAMILY	Moschidae

Of all the musk deer the **Siberian musk deer** *M. moschiferus* has the widest distribution by a very great margin and is considered to be the typical species within the family *Moschidae*. Most of the preceding species are classified as Endangered, though some are perilously close to being reclassified as Critically Endangered. Only the Siberian musk deer is considered to be Vulnerable, although like all of the musk deer it appears to be declining throughout its range. There are six subspecies, four of which occur in Russia: *M. m. moschiferus* (Siberia), *M. m. turovi* (Russian Far East), *M. m. arcticus* (Verkhoyansk Ridge) and *M. m. sachalinensis* (Sakhalin Island). Elsewhere *M. m. moschiferus* occurs in the forests of various northern and eastern Mongolian mountain ranges (the northern Altai, Hangai, Hentii and Hövsgöl) as well as in China (Xinjiang, Nei Mogol and Heilongjiang). *M. m. parvipes* is found around the Chinese border region from where its range extends across both Korean countries.

▲ A Siberian musk deer, pictured at rest in the Land of the Leopard National Park, Primorsky Krai, Russian Far East.
Photograph: Christian Langner

▼ A female Siberian musk deer in San Diego Zoo, showing the chest markings.
Photograph: Alexander F Meyer

The Siberian musk deer is generally a dark brown in colour, though colouration can vary between a lighter yellow-brown and almost black. A pair of place stripes extend down from the chin, along the neck and as far as the belly. The subspecies found on Sakhalin Island, off the far eastern coast of Russia, is said to be the darkest of all the musk deer and is somewhat smaller than the other subspecies. While the Siberian musk deer is the most numerous of the subspecies, there is no firm estimate available of numbers, but the overall picture is at best a steady decrease with ranges contracting.

Clockwise from top
▲ The coat of all newly born musk deer is liberally spotted. This is a Siberian musk deer fawn.
Photographs: Klaus Rudloff

▲ Skull of a male Siberian musk deer.

▲ The musk gland or 'pod' of a musk deer. Only mature males have them.

Distribution	China, Kazakhstan, DPR Korea, Republic of Korea, Mongolia and Russia
IUCN Red List Status 2022	**Vulnerable**, decreasing (last formal assessment 2014
Also known as	Chinese *Ma-she*; Mongolian *Badgana khuder*; Korean *Sahyang noru*; Russian *Kabarga*

Although there is legislation protecting most of the musk deer species across their native ranges, enforcement is generally poor and poaching is rampant. As numbers decrease and become more difficult to harvest for the lucrative black-market musk trade, the effect is inevitably to increase their value. All of the species are in decline and will continue to be so as long as such widespread and indiscriminate hunting is permitted to continue.

DEER SPECIES | TRAGULIDAE

Tragulidae

Chevrotains *or* mouse deer

ORDER	Artiodactyla
SUBORDER	Ruminantia
INFRAORDER	Tragulina
FAMILY	Tragulidae

◄ A Javan chevrotain.
Photograph: Alexander F Meyer

ALTHOUGH THEY BEAR a superficial resemblance to the true deer of the *Cervidae*, the diminutive chevrotains or tragulids are actually only distant relatives, and it is just their general appearance and size which led them to be called mouse deer. Though both they and the true deer belong to the Artiodactyla, the even-toed ungulates, they are actually more closely related to the giraffe and antelope families and should not really be referred to as deer at all; they are included in these pages purely for completeness.

The more accurate common name of chevrotain is derived from the French *chevrot* meaning a kid, itself coming from *chèvre* or goat. The scientific description *Tragulus* comes from the Greek *tragos*, a he-goat, and the *-ulus* suffix is used as a diminutive, reflecting the small sizes of the various species. There is often a popular tendency to refer to those animals with spotted or striped coats as chevrotains and those with plainer pelage as mouse deer, although the terms are often treated as interchangeable. Chevrotain or tragulid is, however, more accurate than 'mouse deer' and less likely to cause unnecessary confusion.

Chevrotains are shy, retiring, delicately built creatures and they include the smallest hoofed animals in the world. Of the ten known species, only one is found in Africa while the remainder inhabit the forests of Southeast Asia. They are almost entirely herbivores although the water chevrotain is known to forage more widely on animal matter. There are many physical and behavioural differences between chevrotains and the more evolved *Cervidae*. Although they have four-chambered stomachs like all ruminants, one of these (the omasum) is poorly developed and they ruminate very little. Their skull structure and dentition are different, and so is the bone structure of the feet. Unlike deer, chevrotains do possess gall bladders; but they never produce antlers, although both sexes bear canine tusks, which are more pronounced in the male.

Chevrotains have short, thin legs and powerful hindquarters, the rump raised higher than the shoulders, often suggesting a hunched appearance. The narrow and quite pointed head is generally held low when walking, the gait characterised by cautious, almost bird-like steps. They usually live singly or in pairs. There is only slight sexual dimorphism, males tending to be slightly larger than females, but with the notable exception of the water chevrotain (*see opposite*). Most live in wet, dense evergreen forest where the close proximity of a water source is usually important and most are seldom found far from it.

Habits are broadly similar across the family; chevrotains tend to be mostly nocturnal, resting up in thick cover during the day and emerging to forage for food at night. Fallen fruits, herbs and shrubs are important foodstuffs. They live in small territories which may extend to 24 hectares (59 acres) but are often much less. These are fiercely defended and fighting, especially between males using their longer canine tusks, is common though usually brief in duration. A single young is usual and might be born at any time of year, although there are often seasonal peaks in breeding.

Though chevrotains lack many of the scent glands possessed by their more evolved cousins the true deer, they do have chin glands which are used in territorial and mating behaviour, and preputial glands in the groin area for marking territory. They make a variety of vocalisations, which can include alarm barks, chattering, or screaming when injured or distressed. Being small, they are prey to a wide variety of predators, ranging from the larger cats to birds of prey, crocodiles and some snakes. If threatened, they tend to freeze to avoid being spotted before fleeing with an explosive, if short-lived, burst of speed. For such small animals they can be surprisingly long-lived, and although eight years or so is probably more usual this may extend to as much as 14 years.

There are currently believed to be ten species which are divided into three subfamilies, Hyemoschus, Moschiola and Tragulus.

Hyemoschus aquaticus
Water chevrotain

ORDER	Artiodactyla
SUBORDER	Ruminantia
INFRAORDER	Tragulina
FAMILY	Tragulidae
SUBFAMILY	Hyemoschus

The **water chevrotain** *Hyemoschus aquaticus* is the only tragulid native to Africa, where it inhabits the central and western tropical regions. It is the only member of the subfamily *Hyemoschus*. It seldom stands more than about 40 cm (16 in) high at the shoulder and unusually among the *Tragulidae* a female, which can weigh up to about 14 kg (31 lb), may be as much as 2 kg (4½ lb) heavier than a male. It is the largest of the chevrotains by a considerable margin, though still diminutive when compared to most of the true deer. The red-brown coat is strongly marked with white spots and horizontal stripes along the flanks. As its name suggests, it is never found far from a water source and seeks to live close to streams or rivers. While its primary diet is fallen fruit, it has also been recorded feeding on insects and crabs and scavenging fish and meat. It is most threatened by habitat loss and hunting for bushmeat; in the Ituri Forest of the Democratic Republic of Congo, it represents around 5 per cent of the regular catch of local net fishermen. With an estimated population of some 280,000 animals, it is currently considered to be of Least Concern, although numbers appear to be declining and this status may yet change.

The distribution map shows the African range of the water chevrotain.

▼ Portrait of an adult female water chevrotain.
Photograph: Brent Huffman

Distribution	Cameroon, the Central African Republic, Congo, Congo (DR), Côte d'Ivoire, Equatorial Guinea, Gabon, Ghana, Guinea, Liberia, Nigeria, Sierra Leone and Togo
IUCN Red List Status 2022	**Least Concern**, decreasing (last formal assessment 2016)
Also known as	French *Chevrotain aquatique*; Spanish *Antilope amizclero enano de agua*, *cervatillo de agua* or *ciervo ratón de agua*; German *Hirschferkel*

Moschiola indica

Indian spotted chevrotain

ORDER	Artiodactyla
SUBORDER	Ruminantia
INFRAORDER	Tragulina
FAMILY	Tragulidae
SUBFAMILY	Moschiola

Photograph: Haneesh K M

All of the remaining species occur across India and Southeast Asia. The **Indian spotted chevrotain** *Moschiola indica* is by far the most widely distributed and occurs across most of India. It may also occur in the lowlands of Nepal but this has not been confirmed by any specific research. The larger of the three species which make up the subfamily *Moschiola*, it stands up to 33 cm (13 in) at the shoulder and averages around 3kg (6½ lb) in weight – although weights of almost 5.5 kg (12 lb) have been recorded. It was once considered to be the only species in the subfamily but a 2005 reclassification split *Moschiola* into three, with the other two species found in Sri Lanka. The Indian spotted chevrotain is a dull brown in colour with patterns of pale spots or stripes and one or two white bands on the throat; these patterns are unique and are often used to identify individuals from camera trap images. The top of the head is a dark brown.

▼ A group of Indian spotted chevrotain, pictured in Leipzig Zoo.
Photograph: Klaus Rudloff

Distribution	Widespread across much of India Presence uncertain in Nepal
IUCN Red List Status 2022	**Least Concern**, unknown (last formal assessment 2014)
Also known as	Bengali *Benkurang* or *Gandwa jitra hurin*; Gond *Turi-maoo*; Hindi *Pisera* or *Pisuri*; Kannada *Barka*; Konkani *Barinka*; Malayalam *Khooran*; Marathi *Pisora* or *Pisura*; Tamil *Sarukumān*; Telugu *Jarini pandi* or *Kurupandi*; Uttar Pradesh *Mugi*

DEER SPECIES | TRAGULIDAE – MOSCHIOLA

Moschiola meminna — White-spotted chevrotain

Photograph: Yu Ching Tam

ORDER	Artiodactyla
SUBORDER	Ruminantia
INFRAORDER	Tragulina
FAMILY	Tragulidae
SUBFAMILY	Moschiola

Distribution

Sri Lanka

IUCN Red List Status 2022

Least Concern, unknown (last formal assessment 2014)

Also known as

Sri Lankan spotted chevrotain

French *Tragule d'Inde*; Sinhalese *Meeminna*, *Meiminna* or *Memminna*; Tamil *Kooran panni*, *Kurampani*, *Kuruman Sarukumān*, *Sarugoo maru* or *Ukkalan*

Found in Sri Lanka, **the White-spotted chevrotain** *Moschiola meminna* is only slightly smaller than the Indian spotted chevrotain and similar in colour, although the white spotting is less prone to merge and form distinct stripes. It is found across the dry zone of the island which forms the majority of the land mass apart from the central mountain range and southern parts. As well as being a forest species, it is also reported frequently in gardens and coconut plantations. Despite a 20-fold rise in the human population of Sri Lanka over the last century or so, this species is still considered to be fairly common and widespread – although it is hunted heavily for food and the true status of the population is unknown.

Moschiola kathygre — Yellow-striped chevrotain

Photograph: Klaus Rudloff

ORDER	Artiodactyla
SUBORDER	Ruminantia
INFRAORDER	Tragulina
FAMILY	Tragulidae
SUBFAMILY	Moschiola

Distribution

Sri Lanka

IUCN Red List Status 2022

Least Concern, unknown (last formal assessment 2014)

Also known as

French *Tragule d'Inde*; Sinhalese *Meeminna*, *Meiminna* or *Memminna*; Tamil *Kooran panni*, *Kurampani*, *Kuruman Sarukumān*, *Sarugoo maru* or *Ukkalan*

The third member of the *Moschiola* subfamily is the **Yellow-striped chevrotain** *Moschiola kathygre*. It is the smallest of the three, though by only a very small margin, and a fully grown adult is unlikely to exceed 3 kg (6½ lb). It too lives on Sri Lanka, though its habitat requirements are different and its range covers the more restricted wet zone in the south. It has a slightly different appearance, being a dark, golden-brown marked with yellowish spots which typically merge into stripes on the flanks with two further stripes across the haunches. The hind legs are also slightly shorter than those of the other species. Apart from the secondary forest it prefers, it has been seen regularly entering rice paddies and is a common resident of human gardens and rubber plantations and seems more tolerant of habitat degradation.

Tragulus javanicus
Javan chevrotain

ORDER	Artiodactyla
SUBORDER	Ruminantia
INFRAORDER	Tragulina
FAMILY	Tragulidae
SUBFAMILY	Tragulus

Photograph: Roland Wirth

Distribution map – Note presence is uncertain on Bali

The remaining six species of chevrotain belong to the subfamily *Tragulus*. The **Javan chevrotain** *Tragulus javanicus* occurs across Java and possibly also on Bali but reported sightings on the latter have not been verified. Standing just 30 cm (12 in) high and weighing about 2 kg (4½ lb) it ranks among the smallest of the ungulates. It is currently assumed that it is the only species of chevrotain on Java, although the possibility that there might be more, or even subspecies, has not been entirely ruled out. None of the *Tragulus* family have the more striking body markings of the other chevrotains, and the body of the Javan chevrotain is an overall reddish-brown. The underparts are white, and there are white markings on the throat and chest. Although it can also be found at lower elevations, it appears to prefer higher ground of over 700 metres above sea level: there it makes tunnels through the thick vegetation to link resting to feeding areas. Javan chevrotains are both hunted and trapped to be kept as pets and are frequently seen in markets both alive and dead; they are especially vulnerable to being hunted at night because of their habit of freezing when caught in a spotlight's beam.

▼ A family group of Javan chevrotain (male on right) pictured at Poznań Zoo, Poland
Photograph: Klaus Rudloff

Distribution	Java Presence uncertain in Bali
IUCN Red List Status 2022	**Data Deficient**, unknown (last formal assessment 2014)
Also known as	Kanchil or lesser mouse deer French *Chevrotain de Java* or *Petit tragul malais*; Indonesian *Kanchil, Sunda Peucang*

DEER SPECIES | TRAGULIDAE – TRAGULUS

Tragulus kanchil

Lesser Oriental chevrotain

ORDER	Artiodactyla
SUBORDER	Ruminantia
INFRAORDER	Tragulina
FAMILY	Tragulidae
SUBFAMILY	Tragulus

Photograph: Klaus Rudloff

Until recently, the *Tragulus* subfamily consisted only of the Javan chevrotain and the relatively larger Greater Oriental chevrotain, but a review in 2004 recognised a further four species which were once thought to fall within these. The **Lesser Oriental chevrotain** *Tragulus kanchil* has a much wider distribution than all of the others and occurs both on the south-east Asian mainland as well as much of Malaysia where its range largely overlaps that of the Greater Oriental chevrotain. It is very similar in colouration to the Javan chevrotain (although on some of the smaller islands there seems to be a tendency towards melanism) but is distinguished from the Greater Oriental chevrotain by its smaller size, standing at about 30 cm (12 in) and weighing 2.5 kg (5½ lb). It has less pronounced facial markings and there are usually only three white throat stripes. There seems to be little interaction between the species where they coexist.

Distribution map – purple: possibly extant.

▼ Lesser Oriental chevrotain, showing throat markings.
Photograph: Alexander F Meyer

Distribution	Brunei, Cambodia, Indonesia, Laos, Malaysia, Myanmar, Singapore, Thailand and Vietnam
	Presence uncertain in China
IUCN Red List Status 2022	**Least Concert**, unknown (last formal assessment 2014)
Also known as	Lesser Malay chevrotain or Lesser mouse deer
	Chinese *Xi-lu*; French *Chevrotain kanchil*, *Petit tragul malais*; Indonesian *Kanchil*

Tragulus napu

Greater Oriental chevrotain

ORDER	Artiodactyla
SUBORDER	Ruminantia
INFRAORDER	Tragulina
FAMILY	Tragulidae
SUBFAMILY	Tragulus

▲ Greater Oriental chevrotain, adult female.
Photograph: Brent Huffman

The **Greater Oriental chevrotain** *Tragulus napu* is found in the forests of the mainland Thai-Malay peninsula, Borneo, Sumatra and many of the smaller islands that surround them. It stands no more than 35 cm (14 in) high and weighs up to 4.5 kg (10 lb). Its pelage is an orangey-brown and it has a slightly grizzled appearance. There are considerable variations in colouration but typically the throat is marked with five white bands, and on the face a dark line extends from the front of the eyes to the nose which, coupled with a dark forehead, gives a distinct masked impression with ginger 'eyebrows'. The underparts, lower surface of the tail and chin are white.

Distribution	Brunei, Indonesia (Kalimantan, Sumatera), Malaysia (Sabah, peninsular Malaysia, Sarawak), Myanmar, Singapore and Thailand
IUCN Red List Status 2022	**Least Concern**, unknown (last formal assessment 2014)
Also known as	Larger Malay chevrotain, Larger mouse deer or Napu
	French *Chevrotain napu* or *Grand tragul malais*; Indonesian *Napu*, *Pelanduc* or *Kantjil*; Malay *Napoh*

Tragulus williamsoni

Williamson's chevrotain

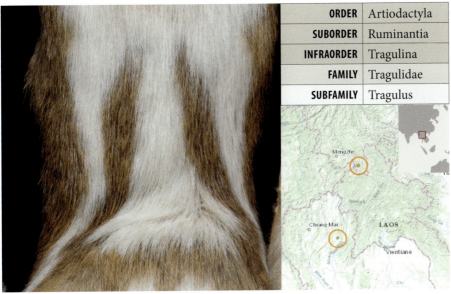

ORDER	Artiodactyla
SUBORDER	Ruminantia
INFRAORDER	Tragulina
FAMILY	Tragulidae
SUBFAMILY	Tragulus

◂ The neck markings of Williamson's chevrotain (head uppermost) from a specimen held by the Natural History Museum, London.
Photograph: Christian Ching. Courtesy of the Trustees of the Natural History Museum

Known only from inadequate records originating in Thailand, and possibly also from Laos and China, our knowledge of **Williamson's chevrotain** *Tragulus williamsoni* has been limited by its description only recently as a separate species from, rather than a subspecies of the Lesser Oriental chevrotain. For over 100 years, its status was based on just a single skull and skin collected in northern Thailand. There is still debate over its true classification, which is probably better regarded as provisional. It is very possible that, unaware of the distinction, the species has been overlooked by researchers when they came across it prior to its recognition and perhaps there may yet be further existing records that have been misidentified as the Lesser Oriental chevrotain. Certainly the two species are very similar, though Williamson's chevrotain is considered to be somewhat larger and more of an orange-brown in colour. For now, its presence is only thought to have been confirmed in northern Thailand and China's Yunnan Province, where it is possible that it may be restricted to evergreen forests at higher elevations, though this is purely speculative. Until more is known about it, the true status of Williamson's chevrotain cannot be fully ascertained across its potential Southeast Asia range.

Distribution	Thailand
	Presence uncertain in China and Laos
IUCN Red List Status 2022	**Data Deficient**, decreasing (last formal assessment 2014)
Also known as	Northern chevrotain
	French *Chevrotain de Williamson*

Tragulus nigricans
Balabac chevrotain

ORDER	Artiodactyla
SUBORDER	Ruminantia
INFRAORDER	Tragulina
FAMILY	Tragulidae
SUBFAMILY	Tragulus

▲ Balabac mouse deer, Avilon Zoo, Philippines.
Photograph: Alexander F Meyer

Distribution map – blue: introduced.

▼ Balabac mouse deer showing chest markings, Chester Zoo, England.
Photograph: Alexander F Meyer

The **Balabac chevrotain** *Tragulus nigricans* is endemic to the islands of Balabac, Bugsuk and Ramos, which represent a total land mass of just a few hundred square kilometres and lie off the southern tip of Mimaropa in the western Philippines. It has also been introduced to the similarly small Apulit and Calauit Islands, on the latter by accident after a few captive animals escaped from their enclosures in a zoo and now appear to be breeding successfully in the wild. Another of the more diminutive tragulids, it is variously described as standing between 18 and 35 cm (7–14 in) tall but is probably unlikely to exceed 30 cm (12 in) at best. It is darkly coloured for a chevrotain with lighter, ginger-brown markings above and below the eyes, on the nape of the neck and similarly coloured legs. The chin, underparts and inner surfaces of the front legs are white, and there are three prominent white stripes on the throat. It is threatened by habitat loss as its environment is increasingly converted for coconut plantations and other purposes, and also by poaching despite being fully protected under Philippine law; its meat is considered a local delicacy. There is also a continuing trade in live animals being captured for local zoos and private collections. The last meaningful population survey was almost 40 years ago, at which point numbers were thought to be stable, but anecdotal reports from hunters have since suggested a decline as capture has become more difficult. More research on this species is urgently needed to ensure that effective conservation measures can be put into place within a range which is severely limited.

Distribution	Philippines (Balabac, Bugsuk and Ramos Islands); introduced on Apulit and Calauit Islands; presence uncertain in Malaysia
IUCN Red List Status 2022	**Endangered**, decreasing (last formal assessment 2014)
Also known as	Balabac mouse deer or Philippine mouse deer French *Chevrotain de Balabac*

Tragulus versicolor
Silver-backed chevrotain

ORDER	Artiodactyla
SUBORDER	Ruminantia
INFRAORDER	Tragulina
FAMILY	Tragulidae
SUBFAMILY	Tragulus

The **Silver-backed chevrotain** *Tragulus versicolor* is very poorly understood because of a lack of meaningful survey work and research, and it is largely known only from a handful of museum specimens. Originally feared to be extinct, it was only in 2018 that the first photographs of a living animal were captured by a remote camera trap in south-eastern Vietnam and more have followed, although a live specimen has yet to be examined properly by a biologist. It is thought to be smaller than the Lesser Oriental chevrotain and to weigh no more than 2 kg (4½ lb). The grey hindquarters of the pelage provide its name, while the head, neck and shoulders are a contrasting orange-brown. Those areas of Vietnam where it is thought to exist are subjected to high levels of indiscriminate hunting, and its habitat may well be subject to degradation and fragmentation. When more data eventually becomes available, it is highly likely that this species will be placed into a higher-risk category by the IUCN, although it is hoped that it will prove to have a wider range than the one currently recognised.

A Silver-backed chevrotain captured on a camera trap in Vietnam.
Photographs: GWC SIE NCNP

Distribution	Vietnam
IUCN Red List Status 2022	**Data Deficient**, decreasing (last formal assessment 2014)
Also known as	Vietnamese mouse deer French *Chevrotain du Vietnam*; Annamese *Nai pa Xuong*

Photograph: David Boston

7 Conclusion

A Future for Deer

A GLANCE AT the cave drawings of ancient man will immediately underline just how important deer were to our ancestors. As a precious natural resource that provided us with food and a wide range of other materials essential for survival, they were revered and appreciated. This tradition is continued by several indigenous cultures even today, but sadly the fortunes of deer have declined elsewhere, being over-exploited, deprived of their habitat or actively persecuted as competitors to human interests.

A glance through the IUCN Red List categories can make for depressing reading. Too many of the deer species are designated as Vulnerable or worse, but do not attract the international concern that reduced numbers of other more iconic species might. Snow leopards, cheetahs and leopards may also be classified as Vulnerable, but there is far less public recognition of the plight of the even more Endangered Eld's deer, Persian fallow, huemul or Balabac chevrotain, let alone the Critically Endangered Bawean deer, or the Père David's deer which is listed as Extinct in the Wild. A full six of the seven musk deer are in the Endangered category, and the remaining one is itself Vulnerable. While many higher profile animal species have been extensively studied, far too many of the deer are still so poorly understood that we have no real idea of their true status. Some are in danger of going the same way as the Schomburgk's deer, abundant on the swampy plains of Thailand just over a century ago but hunted to extinction in the space of just a few decades.

All too often, deer feature only in supporting roles in the wildlife dramas played out on our television screens and we are perhaps guilty of giving them little further thought. Despite this, and although there is no denying that they may present problems in places, for most of us sighting a deer is still a welcome and even a magical encounter. Our children and grandchildren may not be so lucky. Dropping the conservation ball now may lead to irreplaceable, inexcusable losses.

Deer are a vital part of the world's ecosystems, and we would be far worse off without them. Lacking such animals, the predators that depend on them will decline, while their natural levels of grazing and browsing help to ensure that habitats are maintained and regenerated. In many places they offer a real and tangible value to local economies, representing a genuinely renewable resource to a protein-hungry world if properly managed, and there are many examples of how intelligently regulated hunting can actually be beneficial to a species. Where this happens, or in places where control is necessary to keep numbers in check, it must of course be done with understanding, respect and humanity to achieve a realistic balance.

In far too many situations, deer face multiple challenges to their existence, not least because of the habitat loss forced on them by the most invasive and land-hungry species on this planet – mankind itself. Illegal hunting can also be a real problem. Much of it is driven by greed and a lucrative trade in bushmeat and other body parts, often for some deeply spurious reasons, but a greater challenge may exist in those parts of the world that are beset by genuine poverty and associated subsistence hunting.

All wildlife needs somewhere to live, which means that habitats must be preserved with meaningful levels of policing in place to ensure that they remain protected. For some species, far greater research efforts are needed to help us understand the lesser-known deer, their habitat needs and their place within the ecosystem. Only then can appropriate measures be put in place. The essential work of conservation organisations such as the IUCN at an international level, and the many national and regional groups which work tirelessly and often for very little reward, continue to make a big difference. All of those involved in this work, be they professional or amateur, deserve our applause and absolute support.

The challenges faced by deer in the modern world are no more than a reflection of those faced by our other fauna and flora. If humans, as the dominant species on this planet, can collectively learn to celebrate our wildlife and treat it with the respect it needs and deserves, it will continue to thrive in the years to come. It is surely now time for the people of all nations to be encouraged to respect the natural world rather than to exploit it. We understand the need for conservation so much more comprehensively than our forebears did, yet we have still seen too many species disappear within living memory. There can be no excuse for further losses. It is a simple but compelling truth that the future of the world's wildlife rests in our hands.

Photograph: Brent Huffman

Photograph: Dave Ranck

Glossary of Terms

Further Resources

Glossary of Terms

The terminology associated with deer can occasionally be confusing; these are some of the more commonly used expressions

Albinism A condition leading to a pale, *skewbald*, *piebald* or white coat caused by under-production of *melanin*.

Albino An animal with extreme *albinism*, characterised by a pure white coat, pink skin, and pink or blue irises of the eyes.

Antler Bone growths on the top of a deer's head which are cast and regrown annually. They are typically produced by adult male deer of the *Cervidae* except the Chinese water deer, though only by the female reindeer. They are not present on any of the musk deer or the chevrotains.

Beam The main stem of a deer's *antler*.

Biome A naturally occurring and distinct community of plants and animals which share a common environment. A biome can encompass a variety of habitats. Some examples include tundra, tropical rainforest, montane forest and arid desert.

Bole scoring The act of a male deer scoring the bark of trees with his *brow* tines; most usually associated with sika deer.

Boxing When deer rear up on their hind feet to flail at each other with their forefeet. Done by male deer still in *velvet*, and also by female deer.

Brow The forward-pointing lower *tine* of a deer's *antlers*.

Browsing Feeding on the leaves, shoots or twigs of a tree or shrub, usually selectively, as opposed to *grazing* on plant material at ground level.

Buck The adult male of some species of deer.

Bull A male caribou, reindeer, elk or moose.

Calf A young deer of some species which is still dependent on its mother. *See also* fawn or kid.

Carnivore An animal that feeds primarily on the meat of other animals.

Cast/casting When a deer sheds its *antlers*.

Cathemeral Feeding at irregular intervals throughout the day and night.

Caudal patch Rump patch.

Clade A group of organisms which share a common ancestor; they might be thought of as sitting close together on the same branch of the tree of life.

Cleaves The two sides of the split hoof of an even-toed *ungulate*.

Cohort The proportion of a population born in a specific year.

Coppice Woodland cut back to encourage new growth for use as firewood, timber or other purposes.

GLOSSARY OF TERMS

Coronet	The base of an *antler* where it joins the *pedicle*.	**Flehmen**	A behavioural response in which some male mammals react to an interesting smell, particularly that of a female in *oestrus*, in which the upper lip is curled up and the head raised, often with nostrils closed and inhaling.
Couch	A deer's bedding place.		
Cow	A female caribou, reindeer, elk or moose.		
Crepuscular	Active during the hours of twilight.		
Crotties	Groups of deer droppings.	**FMD**	Foot and Mouth Disease.
Cud	Food regurgitated by *ruminants* from their first stomach to be chewed at leisure.	**Fray/fraying**	The act or a male deer rubbing its *antlers* against a shrub or tree, usually to mark territory or to remove *velvet*.
Cull	The act of removing surplus deer from a population, usually to balance age and sex groups, to maintain it in proportion to the available habitat, or to meet other set management objectives.	**Frugivore**	An animal that feeds primarily on fruit.
		Grazing	Feeding on grasses, sedges, herbs or lichens that grow at ground level, as opposed to *browsing* on plant material found above the ground.
Dimorphism (sexual)	Where the sexes of the same species exhibit different physical characteristics in size or appearance, in addition to the differences in the sexual organs.	**Hard horn, In**	When a deer has removed the *velvet* from its newly grown *antlers*.
		Herbivore	An animal that feeds primarily on plants.
		Hind	The female of some species of deer.
Diurnal	Active during the day.	**Home range**	The area that an animal habitually travels within during its daily activities; not to be confused with *territory*.
Doe	The female of some species of deer.		
Dorsal tine	A *tine* growing from the back of an *antler*.		
DSG	Deer Specialist Group, a sub-group of the *IUCN SSC*.	**Interdigital gland**	A scent gland situated between the *cleaves* of the hooves.
		IUCN	The International Union for Conservation of Nature.
Fawn	A young deer of some species which is still dependent in its mother. ***See also*** *calf* and *kid*.	**Leucism/leucistic**	Paler than usual colouration caused by under-production of *melanin* (***see*** *albinism*).
Fewmet	A deer dropping.		

Kid	A young deer, more specifically roe, which is still dependent in its mother. *See also* calf and *fawn*.	**Polygamous**	Typically having more than one mate.
Melanin	The chemical responsible for dark pigmentation in animals.	**Polymorphism**	Where organisms occur in several different forms.
Monogamous	Having only one mate at a time.	**Preorbital gland**	A scent gland located just forward of the eye, most associated with territorial marking. Sometimes referred to as the *suborbital gland*.
Morphology	The form and structure of an organism (also the branch of biology that studies such forms and structures).	**Pronking**	A characteristic form of locomotion among some deer and antelope species, in which all four feet leave the ground together as the animal bounces away. Also known as *stotting*.
Nocturnal	Active at night.		
Oestrus	The time during which a female animal is fertile and able to conceive.	**Red List**	The *IUCN* Red List of Threatened Species is a comprehensive list of all animal and plant species around the world which categorises their conservation status.
Omnivore	An animal that feeds on a variety of material of both plant and animal origin.		
		Rumen	The first stomach of a *ruminant*.
Palmation	The spread and flattened surface of the *antlers* of some deer species, such as the fallow or moose.	**Ruminant**	Any of the even-toed *ungulates* that chews the cud regurgitated from its *rumen*.
Pearling	The rough surface on the beam of an *antler*.	**Rut**	The mating season of certain mammals (including deer), most usually *ruminants* but also others.
Pedicle	The bony protrusion on the top of a deer's skull from which the *antler* grows.	**Shed/shedding**	The act of removing *velvet* from newly-grown *antlers*.
Pelage	The fur, hair or wool coat of a mammal that covers its skin.	**Skewbald**	An animal with a coat coloured with brown and white patches.
Piebald	An animal with a coat coloured with black and white patches.	**Slot**	The footprint of a deer.
Poaching	The illegal hunting of game.	**Snare**	A trap, often set illegally and widely employed as a *poaching* method, that uses a loop of wire or other material to catch and restrain a hunted animal around the neck, foot or body.
Polyestrous	Having more than one period of *oestrus* during a year.		

SSC	The Species Survival Commission of the *IUCN*. A worldwide network of volunteer experts, Its major role is to provide science-based information which is fed into the Red List of Threatened Species to drive conservation policy and activities.
Stag	The adult male of some species of deer.
Stotting	*See pronking.*
Suborbital gland	*See preorbital gland.*
Territory	A defined area of habitat that an animal will attempt to claim the exclusive use of, usually for breeding purposes.
Thrash/thrashing	The act of a male deer beating trees or bushes with his *antlers*.
Tine	A branch of growth from an *antler*.
Tush	A downward-pointing tuft of hair at the base of the rump patch of a roe doe. Also an archaic term for the canine tooth of a red deer.
Ungulate	One of a wide and diverse group of hooved quadrupeds which includes odd-toed ungulates such as horses, rhinoceroses and tapirs, and even-toed ungulates typified by deer, cattle, sheep, pigs, camels, and hippopotami. Cetaceans such as whales also technically belong to the latter category even though they do not have hooves.
Velvet	A vascular, sensitive layer covered with hair that protects and nourishes the growing *antler*.
Venison	Specifically the meat of deer, but also commonly used more widely to describe that of other game animals such as antelope.
Vomeronasal organ	An olfactory sense organ in the nasal cavity of certain amphibians, reptiles and mammals (including deer) which detects pheromones and other chemical compounds. Also known as the Jacobson's organ.
Yearling	A young deer of either sex in its first year of life.
Yard	A sheltered place where deer gather in winter to conserve energy (applies more specifically to white-tailed deer).
Yeld	A mature female deer that has not produced offspring but is not necessarily barren.

Further Resources

*There is a multitude of further resources available to anyone who wants to know more about deer, and the list below contains just a few personal recommendations. Some offer a predominantly UK perspective but others have a more international aspect. Some of the books may be out of print but can still be sourced by specialist booksellers such as Coch-y-Bonddu Books in the UK (**www.anglebooks.com**) or Internet sources such as Amazon.*

Books

Geist, Valerius **Deer of the World**
(Swan Hill Press 1999)
A detailed and scholarly examination of deer evolution and behaviour.

Prior, Richard **Deer Watch**
(Swan Hill Press 2007)
An overview of the origins, history and ecology of British deer.

Putman, Rory **The Natural History of Deer**
(Christopher Helm 1988)
A detailed academic overview of deer origins, behaviour and natural history by one of our foremost experts. Out of print but well worth searching for.

Whitehead, G.K. **Deer of the World**
(Constable 1972)
Although our understanding of deer classifications have changed considerably in the 50 years since this was published, it remains an otherwise accurate, informative and thoroughly researched book with important historical insights to the presence, human transplantation and use of deer.

Whitehead, G.K. **The Whitehead Encyclopedia of Deer**
(Swan Hill Press 1993)
An extensive and accessible work covering hunting, biology, history and a host of other aspects relating to deer, this is probably the ultimate in reference material for any deer *aficionado*. For a long time unavailable, but reprinted in 2008 by popular demand.

McShea, J.M. et al **The Science of Overabundance**
(Smithsonian Institution 1997)
An analysis of deer ecology and population management by a number of leading ungulate biologists. Although focusing heavily on white-tailed deer in the USA, this collection of papers has a wider relevance to deer management and is essential reading for anyone with an academic interest in the subject.

Coles, Charles **Gardens and Deer**
(Swan Hill Press 1997)
A clearly written and straightforward guide to deer damage limitation in gardens.

Prior, Richard **Trees & Deer** (Swan Hill Press 1994)
A comprehensive guide to tackling the problems that deer pose in forest, field and garden.

Online resources

Some websites may have greater longevity than others, but those below are active at the time of writing (2022):

Animal Diversity Web
Fact sheets for most deer species, with useful bibliographies included for further research.
www.animaldiversity.org

BioLib
A comprehensive international encyclopedia of plants, fungi and animals containing taxonomies, illustrations, literature and further information. Hosted in Czech but full translation to English available.
www.biolib.cz

FURTHER RESOURCES

The British Deer Society
An informative website that includes a searchable database of zoos, parks and other collections in the United Kingdom that contain deer and are open to the public.
www.bds.org.uk

Encyclopedia of Life
A digital collection of data, media and articles.
www.eol.org

iNaturalist
A social network for naturalists which allows sightings, photographs etc to be freely shared and discussed.
www.inaturalist.org

IUCN Red List
Comprehensive and authoritative listings of all world species of fauna and flora, with an extensive web page for each covering conservation status, distribution (with map), taxonomy, assessment information, population, habitat and ecology, threats, use and trade, conservation actions already in place or needed, and a bibliography.
www.iucnredlist.org

List of Zoos
An online index of zoos around the world.
www.listofzoos.com

Ultimate Ungulate
Reliable information and pictures of the world's ungulate species.
www.ultimateungulate.com

Zootierliste
A huge database, with English and German search options, of the current and former vertebrate inventories of zoos and other public collections across Europe, Russia and further afield. It includes multiple images of most of the deer species.
www.zootierliste.de

There are many sources of Internet information regarding individual species; using the scientific name in the search engine is often more likely to direct you towards relevant and accurate material. Care should always be taken to use reputable sources; some can be unreliable, and peer-reviewed academic papers and similar documents tend to be the most trustworthy.

Photograph: Alexander F Meyer

Index

INDEX

In this index, page references in italics identify where the main illustrations for a particular animal or subject appear.

Acapulco white-tailed deer 129
Alashan wapiti 173
Alaskan moose 81
Alces alces alces
　see Eurasian elk
Alces alces americana
　see American moose
Alces alces andersoni
　see Canadian moose
Alces alces buturlini
　see Chukotka elk
Alces alces cameloides
　see Amur elk
Alces alces caucasicus
　see Caucasian elk
Alces alces gigas see Alaskan moose
Alces alces pfizenmayeri
　see Yakutia elk
Alces alces shirasi see Shiras moose
Alpine musk deer 276, 279, *279*
Altai wapiti 173, 174, 176
Amazonian brown brocket 109, 112, *114*, 116
　antlers 115
　diet 115
　dimensions 115
　distribution 114, 115
　habitat 115
　recognition features 115
　rut and birthing 115
American moose 81
Amur elk 81
Andean deer *see* Taruca
Andean white-tailed deer 129
Anhui musk deer 276, 277, *277*

Annamite muntjac 239, 244
Anthrax 69
Antlers 26–8, 38
Artiodactyla 16–17, 19, 52
Atlas deer *see* Barbary red deer
Avery Island white-tailed deer 129
Axis axis see Chital
Axis axis axis see Indian chital
Axis axis ceylonensis
　see Ceylon axis
Axis calamianensis
　see Calamian deer
Axis deer *see* Chital
Axis kuhlii see Bawean deer
Axis porcinus see Hog deer
Axis porcinus annamiticus
　see Hog deer
Axis porcinus porcinus
　see Hog deer

Bactrian deer *184*, 185, *185*, 187
Balabac chevrotain 294, *294*
Barasingha 20, 22, 60, 246–50, *246*, *247*, 248
　antlers 250
　birthing 250
　diet 249
　dimensions 249
　distribution 246, 249
　habitat 248, 249
　population
　recognition features 249
　rut 250
Barbary red deer 21, 178, 179, *180*
Barbary stag *see* Barbary red deer

Barren ground caribou 147
Bawean deer 20, 157, 160–1, *160*, *161*
　antlers 162
　birthing 162
　diet 162
　dimensions 162
　distribution 160, 161
　habitat 162
　population 161
　recognition features 162
　rut 162
Bedford's deer
　see Manchurian wapiti
Bent-nose syndrome
　see Campylognathie
Black muntjac 214–216, *214*, *215*
　antlers 214, 216
　diet 216
　dimensions 216
　distribution 214, 215, 216
　habitat 216
　recognition features 216
Black musk deer 276, 281, *281*
Blackbeard Island white-tailed deer 129
Back-tailed deer 20
Blastocerus dichotomus
　see marsh deer
Boach (or bogi) *see* Altai wapiti
Boreal woodland caribou
　see woodland caribou
Bornean sambar 270
Bornean yellow muntjac 211–213, *211*, *212*
　antlers 213
　diet 213

　dimensions 213
　distribution 211, 213
　habitat 211–212, 213
　recognition features 213
Borrelia bacteria 37
Bovine tuberculosis 37, 69
Brazilian dwarf brocket *44*, 50–52, 120
Brocket deer 20, 21, 27, 36
Bulls Island white-tailed deer 129
Busk reindeer 147

Calamian deer 20, 157–158 *157*, *158*, 160
　antlers 159
　birthing 159
　diet 159
　distribution 158, 159
　dimensions 159
　habitat 158, 159
　recognition features 159
　rut 159
California mule deer 124, *125*,
Campylognathie 39
Canadian moose 81
Canadian wapiti
　see Roosevelt's elk
Capreolus capreolus
　see European roe deer
Capreolus capreolus capreolus see European roe deer
Capreolus capreolus caucasicus see European roe deer
Capreolus capreolus coxi
　see European roe deer
Capreolus capreolus garganta see European

INDEX

roe deer
Capreolus capreolus italicus
see European roe deer
Capreolus pygargus pygargus
see Siberian roe deer
Capreolus tianschanicus
see Siberian roe deer
Caribou *see* Reindeer
Carmen Mountain white-
tailed deer 129
Caspian red deer 179, *180*
Cedros Island deer 124, 126
Central American red
brocket 122, *122*
Cervidae 16, 19, 22, 28, 32
Cervus canadensis
see wapiti
*Cervus canadensis
alashanicus* see Alashan
wapiti
*Cervus canadensis
canadensis* see North
American elk
Cervus canadensis macneilli
see Sichuan deer
Cervus canadensis nannodes
see Tule elk
Cervus canadensis roosevelti
see Roosevelt's elk
Cervus canadensis sibiricus
see Altai wapiti
Cervus canadensis wallichii
see Shou deer
*Cervus canadensis
xanthopygus* see
Manchurian wapiti
Cervus elaphus barbarus
see Barbary red deer
Cervus elaphus brauneri
see Crimean red deer
Cervus elaphus corsicanus
see Corsican red deer
Cervus elaphus elaphus
see Red deer
Cervus elaphus italicus
see Mesola red deer
Cervus elaphus maral
see Caspian red deer
Cervus elaphus montanus
see Carpathian red deer
Cervus hanglu see Tarim
red deer
Cervus hanglu hanglu
see Kashmir stag

Cervus hanglu yarkandensis
see Yarkand deer
Cervus nippon see Sika
Cervus nippon aplodontus
see North Honshu sika
Cervus nippon grassianus
see Shansi sika
Cervus nippon hortulorum
see Dybowski's sika
Cervus nippon keramae
see Ryuku sika
Cervus nippon kopschi
see South China sika
Cervus nippon mandarinus
see North China sika
Cervus nippon mantchuricus
see Manchurian sika
Cervus nippon nippon
see Japanese sika
Cervus nippon pseudaxis
see Vietnamese sika
Cervus nippon pulchellus
see Tsushima sika
Cervus nippon sichuanicus
see Sichuan sika
Cervus nippon taiouanus
see Formosan sika
Cervus nippon yesoensis
see Hokkaido sika
Chevrotains 16, 17, 18, 19,
26, 285–6
rumination 29
scent glands 32
teeth 30
Ceylon axis deer 153
Chital 20, 22, 35, *152–5*,
antlers 152, 156
birthing 156
diet 153–4, 156
dimensions 156
distribution 152, 155
habitat 156
population 155
recognition features 156
rut 156
Chukotka elk 81
Chiriqui white-tailed deer
129
Chronic Wasting Disease 37
Chukotka elk 81, 82
Cedros Island deer 124
Chiapas white-tailed deer
129
Coiba Island white-tailed

deer 129
Colombian mule deer *125*
Columbian black-tailed
deer 124
Columbian white-tailed
deer 128, 129
communication 48–50
Corsican red deer 179
Coue's white-tailed deer
129, *130*
Crimean red deer 179
Curaçao white-tailed deer
129
Cuvier, Georges 248

Dakota white-tailed deer
129
Dama dama see Fallow
deer
David, Père Armand 208
Dawson's caribou
see Queen Charlotte
Islands caribou
Desert mule deer 124
Dicroceros furcatus 18
Diet 44–5
Disease 37–9
Domestication 65–7
Duvaucel, Alfred 248
Dwarf elk *see* Tule elk
Dwarf red brocket 122, *122*
Dybowski's sika 189, *189*,
190

East Greenland caribou 147
Eastern barasingha 248–9,
248
Eastern moose
see American moose
Echidnas 16
Elaphodus cephalophus
see Tufted deer
*Elaphodus cephalophus
ichangensis* see Ichang
tufted deer
*Elaphodus cephalophus
michianus* see Michie's
tufted deer
Elaphurus davidianus
see Père David's deer
Eld, Lieutenant Percy 251
Eld's deer 20, 22, 251–5,
251, 252, 253, 254
antlers 255

birthing 255
diet 255
dimensions 255
distribution 251, 254
habitat 255
recognition features 254
rut 255
Elk 20
Causasian 83
European 65
see also Moose *and*
Wapiti
Eumeryx 18, 19
Eurasian elk 81, 83, *83*
see also Moose
European elk 81
European roe deer *90–3*
antlers 94
dimensions 94
habitat 90–1, 94
mating 91–2
population 91
recognition features 94

Fallow deer 19, 20, 22, 23,
26, 27, *27*, 195–9, *195,
196, 197*
antlers 199
birthing 199
diet 198
dimensions 198
distribution 195, 198
habitat 198
hybridisation 36
management 62, 64, *64*,
polydactylism 38
recognition features 198
rut 199
swimming 44
teeth 30
Fea's muntjac 217–219, *217,
218*
antlers 219
birthing 219
diet 219
dimensions 219
distribution 217, 219
habitat 219
recognition features 219
rut 219
Fea, Leonardo 217
Federal Aid in Wildlife
Restoration Act (USA)
131

Feeding (*see also* domestication) 68–9
Finnish forest reindeer 147, *148*
Florida coastal white-tailed deer 129
Florida Key white-tailed deer 128, 129, *130*, 131, *131*
Florida white-tailed deer 129
Food *see* Diet
Foot and mouth disease 37
Forest musk deer 276, 278, *278*
Formosan sambar 270
Formosan sika 190, *192*

Giant elk *see* Megaloceros giganteus
Giant muntjac 236–8, *236*, *237*
 antlers 238
 birthing 238
 diet 238
 dimensions 238
 distribution 236, 238
 habitat 237, 238
 recognition features 238
 rut 238
Gongshan muntjac 22, 239, 240–241, *240*, *241*
Grants caribou 147
Greater Oriental chevrotain 292, *292*
Grey brocket *112*, 116
 antlers 113
 birthing 113
 diet 113
 dimensions 113
 distribution 112, 113
 habitat 113
 recognition features 113

Habitats 42
Hainan sambar 270
Hard-ground barasingha *see* Southern barasingha
Hilton Head Island white-tailed deer 129
Himalayan musk deer 276, 282, *282*
Hippocamelus antisensis *see* Taruca

Hippocamelus bisulcus *see* Huemul
Hog deer 20, 35, 157, 160, 163–6, *163*, *164*, *165*, *166*
 antlers 163, 167
 birthing 167
 diet 167
 dimensions 167
 distribution 163, 165, 166
 habitat 167
 recognition features 167
 rut 167
Hokkaido sika 189, *191*, 194
Huemul *see* Patagonian huemul
Hummelism 39, 181
Hunting Island white-tailed deer 129
Hybridisation 35
Hydropotes inermis *see* Water deer
Hydropotes inermis argyropus *see* Korean water deer
Hydropotes inermis inermis *see* Chinese water deer
Hyemoschus aquaticus *see* Water chevrotain
Hypertragulus calcaratus 18

Ichang tufted deer 205
Immunocontraception 63
Indian chital 152
Indian sambar *269*, 270, *270*
Indian spotted chevrotain 288, *288*
International Union for Conservation of Nature (IUCN) 74–5
Inyo mule deer 124
Irish Elk *see* Megaloceros giganteus
Isubra/Izubra *see* Manchurian wapiti
Italian roe deer *91*
IUCN *see* International Union for Conservation of Nature

Jacobson's organ *see* Vomeronasal organ
Japanese sika 189, *190*, *191*, 194

Javan chevrotain 285, 290, *290*
Javan deer 20, 265–268, *265*, *266*, *267*
 antlers 268
 birthing 268
 diet 268
 dimensions 268
 distribution 265, 267
 habitat 268
 recognition features 267
 rut 268

Kamchatkan reindeer 147
Kansas white-tailed deer 129
Kansu deer *see* Sichuan deer
Kashmir musk deer 276, 280, *280*
Kashmir stag 184, *184*, 186, 187
Kerama sika *see* Ryukyu sika
Kopschi sika *see* South China sika

Labrador caribou 147
Leaf muntjac 223–5, *223*, *224*
 antlers 225
 birthing 225
 diet 225
 dimensions 225
 distribution 223–4, 225
 habitat 225
 recognition features 225
 rut 225
Lesser Oriental chevrotain 291, *291*
Lyme disease 37, 69–70, *70*

MacNeill's deer *see* Sichuan deer
Malayan sambar *271*
Mammals, definition 16
Manchurian sika 189, *192*, 194
Manchurian wapiti 173, 176
Manipuri brow-antlered deer 251, 253
Maral *see* Caspian red deer
Margarita Island white-tailed deer 129

Marsh deer 20, 86–9, *86*, *87*, 88
 antlers 89
 birthing 89
 diet 89
 dimensions 89
 distribution 86, 88
 habitat 89
 recognition features 86
 rut 89
Mastreani deer *see* Muntjac
Mazama americana *see* Red brocket
Mazama bororo *see* Small red brocket
Mazama bricenii *see* Mérida brocket
Mazama chunyi *see* Peruvian dwarf brocket
Mazama gouazoubira *see* Grey brocket
Mazama nana *see* Brazilian dwarf brocket
Mazama nemorivaga *see* Amazonian brown brocket
Mazama pandora *see* Yucatan brown brocket
Mazama rufina *see* Dwarf red brocket
Mazama temama *see* Central American red brocket
Megaloceros giganteus 18–19
Menil fallow deer *195*, *197*, 198
Mérida brocket 118, *118*
Mesola red deer 179
Mexican lowland white-tailed deer 129
Mexican white-tailed deer 129
Michie's tufted deer 206, *206*
Miquilhuan white-tailed deer 129
Moose 20, 22, 23, 27, *46*, 80–1, *80–1*, 84
 Alaskan 81, 82, *82*
 birthing 52
 Chronic Wasting Disease 37

INDEX

domestication 65
gestation period 51
hybridisation 36
pelage 34
Shiras 82
speed 42
swimming 44, 82–3
mortality 55–7
Moschidae see Musk deer
Moschiola indica see Indian spotted chevrotain
Moschiola kathygre see Yellow-striped chevrotain
Moschiola meminna see White-spotted chevrotain
Moschus anhuiensis see Anhui musk deer
Moschus berezovskii see Forest musk deer
Moschus chrysogaster see Alpine musk deer
Moschus cupreus see Kashmir musk deer
Moschus fuscus see Black musk deer
Moschus leucogaster see Himalayan musk deer
Moschus moschus arcticus see Siberian musk deer
Moschus moschus moschiferus see Siberian musk deer
Moschus moschus sachalinensis see Siberian musk deer
Moschus moschus turovi see Siberian musk deer
Mountain reindeer 129, 147, *148*
Mountain woodland caribou *see* Woodland caribou
Mouse deer *see* Chevrotains
Mule deer 20, 21, 35, 52, *123*, *124*
    antlers 127
    birthing 127
    diet 127
    dimensions 126
    distribution 123, 125
    gait 123

habitat 127
population 126
rut 127
recognition features 126
Muntiacus atherodes see Bornean yellow muntjac
Muntiacus crinifrons see Black muntjac
Muntiacus feae see Fea's muntjac
Muntiacus gongshanensis see Gongshan muntjac
Muntiacus montanus see Sumatran muntjac
Muntiacus muntjak see Southern red muntjac
Muntiacus puhoatensis see Puhoat muntjac
Muntiacus putaoensis see Leaf muntjac
Muntiacus reevesi see Reeves' muntjac
Muntiacus reevesi jiangkouensis see Reeves' muntjac
Muntiacus reevesi micrurus see Reeves' muntjac
Muntiacus reevesi sinensis see Reeves' muntjac
Muntiacus rooseveltorum see Roosevelts' muntjac
Muntiacus truongsonensis see Annamite muntjac
Muntiacus vaginalis see Northern red muntjac
Muntiacus vuquangensis see Giant muntjac
Muntjac 19, 20, 21, 22, 23
    gestation period 52
    scent glands 46
    management 64
Musk deer 19, 20, 26, *274*, 274–6
    breeding 51
    disease 37
    distribution 274
    poaching 61
    rumination 29
    scent glands 32
    sexual dimorphism 35
    swimming 44
    teeth 30

Natality 54–5
Newfoundland caribou 147
Nicaraguan white-tailed deer 129, *130*
North American elk *see* Wapiti
North China sika 189
North Honshu sika 189
Northern pudu *137, 138*
    antlers 139
    birthing 139
    diet 139
    dimensions 137, 139
    distribution 138
    habitat 137
    recognition features 139
    teeth and tusks 138
Northern red muntjac 220, 231–5, *231, 232, 233, 234*
    antlers 232, 235
    birthing 235
    diet 139
    dimensions 235
    distribution 231–2, 234
    evolution 232
    habitat 235
    recognition features 235
    rut 233, 235
Northern woodland white-tailed deer 129, *130*
Northwestern white-tailed deer 129
Norwegian reindeer *see* Mountain reindeer
Novaya Zemlya reindeer 147

Oaxaca white-tailed deer 129
Odocoileus hemionus californicus see California mule deer
Odocoileus hemionus cerrosensis see Cedros Island deer
Odocoileus hemionus columbianus see Columbian black-tailed deer
Odocoileus hemionus crooki see Desert mule deer
Odocoileus hemionus fuliginatus see Southern mule deer

Odocoileus hemionus hemionus see Rocky Mountain mule deer
Odocoileus hemionus inyoensis see Inyo mule deer
Odocoileus hemionus peninsulae see Peninsula mule deer
Odocoileus hemionus sheldoni see Tiburon Island mule deer
Odocoileus hemionus sitkensis see Sitka black-tailed deer
Odocoileus virginianus see White-tailed deer
Odocoileus virginianus acapulcensis see Acapulco white-tailed deer
Odocoileus virginianus borealis see Northern woodland white-tailed deer
Odocoileus virginianus cariacou see Venado
Odocoileus virginianus carminis see Carmen Mountain white-tailed deer
Odocoileus virginianus chiriquensis see Chiriqui white-tailed deer
Odocoileus virginianus clavium see Florida Key white-tailed deer
Odocoileus virginianus couesi see Coues white-tailed deer
Odocoileus virginianus curassavicus see Curaçao white-tailed deer
Odocoileus virginianus dacotensis see Dakota white-tailed deer
Odocoileus virginianus goudotii see Venado
Odocoileus virginianus gymnotis see South American white-tailed deer
Odocoileus virginianus hiltonensis see Hilton

Head Island white-tailed deer
Odocoileus virginianus leucurus see Columbian white-tailed deer
Odocoileus virginianus mcilhennyi see Avery Island white-tailed deer
Odocoileus virginianus macrourus see Kansas white-tailed deer
Odocoileus virginianus margaritae see Margarita Island white-tailed deer
Odocoileus virginianus mexicanus see Mexican white-tailed deer
Odocoileus virginianus miquihuanensis see Miquilhuan white-tailed deer
Odocoileus virginianus nelsoni see Chiapas white-tailed deer
Odocoileus virginianus nemoralis see Nicaraguan white-tailed deer
Odocoileus virginianus nigribarbis see Blackbeard Island white-tailed deer
Odocoileus virginianus oaxacensis see Oaxaca white-tailed deer
Odocoileus virginianus ochrourus see Northwestern or Rocky Mountain white-tailed deer
Odocoileus virginianus osceola see Florida coastal white-tailed deer
Odocoileus virginianus peruvianus see Andean white-tailed deer
Odocoileus virginianus rothschildi see Coiba Island white-tailed deer
Odocoileus virginianus seminolus see Florida white-tailed deer
Odocoileus virginianus sinaloae see Sinaloa white-tailed deer
Odocoileus virginianus taurinsulae see Bulls Island white-tailed deer
Odocoileus virginianus texanus see Texas white-tailed deer
Odocoileus virginianus thomasi see Mexican lowland white-tailed deer
Odocoileus virginianus toltecus see Rain forest white-tailed deer
Odocoileus virginianus tropicalis see Venado
Odocoileus virginianus ustus see Venado
Odocoileus virginianus venatorius see Hunting Island white-tailed deer
Odocoileus virginianus veraecrucis see Northern Veracruz white-tailed deer
Odocoileus virginianus virginiana see Virginia white-tailed deer
Odocoileus virginianus yucatanensis see Yucatan white-tailed deer
Okhotsk reindeer *see* Kamchatkan reindeer
Osborn's caribou 147
Ozotoceros bezoarticus arerunguaensis see Pampas deer
Ozotoceros bezoarticus bezoarticus see Pampas deer
Ozotoceros bezoarticus celer see Pampas deer
Ozotoceros bezoarticus leucogaster see Pampas deer
Ozotoceros bezoarticus uruguayensis see Pampas deer

Palaeomerycidae 18
Pampas deer 20, 22, *134, 135*
  antlers 136
  birthing 136
  diet 136
  dimensions 136
  distribution 134, 135
  habitat 136
  population 135
  recognition features 136
  rut 136
Patagonian huemul *101, 102, 103*
  antlers 104
  birthing 103, 104
  diet 104
  dimensions 104
  distribution 101, 104
  habitat 101–2, 104
  population 103
  recognition features 104
Peary caribou 147
Pelage 33–5
Peninsula mule deer 124, 126
Père David's deer 20, 22, 23, *23*, 180, 208–210, *208*,
  antlers 28, 210
  birthing 210
  diet 210
  dimensions 210
  distribution 208, 210
  extinction 208
  habitat 209
  hybridisation 35
  recognition features 210
  rut 210
Perissodactyla 16
Persian fallow deer 200–3, *200, 201, 202*
  antlers 203
  birthing 203
  diet 203
  dimensions 203
  distribution 201, 203
  habitat 203
  recognition features 203
Peruvian dwarf brocket *119*
  appearance 119
  distribution 119
Philippine sambar 20, 157, 262–264, *262, 263*
  antlers 264
  birthing 264
  diet 264
  dimensions 264
  distribution 262, 263
  habitat 264
  recognition features 264
  rut 264
Poaching 61–2
Polydactylism 38, *38*
Porcupine caribou *see* Grants caribou
Predators *see* Mortality
Pudu 20
Pudu mephistophiles see Northern pudu
Pudu puda see Southern pudu
Puhoat muntjac 239, 244

Queen Charlotte Island caribou 147

Rabinowitz, Alan 223
Rabinowitz, Selina 223
Rain forest white-tailed deer 129
Rangifer tarandus buskensis see Busk reindeer
Rangifer tarandus caboti see Labrador caribou
Rangifer tarandus caribou see Woodland caribou
Rangifer tarandus dawsoni see Queen Charlotte Islands caribou
Rangifer tarandus eogroenlandicus see East Greenland caribou
Rangifer tarandus finnicus see Finnish forest reindeer
Rangifer tarandus granti see Grants caribou
Rangifer tarandus groenlandicus see Barren ground caribou
Rangifer tarandus osborni see Osborn's caribou
Rangifer tarandus Pearsoni see Novaya Zemlya reindeer
Rangifer tarandus pearyi see Peary caribou
Rangifer tarandus phylarchus see Kamchatkan reindeer
Rangifer tarandus platyrhynchus see Svalbard reindeer

INDEX

Rangifer tarandus sibiricus
  see Siberian tundra
  reindeer
Rangifer tarandus tarandus
  see Mountain reindeer
Rangifer tarandus
  terraenovae
  see Newfoundland
  caribou
Rangifer tarandus valentinae
  see Siberian forest
  reindeer
Red brocket 109, *110*, 112
  antlers 111
  birthing 111
  diet 111
  distribution 109, 110
  dimensions 110–111
  habitat 111
  recognition features 110
  rut 111
  taxonomy 109
Red deer 20, 21, 22, 23, *26*, 178–182, *178, 179, 180, 181,*
  antlers 28, *38*, 181, 183
  birthing 43, 183
  diet 45, 182
  dimensions 182
  distribution 178, 182
  domestication 65, *66*, 148–9, 178
  gestation period 51
  habitat 149, 182
  hybridisation 35–6, *36*
  migration 148
  mortality 57
  recognition features 182
  rut 183
  speed 43
  swimming 44
Reeves, John Russell 226
Reeves' muntjac 107, 221, 226–30, *226, 227, 228, 229*
  antlers 230
  barking 227
  birthing 227
  diet 230
  distribution 226, 229
  dimensions 230
  habitat 230
  recognition features 230
  rut 230

tusks 226
Reindeer 20, 26, *144, 145, 146, 148, 149*
  antlers 28, 48, 146, 151
  birthing 53
  Chronic Wasting Disease 37
  diet 45, 151
  dimensions 144–5, 150–1
  distribution 144, 150
  domestication 65, *65*, 67
  habitat and movement 42–3, *42*, 145–6, 151
  recognition features 150
  rut 151
  sexual dimorphism 35, 150
  swimming 43–4, 145
Relationships 46–8
Rocky Mountain mule deer 124, 126, 127
Rocky Mountain white-tailed deer
  see Northwestern white-tailed deer
Roe deer 19, 29, 22, 23, *26, 68,* 93
  antlers 28, 39, 94
  breeding 52, 55, 94
  diet 94
  dimensions 94
  disease 37, *39*
  domestication 67
  habitat 94
  hybridisation 36
  management 62
  recognition features 94
  swimming 44
  teeth 30, *30*, 93
Roosevelt, Kermit 242
Roosevelt, Theodore 242
Roosevelt's elk 173
Roosevelts' muntjac 239, 242–3, *242,* 243
Rucervus duvaucelii
  see Barasingha
Rucervus duvaucelii
  branderi see Southern barasingha
Rucervus duvaucelii
  duvaucelii see Western barasingha
Rucervus duvaucelii

ranjitsinhi see Eastern barasingha
Rucervus eldii eldii
  see Manipuri brow-antlered deer
Rucervus eldii siamensis
  see Thai brow-antlered deer
Rucervus eldii thamin
  see Thamin deer
Rumination 28–30
Rusa alfredi see Visayan spotted deer
Rusa marianna
  see Philippine sambar
Rusa marianna barandana
  see Philippine sambar
Rusa marianna nigella
  see Philippine sambar
Rusa marianna marianna
  see Philippine sambar
Rusa timorensis see Javan deer
Rusa unicolor see Sambar
Rusa unicolor brookei see Bornean sambar
Rusa unicolor cambojensis
  see Southeast Asian sambar
Rusa unicolor dejeani
  see South China sambar
Rusa unicolor equina
  see Hainan sambar
Rusa unicolor swinhoii
  see Formosan sambar
Rusa unicolor unicolor
  see Indian sambar
Ryukyu sika 190

Sambar 20, 34, 47, 180, 269–273, *269, 270, 271*
  antlers 273
  birthing 273
  diet 272
  dimensions 272
  distribution 269, 272
  habitat 273
  recognition features 272
  rut 273
Sayansk 173
Scent glands 32
Schomburgk, Sir Robert 256
Schomburgk's deer 27, 60, 256–7, *256,* 298

antlers 257
  dimensions 257
  distribution, former 256
  extinction 256
  habitat 257
  recognition features 257
Senses 31–2
Sexual dimosphism 35
Shansi sika 189
Shiras moose 81, 82
Shou deer 173, 176
Siberian elk see Amur elk
Siberian forest reindeer 147
Siberian musk deer 276, 283–4, *283, 284*
Siberian roe deer *95,* 96
  antlers 97
  birthing 97
  classification 95
  dimensions 97
  distribution 96
  food 97
  habitat 95, 97
  migration 95–6
  recognition features 97
Siberian tundra reindeer 147, *148*
Sichuan deer 173
Sichuan sika 189
Sika 20, 21, 22, 188–94, *188,*
  antlers 189, 194
  birthing *52,* 194
  diet 193
  dimensions 193
  distribution 188–9, 193
  domestication *67*
  habitat 193
  hybridisation 35–6, *36*, 191
  management 62, 64
  populations 190–2
  recognition features 193
  rut 194
  swimming 44
Silver-backed chevrotain 295, *295*
Sinaloa white-tailed deer 129
Sitka black-tailed deer 124, 125–126
Sitka mule deer *125*
Small red brocket 116, 117 *117*
Smell, sense of *see* senses

South American white-
    tailed deer 129, *130*
South China sambar 270
South China sika 190
Southeast Asian sambar
    270, *271*
Southern barasingha 247,
    247
Southern mule deer 124
Southern pudu 138, 139,
    140, *141*, *142*
    antlers 140, 143
    birthing 143
    diet 143
    dimensions 140, 143
    distribution 141–2
    habitat 143
    population 141
    recognition features 142
    rut 143
Southern red muntjac 211,
    220-2, *220*, *221*
    antlers 222
    birthing 222
    diet 222
    dimensions 222
    distribution 220, 222
    habitat 220, 222
    population
    recognition features 222
    rut 222
Species, list of 78–9
Spitzbergen reindeer
    see Svalbard reindeer
Sri Lankan sambar
    see Indian sambar
Steinheim (Germany) 18
Stinking deer *see* Pampas
    deer
Sumatran muntjac 239, 245,
    245
Svalbard reindeer 147
Swamp deer 22

Taiwan sika *see* Formosan
    sika
Tarim red deer 20, 21,
    184-7, *184*, *185*
    antlers 187
    birthing 187
    diet 187
    dimensions 186–7
    distribution 184, 186

habitat 187
recognition features 186
rut 187
Taruca 20, *99*,
    antlers 98, 100
    birthing 100
    description 98
    dimensions 100
    distribution 100
    habitat 98, 100
    herds 99
    population 99
    recognition features 100
    teeth 98, 100
Teeth 30-1
Texas white-tailed deer 129
Thai brow-antlered deer
    253, *254*
Thamin deer *251*, *252*, 253
Tian Shan wapiti *see* Altai
    wapiti
Tibetan red deer *see* Shou
    deer
Tiburon Island mule deer
    124, 126
Tonkin sika *see* Vietnamese
    sika
Tragulidae *see* Chevrotains
Tragulus javanicus see Javan
    chevrotain
Tragulus kanchil see Lesser
    Oriental chevrotain
Tragulus napu see Greater
    Oriental chevrotain
Tragulus nigricans
    see Balabac chevrotain
Tragulus versicolor
    see Silver-backed
    chevrotain
Tragulus williamsoni
    see Williamson's
    chevrotain
Truong Son muntjac 22
Tsushima sika 190
Tufted deer 20, 204–7, *204*,
    205, 206
    antlers 204, 207
    diet 207
    dimensions 207
    distribution 204, 206
    habitat 207
    recognition features 207
    rut 207

Tule elk 173, 177

Ungulates, definition 16
Ussuri elk *see* Siberian elk

Valley elk *see* Tule elk
Venado 129, *130*
Vietnamese sika 190, *192*
Virginia white-tailed deer
    129
Visayan spotted deer 20,
    157, 258–61, *258*, *259*,
    260
    antlers 261
    birthing 261
    diet 261
    dimensions 261
    distribution 258, 260,
        261
    habitat 261
    population 259
    recognition features 261
    rut 261
Vision *see* Senses
Vomeronasal organ (VNO)
    32

Wapiti 20, 21, 22, 23, 27,
    172-173, *172*, *173*
    antlers 174, 177
    Chronic Wasting Disease
        37, 176
    diet 176
    dimensions 176
    distribution 172, 174–5,
        176
    habitat 177
    recognition features 176
    rut 177
    speed 43
Water chevrotain 29, 35, 45,
    287, *287*
Water deer 20, 21, *21*, 22,
    105, *106*, *107*
    antlers 105, 107
    birthing 51, 55, 107, 108
    diet 108
    dimensions 108
    distribution 107
    habitat 106, 107, 108
    management 64
    recognition features
        107–108

rut 106, 108
teeth 30
tusks 105, 107
West American wapiti
    see Roosevelt's elk
Western barasingha 246,
    246
Western moose
    see Canadian moose
Whitehead, G. Kenneth 19
White-lipped deer 20,
    168–70, *168*, *169*, *170*
    antlers 171
    birthing 171
    dimensions 170
    diet 170
    distribution 170
    habitat 170
    recognition features 170
    rut 171
White-spotted chevrotain
    289, *289*
White-tailed deer 20, 21, 30,
    34, *128*
    antlers 133
    birthing 52, 133
    dimensions 133
    diet 133
    distribution 128, 132
    habitat 133
    hunting 131–2
    hybridisation 35
    management 63
    population 128, 131–2
    recognition features 132
    rut 133
    speed 43
Williamson's chevrotain 293
Woodland caribou 147, *148*

Yarkand deer 185, *185*, 187
Yellow-striped chevrotain
    389, *289*
Yucatan brown brocket 121,
    121
Yucatan white-tailed deer
    129

Zoonoses 69–70

Charles Smith-Jones

A LIFELONG NATURALIST and countryman, Charles Smith-Jones has always taken a special interest in deer which he has studied and worked with closely for more than 40 years at levels ranging between local issues and national policy. Previously a lecturer in countryside management at Sparsholt College, Hampshire, he currently works freelance as a writer and wildlife consultant, and is Technical Adviser to the British Deer Society. He has written four other books, three of them specifically on deer, and is a regular contributor to national countryside publications. He now lives in Cornwall, England.

Dr Susana González

DR SUSANA GONZÁLEZ is a conservation biologist who has worked as Director of Uruguay's Instituto de Conservacion Neotropical and with the Departmento de Biodiversidad y Genética, Clemente Estable Biological Research Institute, Montevideo. She is Co-Chair of the IUCN/SSC Deer Specialist group. A global champion for deer conservation, she has led efforts to conserve the Uruguayan pampas deer and its habitat for over 30 years for which she has been awarded a prestigious Whitley Award. Her work has also included combining scientific study with community outreach, and she also promotes training in ecotourism with its attendant long-term benefits to local people.

Dr Noam Werner

DR NOAM WERNER holds a B.A. in social sciences from the Hebrew University, an M.A. in Environmental Sciences, and a PhD in Zoology from Tel Aviv University in the field of animal behaviour. A member of the Jerusalem Biblical Zoo's senior management team for over 15 years as a zoologist and general curator, he is currently the director of the Haifa Educational Zoo. He serves as the European Association of Zoos and Aquaria (EAZA) Deer TAG chair as well as Co-Chair for the IUCN/SSC Deer Specialist Group and was also heavily involved with the Jerusalem Zoo's Mesopotamian fallow deer reintroduction project.